# GOVERNING HONG KONG

To kwok-wing chan

# GOVERNING HONG KONG

Administrative Officers from the Nineteenth Century to the Handover to China, 1862–1997

Steve Tsang

I.B. TAURIS
LONDON · NEW YORK

Published in 2007 by I.B.Tauris & Co Ltd
6 Salem Road, London W2 4BU
175 Fifth Avenue, New York NY 10010
www.ibtauris.com

In the United States of America and Canada distributed by Palgrave Macmillan
a division of St Martin's Press 175 Fifth Avenue, New York NY 10010

In China, Hong Kong, Macau, North and South Korea distributed by Hong Kong
University Press

Copyright © Steve Tsang, 2007

The right of Steve Tsang to be identified as the author of this work has been
asserted by him in accordance with the Copyright, Design and Patents Act 1988.

All rights reserved. Except for brief quotations in a review, this book, or any part
thereof, may not be reproduced, stored in or introduced into a retrieval system,
or transmitted, in any form or by any means, electronic, mechanical,
photocopying, recording or otherwise, without the prior written permission of
the publisher.

ISBN: 978 1 84511 525 8

International Library of Colonial History 9

A full CIP record for this book is available from the British Library
A full CIP record is available from the Library of Congress

Library of Congress Catalog Card Number: available

Printed and bound in India by Replika Press Pvt. Ltd
From camera-ready copy edited and typeset by
Oxford Publishing Services, Oxford

# CONTENTS

| | |
|---|---|
| Acronyms and Abbreviations | vii |
| Preface | viii |

1. Governance in a colonial society ................ 1
   *Managing the expatriate community* ........... 3
   *Governing the local Chinese* ................. 6
   *Institutional inadequacies* .................. 9

2. The cadet scheme .............................. 13
   *Origins* ..................................... 13
   *From language cadets to bureaucratic high flyers* ... 19
   *Impact on colonial administration* ........... 23

3. Benevolent paternalism ........................ 27
   *Learning about the Chinese* .................. 29
   *Life and work as a cadet* .................... 33
   *The making of an elite* ...................... 43

4. Effects of the Pacific War .................... 51
   *End of the colour bar* ....................... 52
   *A new outlook* ............................... 58

5. Expansion ..................................... 67
   *From cadets to administrative officers* ...... 69
   *Ever expanding scope of government activities* ... 72
   *The last of the old guard* ................... 75
   *Rapid growth and changes* .................... 84

*Contents*

| | | |
|---|---|---|
| 6. | **Meeting the challenges of a Chinese community** | 87 |
| | *Life and work of a modern district officer* | 87 |
| | *The life and work of a CDO* | 94 |
| | *Life and work at the secretariat* | 99 |
| | *Life and work in departments* | 104 |
| | *Fighting corruption* | 110 |
| 7. | **Localization** | 114 |
| | *Colonial 'retreads' and transferees* | 116 |
| | *Obstacles to local recruitment* | 120 |
| | *Beyond the 'glass ceiling'* | 125 |
| | *End of the gender bar* | 131 |
| | *British mandarins or Chinese officials* | 135 |
| 8. | **Meeting the challenges of modernity** | 139 |
| | *The McKinsey reforms* | 140 |
| | *Accountability without democracy* | 147 |
| | *Preparing for the end of empire* | 152 |
| 9. | **An elite within the government** | 161 |
| | *Esprit de corps* | 161 |
| | *Relations with non-administrative officers* | 167 |
| | *Relations with London* | 170 |
| 10. | **Inhibited elitism** | 181 |
| | *Intellectual brilliance versus good governance* | 182 |
| | *An inhibited political centre* | 188 |
| | *Wider implications* | 191 |
| | Notes | 196 |
| | References | 216 |
| | Index | 223 |

# ACRONYMS AND ABBREVIATIONS

| | |
|---|---|
| AO | administrative officer |
| BAAG | British Army Aid Group |
| CAT | Central Air Transport |
| CATC | Central Air Transport Corporation |
| CDO | City District Officer |
| CNAC | China National Aviation Corporation |
| CID | Criminal Investigation Department |
| CS | Colonial Secretary |
| DCS | Deputy Colonial Secretary |
| EIC | East India Company |
| FCO | Foreign and Commonwealth Office |
| FS | Financial Secretary |
| GATT | General Agreement on Tariffs and Trade |
| HK | Hong Kong |
| ICAC | Independent Commission Against Corruption |
| ICS | Indian Civil Service |
| MAC | Mutual Aid Committee |
| MBE | Member of the British Empire |
| NT | New Territories |
| PAS | Principal Assistant Secretary |
| PRC | People's Republic of China |
| SAR | Special Administrative Region |
| TUC | Trades Union Congress |

# PREFACE

Colonial Hong Kong was a place of contradictions and ironies. It started as a small outpost on the Eastern periphery of the British Empire, but by the time it was handed back to China it had become the last major, most important and most successful British imperial possession. It also, despite never having developed democracy and having been caught up in the politics of the Chinese civil war and in the cold war confrontations of the twentieth century, had earned a reputation for being a well-governed, stable and prosperous place. Right up until the end of the British period it retained its archaic crown colony system devised when Victoria was Queen of England, but it had an infrastructure, economy and life-style that evoked comparison with New York. Thoughtful visitors to Hong Kong are often as intrigued as longstanding residents by what really made Hong Kong tick.

The success of Hong Kong's colonial administration in providing good governance was in fact not a postwar creation, though Hong Kong suffered from poor governance in the early decades of its existence as a crown colony. By the latter part of the nineteenth century the quality of governance had changed so much that the founding father of the Chinese Republic, Sun Yat-sen, acknowledged this in public. When he addressed students at his alma mater, the University of Hong Kong, just over a decade after his republican revolution ended the Manchu Dynasty in China he said: 'Where and how did I get my revolutionary and modern ideas? I got my ideas in this very place, in Hong Kong. We must carry the English example of good government to every part of China.'

What really could be held to be responsible for the good governance of Hong Kong? As it turned out, it started with the appointment

*Preface*

in 1861 of three young British graduates as cadets to the Hong Kong government.

In this book I address that question. The central importance of the administrative officers, who were called cadets until the 1950s, was apparent to me as I conducted research for other books on Hong Kong in the last quarter of a century. But how important they really were and how they delivered good governance was not entirely clear to me when I decided to embark on this project.

The administrative officers made a huge difference to the quality of governance in Hong Kong. Individually, while most of them might not have been intellectually brilliant, they were mostly highly able and dedicated public servants. Collectively, they added up to more than the sum total of their individual efforts and abilities. Team work and a strong *esprit de corps* enabled them to work together for the general interest of the Hong Kong community (the meaning of which changed in the 'official mind' over time) and, though opportunities for graft existed aplenty, by and large they resisted the temptation of corruption.

This leads to a particularly intriguing and important conclusion of this book. It is that if Hong Kong's experience of administrative officers is any guide, there is no need to fill senior governmental posts with the intellectually brightest or most brilliant officers to secure good governance. Indeed, if intellectual brilliance were to be the key, the leading universities of the world should *ipso facto* be models of good governance – an extremely dubious claim if made. The Hong Kong experience shows that other factors matter more and that to deliver good governance one only needs able and dedicated civil servants who are willing to accept limits in exercising their power to govern.

The administrative officer's successful search for good governance is an important lesson for many – not least for the people of the Hong Kong Special Administrative Region and for the Chinese government. Both have a vested interest in ensuring that the high standard of governance should be maintained and improved in Hong Kong. This book can be seen as a judicious attempt to examine the roles administrative officers played in searching for and securing good governance in colonial Hong Kong. Although it is about the ethos of the colonial government in Hong Kong and its search for good governance, it is above all about the people who played key roles in this

*Preface*

process. This is also a book that should make an interesting comparison and contrast with the record of colonial governance in other parts of the once mighty British Empire.

\*\*\*

In undertaking the research and writing of this book I have received generous support and assistance. Above all, encouragement has come from a group of distinguished former administrative officers, Selwyn Alleyne, Trevor Clark, Sir Philip Haddon-Cave, Eric Peter Ho, Ian Lightbody, Kenneth Topley, Robert Upton, Bernard Williams, Brian Wilson, and Kai-yin Yeung. Over almost a decade they have given unfailing support and assistance in all sorts of ways, not least in answering specific queries and in reading and commenting on the book in draft. Some of them also shared with me their own private memoirs, personal communications and documents not otherwise available to researchers. Through their good office I have also received generous financial support from The New World Development Company Limited and Chun Wo Holdings Limited, which have been invaluable in enabling me to conduct the research and to prepare for a Chinese edition of this book to be published. In their usual responsible way while they reassured me that the financial support came from highly respected sources I was not in fact told of the name of the sponsors until the entire book was completed in draft. It is only fair for me to admit that this book would not have been written, let alone completed, without the generous support and encouragement I have received from them all.

I am also deeply indebted to others who have kindly offered me assistance in my research. Dame Anson Chan allowed me to tape an interview with her about her experience as an administrative officer specifically for this project. Dr James Hayes generously made available to me some of his research material and allowed me a preview of his latest book, *The Great Difference: Hong Kong's New Territories and its People 1898–2004*, before it was put into production. Trevor Clark and Eric Ho shared with me their writings before they were published. Mrs Penny Jordan gave me permission to make free use of the very lengthy transcript of interviews I conducted with her late husband David Jordan over a decade ago but its use is still under restriction unless specifically exempted. Likewise, Sir Donald

Luddington allowed me to quote from the record of confidential interviews I had with him, and the late Sir John Cowperwaithe permitted me to use material from another confidential interview I conducted with him. Graham Barnes, Rachel Cartland, G. K. Fawcett, Peter Lloyd, Jeremy Marriott, Ian Macpherson, Gareth Mulloy, Roderick MacLean , Ian Strachan, Simon Vickers, Patrick Williamson, and Michael Wright either wrote to me at length about their service or provided memoirs of their service in Hong Kong. Mrs Ann Partridge and Mrs Sheena Recaldin generously made available to me some private papers of their father David MacDougall that had not been made available to non-family members previously.

Many administrative officers of Hong Kong, some retired and some still in service, also gave me the benefit of their views by returning a questionnaire. As a majority of them have chosen to remain anonymous I shall refrain from naming only those who provided me with their names. When I ran the Oxford University Hong Kong Project in the late 1980s and early 1990s, I also interviewed at length about 20 retired top level administrative officers. Many of those interview transcripts are still subject to time bans and have therefore not been quoted or cited, but I have benefited greatly from speaking to them and cannot unlearn what I had learnt. A few of these transcripts are now open to the public and to those I owe an intellectual debt and they are acknowledged in the endnotes. Those whose interview transcripts are still subject to a time ban shall remain unnamed but to them and to those who returned the questionnaire, I thank them for their kindness and insights.

The staff at the Public Record Office in Kew, St Antony's College Library, Rhodes House Library, and University of Hong Kong Library also gave me excellent assistance and help. In particular Ms Carmen Tsang at the Hong Kong University Library went beyond the normal call of duty in helping me with my research.

I am further indebted to the following for kindly providing photographs for this book, most of them have never been published before. They are:

- Frances Coakley of www.manxnotebook.com for providing a copy of Sir James Stewart Lockhart's photograph;
- Ian Lightbody for three photographs: two of himself and a group photograph of cadets in 1957;

*Preface*

- Selwyn Alleyne for three photographs: one of himself, just retired as Commissioner in London greeting Prime Minister Thatcher on 8 June 1989; one of himself accompanying Governor Grantham who received a petition from a resident of the Taihangtung Estate; and the photograph of the farewell dinner for Governor Grantham in December 1957;
- Denis Yue for the photograph of Anson Chan;
- Andrew Tsui for the photograph of Paul Tsui in dress uniform and the group photograph of the local administrative officers on the occasion of Paul Tsui's retirement in 1973;
- Lady Holmes for the photograph of Sir Ronald Holmes in dress uniform taken by Frank Fischbeck;
- Mrs Ann Partridge for the photograph of David MacDougall;
- Mr G. K. Fawcett for the group photograph after a game of cricket in the early 1960s;
- Mr Edward Yau and the Information Service Department for four photographs: the Queen on inspection with Secretary for Housing Ian Lightbody in 1975, the Queen with Secretary for Municipal Services Augustine Chui and film star Jackie Chan (1986), the opening of the Cross-harbour Tunnel, and the group photograph of Po Leung Kuk directors with James Stewart Lockhart at the opening of a new hospital (1900).

Steve Tsang
Summer 2007

*Chapter 1*
# GOVERNANCE IN A COLONIAL SOCIETY

In sharp contrast to what became of the government towards the end of British colonial rule, governance in the formative years of British Hong Kong was not a matter of pride for either the colonists or the British Empire. Immediately after it was founded as a crown colony in 1843 this easternmost outpost of the British Empire in Asia attracted few well educated individuals, highly qualified professionals, well-trained administrators or highly respected merchants not engaged in the opium trade. Most of the Europeans who went to Hong Kong in the mid-nineteenth century were adventurers, smugglers, merchants dedicated to making a quick profit, and sailors or soldiers who took discharge in the Orient. Even after the initial administration had been passed on from Sir Henry Pottinger, a career soldier who founded the colony, to Sir John Davis, a learned man known for his scholarship on the Chinese, governance remained a problem. Indeed, the situation did not improve substantially in the first two decades of British rule. There were few talents or qualified professionals among the colonists who could be recruited by the colonial administration to provide a high standard of government service.

The candid admission in a weekly newspaper, the *Hong Kong Register*, that early colonial Hong Kong was 'one of the most unenviable transmarine possessions belonging to her most Gracious Majesty', Queen Victoria, reflected the prevailing British view of Hong Kong in its infancy.[1] The reputation of this nascent colony did not improve much in the following decade. In the course of the

*Governing Hong Kong*

second Anglo–Chinese War, *The Times* still described it in terms of being 'always connected with some fatal pestilence, some doubtful war, or some discreditable internal squabble; so much so that, in popular language, the name of this noisy, bustling, quarrelsome, discontented, and insalubrious little island, may not inaptly be used as an euphonious synonym for a place not mentionable to ears polite.'[2]

The problems of governance in this British imperial outpost at the edge of the Chinese Empire were augmented by the non-existence of an established local elite. In most parts of Queen Victoria's steadily expanding empire, the local elite generally provided a ready-made network of collaborators that enabled a small number of British colonists to govern under some form of indirect rule. This did not apply to Hong Kong in its early years as it was itself originally a remote part of the Chinese Empire. Before the British arrived Hong Kong did not have in place either a formal local government or a well entrenched group of scholar gentry who would, as happened elsewhere in the Chinese Empire, constitute the local elite and provide informal government at the sub-county magistrate level. The rapidly rising Chinese population that followed British occupation consisted largely of new immigrants. By and large, they came from neighbouring Guangdong province and were mostly small shopkeepers, labourers, other economic migrants, the destitute, pirates, and people generally deemed to have come not from an honourable background. On the whole, respected and wealthy Chinese did not in this period have any desire to migrate to live under alien rule.

As a result the small colonial administration had to rely in its early years on ethnic Chinese collaborators who did not initially command high respect in either the small indigenous or the much bigger immigrant Chinese community.[3] Their collaborators were Chinese who 'chose to follow the British to Hong Kong, which offered lucrative opportunities for collaboration'.[4] They only emerged as the local elite after they had profited from the collaboration and acquired the means to rise above the labouring class.

In short, the challenge the colonial administration had to face was to get a few poorly trained or unqualified administrators to provide a decent level of governance in a multicultural, multiethnic and largely transient society. It had to govern the Chinese community as well because the latter could not be left to its own local elite. These demands were made more difficult because the hope that Hong

*Governance in a colonial society*

Kong would turn into a prosperous port supporting British trade in China did not materialize quickly. This meant that the colonial government had to operate within severe financial restraints, for it was financially dependent on the British Treasury for a subsidy and was therefore subject to tight Treasury control. Importing experienced and able administrators from Britain or elsewhere within the British Empire to rectify this situation was not an option, except at the top level. Governance in the first two decades of British rule had to operate within these constraints.

## Managing the expatriate community

The number of expatriate British residents in Hong Kong was small, and merely increased from 158 when the British first took possession in 1841 to 618 in 1847.[5] It did not exceed 1000 in the first decade of British rule and only got near 2000 in 1860. Despite their small number their assertiveness meant that they formed the focus of attention of the tiny colonial administration. The main driving force behind the British mercantile community's political activism was self-interest.

As a new colony, Hong Kong needed to raise an income locally to support government services and development, and to build a basic infrastructure. Although it already received a subvention from the British Treasury and would continue to do so for almost two decades, its nature as an imperial outpost rather than a settlement colony gave the colonists justifiable grounds to argue that it should receive a significant subsidy from the imperial government. The case of the expatriate mercantile community was that since Hong Kong was founded primarily as a military and naval station to support imperial interests connected with the whole of the China trade rather than to serve their local interests, the British government should pay a significant proportion of the cost of maintaining this imperial outpost.[6] Armed with such an argument they petitioned the home government in 1845 to call for some form of municipal self-government so that they could better resist Governor Davis's attempt to raise local revenue by introducing rates.[7]

The British government rejected the mercantile community's requests. Secretary of State for the Colonies William Gladstone ruled that since Hong Kong was occupied 'solely and exclusively with a view to commercial interests' the introduction of rates and other measures to enable the colonial government to raise revenue locally to finance the administration was justified.[8] This put an end to the colonists' immediate demand for municipal self-government. It did not, however, change the political reality. It was the British colonists not the Chinese community that could secure the attention of metropolitan Britain and thus the focus of the colonial administration.

To put in perspective the nature of governance in early colonial Hong Kong it is important to recognize that both the colonial society and the government were very small. The expatriate community numbered in the hundreds and the administration consisted of about 50 officials in its first decade.[9] Thus, despite the grand title of certain offices and references to colony-wide interests, governance and administration of justice among the expatriates closely resembled that of a very small township. Thinking of Hong Kong as a crown colony being run by His Excellency the Governor, supported by his Executive and Legislative Councils and a civil service in the capital city of Victoria, gave a distorted picture of what colonial life and politics were like in the mid-nineteenth century. The colonial community of expatriates in the infancy of Hong Kong was in fact so small that everyone could have known everybody else had they not been divided by strict class barriers. Colonial society in the early decades of British Hong Kong was characterized by the politics of a small community, with all the pettiness, interlocked interests, personal feuds, jealousy and rivalries this entailed. These were exaggerated by the claustrophobic environment of this small island outpost, the inflated egos of officials intoxicated by their grandiose titles, and by the colonists whose sense of superiority *vis-à-vis* the local Chinese cultivated arrogance and pomposity.

The contempt in which a learned man like Governor Davis held the merchants, who were almost all birds of passage associated with the opium trade, was unsurprisingly reciprocated. They detested him and when he left office in 1848 members of the mercantile community ignored him.[10] The animosity that existed between some senior officials and merchants was relatively mild compared with the intensity of hatred and feud that existed among some top officials. Governor Davis forced his colonial treasurer Robert Montgomery Martin to leave office and Hong Kong because the latter not only took a despondent view of the future of the colony but also sought to appeal over the governor's head to London to advocate abandoning

Hong Kong in favour of the more northern island of Zhoushan.[11] A quarrel between Davis and the first Chief Justice J. W. Hulme, which originated over the duration of leave that Hulme had allocated himself, eventually turned into a long-running feud and contest of will. The result was Davis resigning from his office after unsuccessfully seeking Hulme's removal by accusing the latter of habitual drunkenness though he could not prove it.[12]

The intense politics of personal rivalries was not the preserve of Governor Davis's tenure. Almost two decades from its founding, similar discord in high office continued to cause havoc within the administration. Hong Kong again lost two top level officials in quick succession after they locked horns. They were Attorney General T. Chisholm Anstey and Registrar General Daniel Caldwell.[13] They served under Governor Sir John Bowring, another learned man who made himself so unpopular among the colonists that his departure in 1859 was greeted with silence and disregarded by the colonists. Early colonial Hong Kong did not produce an environment conducive to efficient administration or team work within the government.

The smallness of the expatriate population and lack of fully qualified professionals meant that the line between public service and private practice was often blurred. What today would be deemed basic requirements for good practices were simply unaffordable in early colonial Hong Kong. The lack of officers with adequate command of the Chinese language meant that for years the assistant superintendent of police had to act as the interpreter in court for 'cases that he and his network of informants had played a leading role in bringing to court'.[14] The inherent conflict of interest in such a practice made a mockery of any modern principle of good governance or administration of justice.

Even at the highest level in the administration of justice, a shortage of qualified barristers meant that a leading barrister with a private practice, W. T. Bridges, was at different times in the 1850s appointed to serve as both attorney general and colonial secretary.[15] While allowing the attorney general to run a private practice was also allowed in England at the time, in a small community like Hong Kong it allowed questions to be raised about the loyalty and integrity of the barristers concerned. This and other efforts to maximize the value of the limited supply of qualified human resources affected the quality of both governance and the independence of the judicial officers.

Indeed, the personal integrity of senior officials in early colonial Hong Kong was not beyond reproach. Some were known to have speculated in land, taken bribes, colluded with opium farmers or been involved with criminals guilty of extortion and piracy. They included individuals who reached the higher echelons of government like Administrator of the Colony A. R. Johnston, Lieutenant Governor William Caine, Colonial Secretary W. T. Bridges, Registrar General Daniel Caldwell, and Police Superintendent Charles May.[16] Such personal failings of senior officials neither contributed to good governance nor enhanced the prestige and credibility of the colonial administration.

Given its small expatriate population, what made early Hong Kong more than a village or little township was its rapidly expanding Chinese population. Although the original Chinese inhabitants at the time of the British occupation in 1841 numbered roughly 7500 they were quickly outnumbered by a steady influx of immigrants or temporary workers.[17] By 1847, the Chinese population had reached 20,000; it had grown to almost 90,000 by 1860, but then, with the acquisition of Kowloon peninsula, shot up dramatically to almost 120,000 within a year.[18] This expanding Chinese population not only provided the manpower to build a new city-state but also generated many of the economic activities and much of the revenue to sustain the colonial government. In 1855, for example, among 1999 residents who paid rates at or above £10, 1637 were Chinese, while 410 out of 772 who paid rates at or above £40 were Chinese.[19] Although the rapid expansion of the Chinese community was what really enabled Hong Kong to become financially independent and therefore a sustainable colony, it was the expatriate community that continued to receive the overwhelming attention of the administration.

**Governing the local Chinese**

Despite Hong Kong having been founded as a free port to which people of all nationalities were welcomed, there was little mixing between the expatriate and Chinese communities. By and large, Chinese and non-Chinese chose to live among their own people as the language and cultural gaps between them were substantial. While the parallel existence of the two communities was generally peaceful, the modality of contact between them did pose challenges to good governance and to the administration of justice.

*Governance in a colonial society*

In the mid-nineteenth century, the relationship between an expatriate colonist and a Chinese person was an unequal one. The fact that the vast majority of Chinese who lived in British Hong Kong had little direct dealings with the expatriates did not change this reality. The overwhelming majority of those who had regular contact with members of the expatriate community did so as the latter's servants or employees for menial jobs. A tiny minority of the successful Chinese served as compradors in expatriate owned firms and were charged with dealing with their employers' Chinese trading partners, subcontractors and menial employees. Even though some compradors became highly successful and a few built fortunes that rivalled those of their expatriate employers within a generation, their relationship with their employers was still not that among peers. In its early years as a colony, Hong Kong did not have laws that discriminated against the Chinese, but there was never any doubt that the British colonists saw themselves as superior to the Chinese.[20] Discrimination against the local Chinese by the expatriates was so much taken for granted in this early stage of British Hong Kong that no thought was given to providing a legal basis.

For the expatriate community and colonial government, those Chinese who were not in their employ but occasionally came into contact with them were generally treated as actual or at least potential troublemakers. The main causes for contact beyond the provision of service were related to crimes or a breach of the law. Although it was extremely rare for a Chinese person to commit a crime against a European, the Chinese were widely seen as primarily responsible for crimes against expatriate-owned property.[21] The Chinese also fell foul of the law as some of the activities they practised regularly were proscribed by law under the British. What a Chinese person saw as an enterprising way of making a living, for example as a street trader, became unlawful obstruction of a public highway and unlicensed hawking. In other words, many Chinese were treated as criminals because some of their normal pursuits had been criminalized.[22] As far as government officials were concerned, the most likely reason why they would need to contact a Chinese person was when the latter had violated the law or some government regulations and had to be arrested and brought to the magistrate's court. In other words, governance of the Chinese community was seen largely in terms of maintaining stability and good order among an alien population that did not fully understand or routinely respect the law of the land.

Given that the *raison d'être* behind the founding of Hong Kong was commercial gain, the British were at first happy to leave local Chinese to their own devices so long as they did not break the law or otherwise disturb the peace. Instability or disorder was bad for business or would at least increase the cost of administration. It was with this in mind that the colonial government imported the Chinese social control arrangement known as the *baojia* system. Chinese constables appointed for this purpose were made peace officers with 'the same authorities, privileges and immunities as any constable'[23] and subjected to the general oversight of the police magistrate. They were introduced because the mainly non-Chinese police during Hong Kong's formative years were unable to dampen criminal activities among the Chinese population. However, since they had been abolished by 1861, one must question their effectiveness, especially since there is little record of their achievements.[24]

As Chinese peace officers failed to establish themselves as an effective auxiliary to the colonial government, the expanding Chinese community gradually produced notables to whom other Chinese increasingly would turn for mediation and arbitration of disputes among themselves. This was tacitly encouraged by the colonial administration as it had no interest in taking on settling disputes among the local Chinese.

Important local leaders in the early days like Loo Aqui and Tam Achoy had generally profited from working for the British in founding Hong Kong, or made fortunes as compradors or in the entrepôt trade.[25] They were not just British collaborators, but differed from traditional Chinese leaders because of their humble and non-gentrified backgrounds.[26] Loo, for example, was a Tanka, a kind of outcast boat people, which would normally have stopped him becoming established as a leader of the local Cantonese. Since Hong Kong did not have an established scholar-gentry class, the wealth Loo amassed from provisioning the British put him in a position to try to rise above his lowly origins.[27]

People like Loo and Tam came to be accepted as community leaders after they used their personal wealth to support local good causes. The landmark development in this connection was the building of the Man Mo Temple on Hollywood Road in the heart of

*Governance in a colonial society*

the Chinese community in 1847. As a temple it was dedicated to the deities for the fortunes of men seeking advancement through the Chinese imperial examinations, and for loyalty and righteousness particularly among warriors. But it was much more than just a temple for the local Chinese. It quickly 'became the main social centre for Hong Kong's Chinese population, regardless of their regional or occupational affiliation'.[28]

By the start of the 1850s the temple administrators had evolved into a *de facto* local governing board among the Chinese. They 'secretly controlled native affairs, acted as commercial arbitrators, arranged for the due reception of mandarins passing through the Colony, negotiated the sale of [Chinese] official titles, and formed an unofficial link between the Chinese residents of Hong Kong and the Canton Authorities'.[29] With neither the wish nor resources to get deeply involved in governing the local Chinese, the colonial government gave benign blessings to this state of affair.

While the local leadership that sprang up around the temple enabled Chinese locals to enjoy *de facto* self government in most everyday affairs, it did not absolve the colonial government of normal policing and public order functions. This was because law and order were matters of serious concern to the expatriate community on which the colonial government focused its attention. When local Chinese broke colonial laws or regulations, they were put before the police magistrate or, in more serious cases, the Supreme Court. Lack of resources, particularly honest officials with sufficient command of the Chinese language to communicate with local Chinese brought in front of the executive or judicial authority, posed a major problem. The relationship between the British governors and the Chinese residents could not be put on a satisfactory footing as neither could communicate effectively with the other.

## Institutional inadequacies

The quality of governance the Hong Kong government could offer its residents towards the end of its first two decades of rule was thus very low by the standards of the late-twentieth century, when the Union flag was finally lowered for the last time. The meaning of good governance had also changed over this century and a half. While the government saw meeting the needs of the local Chinese, who always constituted the overwhelming majority of the population in Hong Kong, as its primary task towards the end of the twentieth century, its predecessor did not do so.

In the nineteenth century the colonial government looked at the Chinese community largely in terms of maintaining law and order and of securing an important source of public revenue through the imposition of rates and other licence fees. Likewise, to the local Chinese, who were used to the traditional Chinese political practice and unfamiliar with modern British concepts, good governance under alien rule meant good order, non-intrusive administration or enforcement of government regulations, low taxation and scope for them to do whatever they could to earn a living.[30] Indeed, even in the United Kingdom, which took a leading part in introducing a professional modern civil service, the mid-nineteenth century was a turning point. In the first part of this century, government offices were still as a general practice, 'shared out [to] the correctly named "offices of profit under the Crown"'.[31] This was hardly surprising since it was normal in preindustrial states for individuals to go 'into government service in order to make money out of it'.[32] The idea of a selfless and devoted modern civil service was only germinating in the early part of the nineteenth century in Britain. It was therefore unexceptional that in Hong Kong, neither the colonial government nor the local Chinese saw their relationship as one between government and citizens.

The inadequacies in governance that existed in mid-nineteenth century Hong Kong were of not much concern to local Chinese primarily interested in being left alone to make a living. They did not think that airing their grievances would reduce abuse by government officials or members of the expatriate community. The colonial government and its magistrates were in any event inherently discriminatory in their dealings with the Chinese. The saving grace for the local Chinese was that the smallness of the administration and the lack of will to interfere in the daily affairs of the local Chinese meant that the government was not generally oppressive. This applied particularly when the failings of the colonial administration were compared with those that prevailed across the border in Guangdong province.[33] Given that stability and good order prevailed and most Chinese were allowed to go about their own affairs as best as they could, they were not dissatisfied with the standard of governance, such as it was.

The institutional inadequacies that existed were largely a matter that interested the colonial administration but not the colonists, for most members of the expatriate community were part of the colonial establishment and thus enjoyed ready access to the government. What was inherently unsatisfactory to the government was the inability of its higher echelons to communicate directly with the overwhelming majority of the population – the Chinese. The problem was summed up in the remarks of Governor Bowring: 'We rule in ignorance, they obey in blindness.'[34]

As revealed in the case laid against Daniel Caldwell, the Chinese speaking registrar general who had previously played crucial roles as a police officer and the chief interpreter for the police and the courts, the administration's heavy reliance on a handful of individuals who happened to know the Chinese language provided wide scope for the abuse of power.[35] Caldwell was appointed the first protector of the Chinese in conjunction with his office as registrar general because Governor Bowring was keen to reduce the abuses the expatriate community perpetuated against the local Chinese. With so much power being concentrated in his hands by virtue of his monopolistic command of the Chinese language at a high level of government, Caldwell could not resist the temptation. He used his office to give patronage to one of the most notorious local pirates Wong Machow and otherwise used his position to further his personal gains. In the Wong case, Caldwell's patronage 'invested him with immense power' so much so that Wong became 'a terror to the bulk of the community, and tyrannized over the lower orders of Chinese, without their daring to complain' as Caldwell was the only channel by which they could do so.[36] With the government's relations with the majority of the people at the mercy of a man whose personal integrity was not beyond doubt, good governance for Hong Kong as a colony was more an aspiration than a reality.

By the end of the 1850s, when social tension was at times raised as a result of the second Anglo–Chinese War (1856–60), as during the trial of the leading Chinese baker who was alleged to have attempted to poison the entire expatriate community, Hong Kong had recognized the need to ameliorate this institutional inadequacy. Governor Bowring considered a positive development would be the recruitment into the colonial government of able, well-educated young officers who could be groomed to become competent administrators able to communicate with the local Chinese community. But he was unable to push for such a reform, for he was not an effective governor and the Treasury control over Hong Kong's finance meant he did not have a lot of scope for increasing public expenditure.[37]

The Hong Kong government had muddled through its first two decades without an adequate means of communicating with the bulk of the local population. This was an undesirable state of affairs that needed to be rectified, particularly once the local economy was doing sufficiently well to allow the government to seek a remedy. As British Hong Kong entered its third decade, the colonial government started to search for a new modality of government. This started in response to the needs of the time but ended up being the beginning of a long search for good governance.

*Chapter 2*
# THE CADET SCHEME

**Origins**

Towards the end of its second decade as a crown colony, Hong Kong expanded and matured. Physical extension was mainly a side effect of the second Anglo–Chinese War (1856–60), which allowed the colonists to seize the opportunity to incorporate the tip of Kowloon on the mainland opposite Hong Kong Island.[1] The maturing of the colony was the result of economic growth and expansion of the population base. These factors enabled Hong Kong to shake off Treasury control from London and gain financial autonomy in 1858, after the local economy had proved it could generate sufficient income to cover public expenditure on a sustainable basis.[2] This meant that the colonial government no longer had to submit its annual budget to the British Treasury for scrutiny, changes and approval before it could be adopted. The local Legislative Council enjoyed for the first time the authority to discuss and debate the annual budget before it was then presented to the Colonial Office for further scrutiny and formal approval. The really important result in practice was that the Hong Kong government now enjoyed much greater freedom in expanding the administration to meet the needs of the colony, as its wage bill ceased to be paid in part by a subvention from Britain.

The recognition in Hong Kong during Governor Bowring's term of office (1854–59) that there were serious institutional inadequacies in its administration roughly coincided with major administrative reforms in Britain. In 1855 the British government introduced a civil service commission to recruit and promote a portion of officials on the basis of competitive examination rather than patronage. Its leading ministerial sponsor, the chancellor of the exchequer William Gladstone, meant this to be 'a guarantee of greater efficiency and ... a simple act of justice' in an era where ministerial patronage was still seen by many as 'an essential part of the political system and its loss' a factor that 'would weaken the executive'.[3]

This important development was the result of 'the growth of competition to replace patronage; changes in recruitment elsewhere, especially for the Indian Civil Service (ICS); the influence of a small group of leading personalities; and the need to rectify administrative inefficiency'.[4] It was also inspired by the Crimean War (1853–56). Had the dreadful results of poor leadership and mismanagement of the welfare and the deployment of troops in the war by non-competitively selected officers not caught public imagination in Britain Gladstone would have faced more formidable opposition.[5] The substance of this reform was based on the recommendations of a commission of inquiry led by Stafford Northcote and Charles Trevelyan a year earlier. They suggested 'the best method of getting good civil servants, and of making the most of them after they were recruited, was to train young men carefully selected by examination and whose permanent appointment would be confirmed only after the satisfactory completion of a short period of probation.'[6]

The original model for selecting civil servants on a competitive basis had come from a civil service reform in India. There the East India Company (EIC) had the 'most effective and best-recruited group of government servants' in the British Empire, particularly after it 'restricted all its posts to successful competitors in written examinations'.[7] The first step towards putting recruitment to the ICS on a competitive basis was taken in 1806 when the Haileybury College was founded 'to provide suitable education for young men nominated to join' the ICS.[8] After some further changes the breakthrough came with the Government of India Act of 1853, under which patronage by directors of the EIC was abolished and the ICS had to be filled by open competitive examination.[9]

In Britain, the Northcote–Trevelyan reform did not in fact result in the recruitment of all senior civil servants to the home civil service on a competitive basis until 1870, after Gladstone became prime minister.[10] Nevertheless, it was a landmark event that incorporated the idea of a meritocracy into the British approach to building a modern civil service.

As far as Hong Kong was concerned, Governor Bowring, who was a member of parliament before he went to China to serve as British consul in Canton in 1849, had noted the unsatisfactory state of affairs whereby the overwhelming majority of government officials could not communicate with the bulk of the population. It was during his term as governor that the inadequacies of the colonial government and the abuses of Registrar General Daniel Caldwell came to the government's attention. In the meantime, the gap between the English governors and the Chinese governed was so great that it even attracted the attention of the British government. As a result, Secretary of State for the Colonies Lord John Russell ruled in 1855 that 'no application for an increase of salary in the civil service of Hong Kong was to be made for any person who had not learnt Chinese.'[11] This inadequacy became more acute after Kowloon was added to the colony, for it dramatically increased the Chinese population from fewer than 90,000 in 1860 to almost 120,000 in 1861.[12] The need to ensure that the colonial government had the capacity to maintain stability and good order in this overwhelmingly Chinese populated imperial outpost meant that it must have senior officials who could understand and communicate with the bulk of the local population.

The term of Bowring's office also suffered from more general administrative malaise. Despite his good intentions, liberal views and imagination over administrative reform, Bowring was not an able governor.[13] Although he secured an end to Treasury control and increased the number of government servants, he failed to lead his expanded group of officials to work together to produce an efficient and effective government. The colonial administration was therefore in an unsatisfactory state of affairs when he handed over to his successor Sir Hercules Robinson in 1859. This was due partly 'to Bowring's own apparent inability to exercise discipline', partly 'to the fact that he had as his chief legal adviser an attorney general whose advice and actions did little towards overcoming difficulties, but rather added to them', and partly to the method of recruitment of public servants, by which 'a number of the leading officials were allowed private practice'.[14]

Bowring's succession by a 35-year-old army officer turned career colonial administrator not only delivered an energetic governor but also a major new development in the administration. From its foundation as a crown colony in 1843, the British government combined the office of governor of Hong Kong with the head of the British diplomatic and trade mission to China. It was in the course of the second Anglo–Chinese War (1856–60) that the British government separated the two offices. Thus, when Robinson succeeded Bowring, he became the first governor whose responsibilities were focused entirely on governing the colony.

It was also during Robinson's term that the problems of Caldwell, the only senior official who could speak Chinese resurfaced. A second inquiry into his conduct, known as the Civil Service Abuses Inquiry, overturned the findings of the previous investigation conducted during Bowring's tenure. On this occasion the council of inquiry concluded that Caldwell's 'long and intimate connexion with the pirate, Machow Wong, was of such a character as to render him unfit to be continued in the public service'.[15] With Caldwell dismissed the colonial government lacked any reliable means to communicate with its Chinese subjects. This was the situation as the 'nine or ten interpreters at present in the employment of the local government ... have neither education nor sufficient knowledge of the English language to qualify them' to take over the duties of Caldwell or serve as a reliable government interpreter.[16]

This unsatisfactory state of affairs did not diminish Robinson's determination 'to make sure ... that the Chinese should be fully and correctly informed of the nature, purport and details of every Government measure affecting their interests'. He was also keen to ensure that 'the Government should be accurately informed of what the Chinese ... really wanted or needed or wished to say'.[17] For these purposes and following the precedent elsewhere within the British Empire, Robinson adopted an idea first mooted by his predecessor. It was to recruit young cadets with a good general education in the United Kingdom to go to Hong Kong to be trained in the Chinese language before being employed as government servants on a fast track to senior offices.[18] This line of thinking was very much in line with the spirit of the Northcote–Trevelyan reform, which 'delineated a hierarchy within the civil service parallel to the social and educational hierarchy'.[19]

Robinson could push hard because Hong Kong could by then afford this expensive initiative without prior approval from the British Treasury. He set out the rationale for his proposal:

With a view to supply the Civil Service in Hong Kong with an efficient staff of Interpreters and also to afford the Government an opportunity of selecting for some of the higher appointments as they become vacant Gentlemen acquainted with the Chinese language, I propose that a certain number of Cadetships be established, the holders of which shall devote themselves for a certain time after their arrival in the Colony solely to learning the language. I recommend 1st that three Cadetships be at once offered for competition by public examination to the Students of such *three or more* Colleges or Schools as Her Majesty's Government may select [emphasis in original].[20]

Robinson's plan was well received in the Colonial Office. Indeed, the secretary of state, the Duke of Newcastle, thought it was 'of such vast importance to the good government of the Colony that ... no time should be lost in putting effect to the scheme proposed'.[21] When it reviewed Robinson's proposal, the Colonial Office took into account parallel developments within the empire as a whole. They were the introduction of competitive examinations for recruitment to the Colonial Office as part of the home civil service, for the civil service in Ceylon and for recruiting language cadets for the Foreign Office's China consular service.[22] Significantly, the last was itself an initiative that came to fruition when Governor Bowring served concurrently as the British chief superintendent of trade in China. Unlike a cadet scheme for Hong Kong, the China consular service was funded by the Foreign Office to further British economic, diplomatic and consular interests and its viability was not dependent on the resources of the colony.

The Hong Kong cadet scheme was one of the earlier attempts to institutionalize the recruitment of senior civil servants by competitive examinations within the British Empire as a whole. It preceded similar schemes for the Straits Settlements and British Malaya, not to say most African colonies. Recruitment by competitive examination was only introduced to the Straits Settlements' civil service in 1869 and at a much later date in Malaya. A combined examination for the three main Eastern colonies, Ceylon, Hong Kong and the Straits Settlements, was introduced in 1882, to which Malaya was later included.[23] Hence, from the early 1880s onwards recruitment for Hong Kong was conducted as part of the examination administered by the civil service commissioners in London for the Eastern cadets, and the successful candidates were able to express a preference for service in one of these colonies in Asia.

When British officials deliberated over this new initiative for Hong Kong they paid no attention to the fact that China had an imperial civil examination system for recruiting government officials that dated back to the Sui dynasty (581–618). Although by the mid-nineteenth century the Chinese system had suffered many abuses, it was still the world's most sophisticated system for recruiting government officials on the basis of open competition through a series of written examinations.[24] Whether through ignorance or imperial arrogance, neither the governor nor any officials in the Colonial Office referred even to the mere existence, not to say the strength and weaknesses, of the Chinese system. There is no evidence to suggest that the British made any attempt to learn from the long experience of China, or to understand what pitfalls such a system might entail, even though the British presence in Hong Kong offered them an opportunity to benefit from the Chinese experience.

Deliberations at the Colonial Office focused instead mainly on the practicalities and advisability of Robinson's specific proposals. They proposed to increase the age for appointment from below 20 to between 20 and 23 and also examined the basic academic curriculum that candidates would be expected to have followed. Of eight subjects initially identified as pertinent, most emphasis was laid on handwriting, arithmetic, Latin, one other foreign language and English composition. Other subjects for which candidates were expected to be examined included at least two of the following: pure mathematics, history and geography, constitutional and international law, as well as natural science.[25] In other words, the main emphasis was laid on a good general education and an aptitude for learning languages. There was not the same high expectation, which the founders of the ICS had, in expecting the bulk of new recruits to come from among bright young gentlemen graduated from the ancient universities of Oxford and Cambridge.[26] What was left unmentioned at this stage, but taken for granted, was the ethnicity requirement. All candidates would have to be 'natural born British subjects', a requirement that became formally incorporated into the terms of reference for the cadetship at the turn of the century.[27]

With strong support from the British government and funding

*The cadet scheme*

from local sources, the colonial government was able to implement this scheme quickly. As with civil service reforms in Britain and British India in the 1850s, there was a feeling in Britain that it was more important to reform the civil service in India than in Britain, even though Britain's service was in a worse state than India's. India was given priority because 'the Indian civil servant exercised a power for good or evil which no English civil servant ... possessed'.[28] While Hong Kong was far less important to Britain than India, British policy makers generally associated it (along with the other Eastern colonies) with the way in which peripheral parts of the empire in India were run.[29] More importantly, reforming the civil service in an outpost like Hong Kong was easier because it did not generate resistance from those who had a vested interest in the old patronage system within the establishment in Britain. What constituted good governance was not clearly defined. Indeed, the meaning of good governance evolved, in colonial Hong Kong as it did in the rest of the world, as modernity and people's expectations impacted on each other raising the standard of what would be accepted by a community as good governance in the spirit of the time.

The British civil service commissioners selected the first three Hong Kong cadets on the basis of competitive examination among candidates nominated by the secretary of state.[30] They were Walter Meredith Deane, Cecil Clementi Smith and Malcolm Struan Tonnochy, all graduates of public schools and Cambridge University. Their arrival in Hong Kong in September 1862 marked a major change in the development of the administration.

**From language cadets to bureaucratic high flyers**

Although the first batch of three officers was recruited as young and impressionable language cadets, it was always intended that they would rise rapidly in the civil service after a period of tutelage superintended by the governor. This approach was inherent in Governor Robinson's thinking. His rationale was set out clearly in the original proposal he submitted to the Colonial Office:

- That each candidate shall be under 20 years of age.
- That the regulations for the examination shall be determined by Her Majesty's Government *that a knowledge of Chinese be not necessary* but that a preference be given to Candidates who have

proved an aptitude for acquiring languages [emphasis in original].
- That each Cadet shall receive on appointment £100 (one hundred pounds sterling) towards defraying his passage to the Colony and outfit; that he be paid a Salary of £200 per annum to commence from date of arrival in Colony, and that quarters, Teachers, and books be provided for him at the public expense while studying the language.
- That for two years after their arrival in China, the Cadets shall apply themselves to learning Chinese.
- That at the end of two years' study, or as soon afterwards as they shall be declared qualified by a Board of competent examiners, the Cadets shall be appointed Government Interpreters and be employed in each of the Departments as may require their services at Salaries of £400 per annum each, without other allowances.
- That after two years' approved service as Interpreters, the Salary be increased to £500, and after three years Service as Interpreters to be considered eligible, in the event of suitable vacancies occurring for promotion in the Civil Service, and '*ceteris paribus*' be preferred to other candidates.
- That the Cadets while studying Chinese shall be under the Control and supervision of the Governor who shall frame regulations for their hours of study and general government. That their progress shall be tested by half yearly examinations – and that every Cadet shall be liable at any time to be sent home to his friends if his conduct or progress should be considered by the Governor and Executive Council to be so unsatisfactory as to render such a step desirable.
- That a bond be entered into by the Cadets and his friends at home with the Agents General to secure the repayment of the £100 given on appointment, and for cost of passage home, in the event of the Cadets' dismissal before appointment as Interpreter.
- That after the disposal of the first three Cadets as Interpreters, the number be maintained permanently at two by fresh appointments and that the mode of selection and course of examination for subsequent Cadetships shall be determined by the experience gained in the selection of the first appointments.[31]

*The cadet scheme*

As the proposed terms of employment suggest, from the beginning cadets were sufficiently well remunerated to remove the temptation for corruption.[32] To put the value of their salary into context, the cost of employing a Chinese servant in a European household was about £15 per annum, a bottle of wine about three shillings, a pound of cheese about two shillings, and a pound of pork only about three pence. In the same period a senior official like the registrar general received a salary of £700, and the second most senior civil official, the colonial secretary a salary of £1500.[33] Although the remuneration of cadets was lower than that offered in the commercial sector, it was sufficient to maintain the standard of living as young gentlemen in the colony.

The original intention that cadets would be put on a fast track in the civil service materialized quickly. In fact it happened much earlier than anyone expected. Robinson's term coincided with the departure of several senior old-timers. This meant that Hong Kong suffered not only from a shortage of good officials but also of senior officials. It provided a great opportunity for the new cadets to advance their careers because they were deployed in government service, albeit in an acting capacity at first, as quickly as it was practicable.

Robinson's bold initiative was vindicated as 'the first recruits showed promise' and soon proved their worth.[34] Two of the three cadets were promoted to head of departments much sooner than originally envisaged. The ablest of them, Smith served as registrar general, a senior post, as early as 1864, only two years after he had arrived in Hong Kong. He left the colony in 1878 upon promotion as colonial secretary of the Straits Settlements, where he later rose to take over the administration as governor. He ended his colonial career as high commissioner for Borneo and Sarawak, and was subsequently appointed a privy councillor. Deane also acquitted himself well and took charge of the police as captain superintendent in 1867, an office he held until he resigned for heath reasons in 1891. Even the laggard of the lot, Tonnochy, gained promotion to head the Victoria gaol as its superintendent 13 years after arrival, in 1875, an office he occupied until his sudden death at the age of 42 in 1882.

The colonial government's desperate need for competent officials meant that none of the first batch of cadets was in fact employed as an interpreter, as was originally intended. The short duration, the apparently haphazard training in the Chinese language and the *de facto* abandonment of the plan to employ them as interpreters for three years after their language training should suggest that many did not acquire a very strong command of the Chinese language. This was, however, not generally true. Among all 85 cadets recruited between 1861 and the beginning of the Pacific War in 1941, the overwhelming majority gained a sufficient command of Cantonese, and a few, like Alfred Lister, Sir James Russell, Sir James Stewart Lockhart, Sir Reginald Johnston, Sir Cecil Clementi and Kenneth Barnett distinguished themselves in their contribution to the study of either the Chinese language or of Chinese society. Others, like Geoffrey Sayer and Walter Schofield, left their marks on scholarship by doing pioneering work in the history of Hong Kong and in the geology and archaeology of Hong Kong respectively.

The general success or failure of the scheme in training administrative officers can only be meaningfully assessed through a long-term perspective. Among the small number of young men recruited in the first 80 years, it produced three governors for Hong Kong: Sir Francis May (1912–18), Sir Cecil Clementi Smith (1925–30) and Sir Alexander Grantham (1947–57). The same group also supplied six colonial secretaries: Sir James Stewart Lockhart (1898–1902), Sir Francis May (1902–11), Norman Smith (1936–41), David MacDougall (1946–49), Claude Burgess (1958–63) and Edmund Teesdale (1963–66).[35] Beyond Hong Kong, the prewar cadets supplied the rest of the empire with seven governors or high commissioners. They were Sir Cecil Clementi Smith in the Straits Settlements, and later in Borneo and Sarawak, Sir James Stewart Lockhart in Weihaiwei, Sir Francis May in Fiji, Sir Reginald in Weihaiwei, Sir George Fletcher in Fiji, and later Trinidad, Sir Cecil Clementi in the Straits Settlements and Sir Alexander Grantham in Fiji.[36]

Those recruited after the Pacific War did less spectacularly well in career terms. This was partly because the rapid winding down of the British Empire in the 1960s meant there were few top positions available. It was also because a distinguished prewar cadet, Grantham, served as governor in Hong Kong for ten years, though a normal term was only five years. Furthermore, the appointment in 1971 of a career diplomat as governor became a general practice, for negotiations over Hong Kong's future started under Sir Murray MacLehose's decade-long tenure. With the last governor becoming a political appointment as well, no postwar-recruited cadet or admin-

Governor Sir Murray MacLehose, being briefed by Donald Luddington, Secretary for Home Affairs, at the Sau Mau Ping landslide disaster site in June 1972.

istrative officer could rise to the top. Nevertheless, the postwar recruits did provide two chief (colonial) secretaries for British Hong Kong – Sir Jack Cater (1978–81) and Anson Chan (1993–97) – and a high commissioner and later governor of the Solomon Islands in the person of Sir Donald Luddington. They also provided two chief secretaries for the Hong Kong Special Administrative Region (SAR), Anson Chan (1997–2001) and Donald Tsang (2001–2005), as well as one chief executive in Donald Tsang (2005–now). It should also be recognized that while he was not originally recruited as a Hong Kong cadet, Sir David Trench did serve as a cadet in Hong Kong for a decade before being promoted to high commissioner for the Western Pacific prior to his appointment as governor of Hong Kong (1964–71).

**Impact on colonial administration**

The deployment of the first cadets in government service effectively laid the foundation for a modern civil service based on merit in Hong Kong. The building of such a service took a long time, however, not least because of the small intake in the early years. The second batch of three cadets – Lister, James Russell and R. G. Starkey – was recruited in 1865 after the first batch had confirmed the value of the scheme. The actual increase in strength was only two because Starkey left for the commercial sector after only one year. The five cadets were reinforced in 1867 by the appointment of H. E.

Wodehouse, the last cadet to be recruited officially as a student interpreter. Recruitment was then suspended for 12 years as 'a general depression which affected a great part of the world, including the China trade' forced the Hong Kong government to adopt a policy of retrenchment.[37] It was resumed in 1879 with the appointment of Stewart Lockhart. For the rest of the nineteenth century, 14 more cadets were appointed. It meant that by the turn of the century, only a total of 21 cadets had been recruited over a period of four decades. Among them one left early, two died in office, two transferred to senior positions elsewhere in the empire, and one (Russell) changed from the executive to the judicial branch upon appointment as chief justice of Hong Kong.

The number of cadets available for duties in Hong Kong at any one time in the second half of the nineteenth century was therefore very small. The cadets' elitist status, the shortage of senior officials, and arrangements for long leaves in an era when the steamship was a fast means of transport produced two results.[38] The first was the tendency for cadets to be moved around a lot on short-term or acting appointments to fill in gaps or provide cover for offices temporarily left vacant, or asked to serve two offices concurrently. There were of course exceptions, like the appointment of Deane as head of the police for most of his career in Hong Kong. However, the general trend built up and reinforced the idea that cadets should be gifted amateurs or generalist administrators rather than specialists.

The second and closely related impact was that while the cadets were efficient and admired, frequent rotation meant that they were not always able to keep sufficiently well informed to avert abuse within their departments or among their junior officers. A spectacular demonstration of such a failing occurred when the second clerk and accountant at the Treasury systematically embezzled almost $63,000 (more than double the governor's annual salary) over a period of four years between 1888 and 1892.[39] The four cadets who served or acted as colonial treasurer in this period failed to monitor the department and his work well enough to foil this scandal or to catch him much earlier. This failure has been attributed to the short tenure each of them served, which prevented them from getting a real grip of the situation.[40]

Although the cadets were recruited young and were originally meant to be trained as interpreters, they in fact became career administrators. Unlike most senior officials in the first two decades of British Hong Kong, who had come from diverse backgrounds and were recruited because they happened to be available, all the cadets received good educations prior to recruitment. As the cadets developed their skills as career administrators they became dedicated professionals. Slowly but steadily they 'introduced routines and procedures, organized the files, and set the administrative machine into grooves, along which it ran, on the whole, smoothly'.[41] The administrative machinery they set up might have been dull and basic, for it was mainly to manage what in effect was a municipality, but it was generally run efficiently.[42] The codification or institutionalization of procedures and practices that happened after 1862 made a contrast to the more *ad hoc* basis on which the colonial administration had operated previously. Their work marked the building of a professionally and rationally organized modern administration.

In this connection, the one exception among the early cadets, Deane, made an important contribution in helping to lay the foundation for a credible police force for Hong Kong. When Deane was asked to head the police in 1867, it was still in a sorry state after two decades of failed attempts to build it into a respectable force. In the assessment of Sir Richard MacDonnell (governor, 1866–72) 'almost every member' of the police was 'eager to be bribed, and willing to connive for money at infringements of the Law, especially of the Laws against gaming' even though he thought the 'present Inspectors appear already as a body much superior to those' he found when he arrived in Hong Kong a year earlier.[43] As captain superintendent for almost a quarter of a century, Deane presided over the transformation of something that was inefficient, ineffective and utterly corrupt into a reasonably efficient police force – at least by the standards of the time within the British Empire. Deane was able to impress Governor MacDonnell sufficiently for the latter to push hard to recruit officers from police forces in Britain at considerable expense in a period of retrenchment.[44] Deane was not a miracle maker, even less infallible, but his captaincy inspired confidence that none of his predecessors did. With a small group of trained and experienced policemen from England, Deane was able to set about training and building up a modern police force. His overall impact was so positive that the police was put, almost without interruption, under the command of a cadet until 1933.[45] This practice only ended when a professional policeman, T. H. King, the first police probationer or specialist cadet for the police service recruited in 1904, proved ready to take over running the force.[46]

The introduction of Cantonese speaking senior officials in the cadets also rectified one of the key institutional inadequacies that inspired Governor Robinson to introduce the scheme in the first place. It was the lack of capacity of senior officials to communicate with local Chinese and for the government not to be held hostage to the only senior official who could speak the Chinese language. Smith's appointment to act as registrar general in 1862 marked the beginning of a new development. From this time onwards, the government could rely on a professional administrator whose integrity was not in doubt to serve as its main channel of communication with the Chinese community. Even given the slow increase in the number of cadets, by the late 1870s there were 'very few departments where there is not someone who can read a Chinese petition for himself and efficiently check the oral interpretation of the native clerks acting as interpreter'.[47] This implied a sea change in the colonial administration's ability to communicate with its Chinese population.

The successful introduction of a competitive examination as the basis for recruiting civil servants on a fast track for senior offices had another long-term impact. It created a precedent and provided an established record to show that such a principle worked well, and thus removed resistance to applying such a principle to civil service recruitment generally. Against such a background, in 1877 Governor Sir Arthur Kennedy introduced in this faraway imperial outpost a general rule that all civil service appointments (except menial workers) should be made on the basis of competitive examination, merely seven years after Britain accepted such an idea as a general policy.[48]

# Chapter 3
# BENEVOLENT PATERNALISM

The introduction of cadets eventually created in Hong Kong a modern British bureaucratic elite that appeared to share some elements of the Chinese mandarin built on the basis of the imperial examination system and Confucian teachings. The idea of a *fumuguan*, or father and mother official, who would treat the people like his own children is inherent in the idea of what a good official should be like in the Chinese political tradition. In principle, he is expected to look after the welfare of the people in a paternalistic way while they enjoy and appreciate the benefits of such benevolence by getting on with their lives, upholding peace and order, and creating prosperity. In other words, county magistrates in imperial China were tasked to provide good governance at the basic level of the imperial administration, in accordance with what was probably the most sophisticated concept for good governance in the pre-modern world.

When the cadet scheme was introduced, the British had not intended the cadets to mimic Confucian scholar officials and to import ideas of governance from China. Indeed, the cadet scheme was one of the earlier experiments that laid the foundation of a modern civil service in the British Empire. In Hong Kong, as in Britain and elsewhere in the empire, the modern British civil service that emerged after the latter part of the nineteenth century gradually developed seven common characteristics. These were as follows: impartiality, integrity, objectivity, selection and promotion on merit, accountability through ministers to parliament, a sense of public service, and a commitment to the public interest.[1]

It should, however, be recognized that most of these ideas in fact have parallels in the traditional Chinese concept of good governance.

By the Qing period (1644–1912), Chinese officials were supposed to be recruited from among Confucian gentlemen of high integrity, and were expected to behave impartially through the rule of avoidance, by which officials were not normally allowed to serve in their home county or province. Most were competitively selected through the imperial civil service examination and were held accountable to the emperor by government censors. As Confucian gentlemen they were expected to uphold the public interest in order to promote the common good in the realm.

Where the Qing system failed was primarily in two areas. The first was the reservation of a disproportionate number of senior civil and military offices to the Manchus and the deliberate duplication of top level administrative offices, so much so that every ministry would be headed by a Manchu as well as a Han Chinese minister, and all deputy ministerial positions were also duplicated on an ethnic basis. The desire of the Manchu monarchy to secure its control over the majority Han population thus systematically reduced the effectiveness and efficiency of the bureaucratic structure.[2] The other failing rested in the government doing too little to minimize corruption, and its lack of sufficient institutional checks and balances to put a stop to officials abusing their authority. Indeed, the long-established habit whereby officials, including county magistrates, would fund official expenditure from irregular or customary charges, known as *lougui* (the ugly practice), encouraged systemic corruption.[3] This failure of the Chinese system worsened from the 1840s onwards when financial stringency, in an era of widespread rebellions and foreign encroachment, forced the government to increase substantially the sale of official ranks and even positions.[4] This meant that an increasing percentage of officials, including county magistrates, was not being recruited on the basis of the imperial examination or merit. Together they gravely undermined the ideal of the traditional Chinese civil service.

In nineteenth-century Hong Kong cadets were appointed to serve British interests, which required rectifying the institutional inadequacies in the colonial administration. Improving the quality of governance and the channels of communication between the colonial administration and the local Chinese were as much in the interest of the British as in that of the local community. Whatever the original intentions of the founders of the scheme, once in government service, the cadets took on their official duties as they saw fit. They were not concerned with either the Chinese ideal of governance or what would later become basic concepts underpinning the modern British civil service. They were mainly interested in how best to discharge their official responsibilities efficiently and effectively. In the context of colonial Hong Kong in this period, good governance implied little more than maintaining the government's integrity and ability to devise and implement policies that secured government revenue, as well as maintaining good order, social stability and economic prosperity.

With their ability to communicate with local Chinese, cadets were often deployed at the front line in the colonial government's dealings with the Chinese community. In time, as their relationship with the Chinese community developed and as Hong Kong grew and expanded, cadets acquired their own ethos. They could not but be products of their upbringing and did what they thought appropriate in the circumstances and in the spirit of the age, be they the good and progressive or bad and ugly practices of the time. This included putting heavy emphasis on a patronizing but helpful attitude when dealing with the Chinese subjects of this British colony. Even though the origins of this benevolent paternalism should be traced more to Victorian imperialism and the British public school education than to any Chinese influence, its manifestation in a British enclave at the edge of the Chinese Empire cannot but raise the question whether their behaviour was inspired by the idea of the Chinese *fumuguan*.

### Learning about the Chinese

Cadets generally started to learn about the Chinese seriously only after they arrived in the colony. The beginning point was to acquire a reasonable command of the language, with more emphasis at first being put on learning the written than the spoken language. This was later reversed and more stress was laid on the ability to communicate orally than on gaining a command of the written language, which was very difficult to achieve within two years.[5] The earliest cadets were tutored personally by native Chinese speakers in Hong Kong. When the recruitment of cadets was resumed in 1879, after it was held in abeyance for a decade, the new recruit Stewart Lockhart was given nine months of Chinese language instruction at King's College in London before being sent to Hong Kong. From there he moved on to Canton for further instruction in the Chinese language.[6] A new experiment was introduced in the earlier part of the 1880s for sending new cadets to Beijing for their language training.[7] This, too, was quickly abandoned because the spoken Chinese that cadets needed to acquire was not Mandarin or standard Chinese but Cantonese, the lingua franca of the overwhelming majority of the local residents in Hong Kong.

From the late-1880s onwards, a new practice was adopted by which newly recruited cadets were sent to Canton for language training for two years. There they were usually housed in properties owned by the British consulate general, which they shared with British cadets for Malaya and the Straits Settlements. They would usually stay in Canton for two years where they received instruction individually from among half a dozen local Chinese teachers and were examined regularly.[8] This practice continued until Canton fell under Japanese occupation in 1938. It was meant to be revived after the end of the Pacific War, but the arrangement fell by the wayside after 1945, despite an attempt to revive it. Manpower shortages meant that new recruits could not be spared for two years' full-time language training in Canton.[9] Arrangements were made for them to receive instruction in Chinese in Hong Kong. Any prospect of restoring the programme in Canton ended when it came under communist rule in October 1949.

If they passed their half yearly language examinations, the colonial government in Hong Kong did not interfere in the lives of cadets on probation. In Canton they were given a free hand to enjoy themselves and engage in any respectable interest they wished to pursue.[10] This marked a departure from Governor Robinson's original conception because it meant that new cadets could not benefit from having the governor as their mentor during their years as probationers.

How much individual cadets learnt about Chinese society and how well they mastered the language during their two years in Canton varied. In terms of language training, one of the most successful of all cadets and an intake of 1922, Alexander Grantham, had put things in perspective. He 'worked hard' but considered himself 'average in the matter of languages'. After he passed his examinations, he found he could 'do no more than make myself understood when shopping, read the easiest parts of a Chinese newspaper and write a simple letter very ungrammatically'.[11] This was a competence he had failed to retain by the time he rose to become governor after a gap of 12 years serving outside Hong Kong. Grantham was close to the norm.

There were cadets who devoted themselves to learning the language and culture and to understanding the Chinese, and they achieved substantially more. Stewart Lockhart, the sole recruit of 1879, developed a close relationship with his teacher in Canton and a lifelong interest in the teachings of Confucius and Mencius. He was the first cadet to have taken on board the idea of a *fumuguan* seriously.[12] Another of the more distinguished cadets, Cecil Clementi, who joined in 1899, was comfortable making public speeches in Cantonese when he served as governor a quarter of a century later, after a gap of 12 years of service outside Hong Kong. Indeed, his Chinese was sufficiently good for Lu Xun, a renowned Chinese writer of the Republican period (1912–49), to have mistaken one of his speeches that appeared in a Hong Kong Chinese language newspaper for an awkwardly written piece by a former official of the imperial dynasty.[13]

During their probationary or language training years in Canton, some cadets travelled to different parts of China to improve their knowledge of the language and of Chinese customs and society. Others preferred to spend most of their free time fraternizing with fellow cadets and other Britons in the foreigners' compound in Shamian. Most only began to learn seriously about the local Chinese after they started working in the colonial government.

Before the colony was extended to include the New Territories in 1898, Hong Kong was a growing municipality built around the port city of Victoria, with only a few villages and rural areas within its jurisdiction. The only department in which cadets needed to deal with the Chinese using the Chinese language on a daily basis was the registrar general's office. The other offices in which post holders routinely benefited from knowing the Chinese language were the magistracies, for they could check the interpretation rendered in court. In most other functional departments, like sanitation, police, prison and land, there were few occasions when cadets posted there would need to use the Chinese language on a regular basis. This was quite apart from it being highly desirable for these departments to have a senior officer with a good grasp of the Chinese language.

A majority of the cadets were deployed to perform managerial or general administrative tasks quickly after they passed their language examination. As such they were more involved with drafting papers, commenting on them in minutes, and managing their junior colleagues. As the nineteenth century progressed, the colonial administration also recruited from local schools a steadily rising number of junior Chinese officers or clerks who could speak English. Thus, by the earlier half of the twentieth century, those cadets who did not serve for any period of time in the registrar general's office or as magistrates had few opportunities or incentives to improve their language ability. Increasingly, they became professional administrators with an understanding of the language and customs rather than China specialists who were also professional administrators.

The acquisition of the New Territories imposed a significant new requirement in the manpower provided by the cadets. This expansion meant taking on territories ten times the size of the colony at the time. It also involved taking on 100,000 Chinese living in long-established rural communities, villages and market towns on the mainland. To put this in perspective, the size of the additional population should be compared with that of the colony just prior to this extension in 1898, which was merely 254,400.[14]

In the first decade of the New Territories under British rule, the work associated with its incorporation into the colony required the regular deployment of three cadets. Although their titles changed on several occasions they effectively functioned as district officers. After the initial work had been completed, two cadets shared the jurisdiction over the New Territories. District Officer North administered most of the mainland south of the new Sino–British border. District Officer South had the task of administering the southern part of the mainland but north of the Kowloon hills and the many islands acquired as part of the New Territories.[15] This arrangement essentially remained until the earlier part of the postwar period.[16]

In a very important sense, the roles of cadets working as district officers bore a closer resemblance to the work of district officers elsewhere in the British Empire than to that of cadets working in the Colonial Secretariat in the city of Victoria, as Hong Kong's capital was known. As district officers in the New Territories, cadets were put 'in charge of police and the general administration of their districts' and were also required to function as 'police magistrates for their districts' with 'civil jurisdiction to try small debt cases not exceeding $200'.[17] Within the areas of their own jurisdictions, from the perspective of the local population, district officers were to all intents and purposes the personification of the colonial government.

In this sense, they also resembled the county magistrates of imperial China, the archetypal *fumuguan*. In the Qing period a magistrate was given jurisdiction for a region with 'several tens of thousand to several hundred thousand households'.[18] He was charged with 'undertaking religious and other ritual responsibilities, dispensing justice, maintaining order, sponsoring public works, patronizing local scholarship, and all the while collecting taxes for the state'.[19] He also 'had charge of the postal service, salt administration, *pao-chia*, police ... granaries, social welfare' and was required 'to defend the city in an uprising or a foreign invasion'.[20] Given that the Qing dynasty was an alien government headed by a Manchurian emperor, and the rule of avoidance meant that county magistrates often did not speak or understand the local vernacular, the British takeover of the New Territories involved little more than swapping one set of alien rulers for another. It did not cause major upheavals to life there.[21]

At first the residents of the New Territories merely needed to accept the British district officers in terms not fundamentally different from the inevitably remote Chinese county magistrate before the lease of 1898. British thinking at the time was summed up by Stewart Lockhart, who was responsible for putting into effect the takeover of the New Territories. He urged that 'in the future government of the newly leased area, the organization at present in existence should be as far as possible utilized.'[22] Since it was sensible for cadets posted to the New Territories as district officers to deal with the locals in terms the latter would understand easily, elements of the Chinese mandarin tradition were borrowed where they would facilitate their work, provided such practices were not repugnant to British values.

Upholding this British approach in practice was confirmed by the senior district officer who submitted the first administrative report on the New Territories in 1912. He proudly stated: 'A visitor to the Territory of 1899, upon returning in 1912, would find changes to remark in the outward appearance of the country, but he would not find the life or character of its inhabitants greatly altered.'[23]

### Life and work as a cadet
Cadets were individuals who lived on their own terms. It would be misleading to give a general description of how they as a whole lived and worked in the nineteenth century. However, the cases of well-

Sir James Stewart Lockhart.

known individuals do provide pointers to illustrate how some of them had settled into their work, chosen to build their careers, discharged their official responsibilities and lived their life in Hong Kong in the heyday of the British Empire. Some were more colourful figures who left bigger marks than others.

Among the better known and most able of the nineteenth-century cadets was James Stewart Lockhart. As he did not rise to become governor in Hong Kong, which would have put him in a position uniquely different from that enjoyed by other cadets, his entire career in Hong Kong can be used to illustrate the work and life of a cadet. He has also been chosen because he happened to have left a sufficiently long written record of his life and work to be reconstructed.[24] Readers should therefore bear in mind that his case merely highlights the attitude, work pattern and life-style of one of the more able cadets who was particularly devoted to understanding the Chinese.

The picture presented below is not meant to represent the average cadet who, by definition, could not have scaled in career terms the dazzling heights that Stewart Lockhart achieved. Indeed, there was no average cadet except in terms of career progression, for everyone who survived to and stayed on until retirement before 1941 would have at some stage served as the head of a department, whether in a substantive or an acting capacity. This happened because the number of government departments that required a cadet to serve as its head exceeded the number of available cadets at any one time.[25] This meant that even the weaker performers, or a cadet who never gained promotion to become a Class 1 Cadet, after this promotional grade was introduced in the twentieth century, would still have acted as a head of department before retirement. More generally, cadets were their own men[26] and most quickly gained sufficient standing within the bureaucracy to enjoy enough scope to take initiatives within the bounds of established procedures – except for the earliest recruits who had few conventions to follow and were responsible for setting them.

Stewart Lockhart was born into a comfortably well-off family with strong Jacobite associations in the Scottish highlands in 1858.[27] He was educated at King William's College on the Isle of Man and at George Watson's College in Edinburgh before attending Edinburgh University. He applied to join the Colonial Office by examination for service in either Hong Kong or Ceylon in 1878 after failing twice to gain admission to the more prestigious Indian Civil Service.[28] He arrived in Hong Kong in 1879 after learning basic Chinese at King's College in London, and was quickly sent to Canton to learn the Chinese language by immersion. His spell in London was unusual because cadets were usually sent to Hong Kong immediately after being recruited, at least until the creation of a unified colonial administrative service in 1932 when new intakes attended a one-year colonial service course before being posted overseas.

Although he was recalled to perform specific short-term duties in the absence of others while learning Chinese, Stewart Lockhart was able to learn Cantonese, pass the requisite test and gain recognition as a passed cadet in August 1882. Once he had qualified for a substantive appointment in the colonial government, he followed the path of earlier cadets and did not serve as a government interpreter as it was originally intended when the scheme was conceived. Instead, he served in different capacities in rapid succession, as the administration was short of cadets.

His first appointment was chief clerk at the colonial secretary's office, a position that required him to discharge the duties of the clerk of councils as well. After two months he was moved to the registrar general's office, where his Chinese language ability was in demand. Within six months he was made superintendent of opium revenue. He returned in August 1883 to the Colonial Secretariat to take on the newly created post of assistant colonial secretary, an office he held in conjunction with that of the assistant auditor-general. Whether intended or not, the rapid rotation from one office to another gave him good exposure to different aspects of the colonial administration. Since cadets were meant to be put on a fast track for promotion to senior offices as generalist administrators after only a few years of service, this was good preparation for higher office later.[29]

A breakthrough in career terms followed quickly when Stewart Lockhart was deployed to act as registrar general when the substantive holder of this senior office Frederick Stewart went on leave in the summer of 1884. This acting appointment in a senior capacity coincided with the outbreak of a strike against working on visiting French warships that culminated in three days of riots in the course of the Sino–French War (1884–85). This war was fought as the Chinese Empire attempted to defend its suzerainty over Indo-China, which was being colonized by the French.

Stewart Lockhart was put to the test as 'Chinese artisans, coolies, and boatmen refused all offers of pay to do any work whatsoever for the French ships'.[30] Although the month-long boycott did result in riots in October, which reflected heavy-handed handling of the situation by the colonial authorities, this whole incident was also caused by incitement and inducement by the Chinese authorities in Canton.[31] As a young cadet of only 26, Stewart Lockhart acquitted himself well in the eyes of the administration by limiting the damage done to the relationship between the colonial government and the Chinese working men.[32] This positive assessment was no doubt affected by Governor Sir George Bowen's misguided view or exaggerated assessment that this incident represented the outbreak of 'popular nationalism' among the local Chinese.[33]

Stewart Lockhart's sterling record, his by then superb command of the Chinese language and the sheer shortage of able officials marked him out for promotion on the fast track.[34] When Frederick Stewart, the registrar general, was appointed colonial secretary in 1887, Stewart Lockhart was promoted to fill his office. Not yet 30 years old and a passed cadet for only four years, Stewart Lockhart was given the reins of one of the most important departments in the colonial administration. As registrar general he was also officially protector of the Chinese. Given that the expatriate and local Chinese communities lived largely separate though parallel existences in the nineteenth century, the registrar general in effect functioned as the 'Colonial Secretary' for the Chinese community. In the nineteenth and first half of the twentieth century the colonial secretary ran the secretariat and dealt mainly with the English-speaking community. The registrar general was the principal and most senior regular link between the government and expatriate community on the one hand and the Chinese community on the other. While it was his duty to ensure that the Chinese community understood and respected the colonial laws, he was also responsible for 'protecting' the Chinese. On a daily basis he had to 'see that Chinese customs and traditions were respected at all times and that, whenever possible, the ordinances issued by the Government did not upset or contravene the Chinese moral code'.[35]

In his capacity as registrar general, an office he kept until the middle of 1899, even after he became colonial secretary in 1895 and took on the additional role as special commissioner for the incorporation of the New Territories into the colony in 1898, Stewart Lockhart came into his element. Given charge of the Chinese community, he combined his passion for studying the Chinese with working with the Chinese community in Hong Kong. In the bureaucratic realm he worked closely with the local community leaders. In his private life he devoted himself to scholarship on China.

As he had by then acquired a good command of the Chinese language, he studied Chinese folklore and published an article on the subject.[36] His private study further resulted in the publication of two serious scholarly works, *A Manual of Chinese Quotations* (first edition 1893), and *The Currency of the Farther East* (1895). In combining his professional career as a colonial administrator with his passion for studying China, Stewart Lockhart had chosen to work and live as a cadet in a particular direction. It was one that a few of his fellow cadets shared, the most notable among those who joined before 1941 being Cecil Clementi and Kenneth Barnett.

Stewart Lockhart's rapid and early promotion to the most senior office responsible for the Chinese community enabled him to go beyond what colonial or expatriate society would customarily tolerate in terms of socializing with the local Chinese. The spirit of the time was marked by a strong racial undertone. Not only were members of the local Chinese elite not admitted to the Hong Kong Club, even a Caucasian like Frederick Sassoon, a wealthy merchant and member of the Legislative Council, was denied membership because of his Bombay Jewish origins. Stewart Lockhart departed from the conventional practice of his time in that he entertained his Chinese friends, who were members of the local elite, at his own house in addition to his British and European friends. Among those known to have been regular visitors to his home were Wei Yuk,

Robert Hotung, Mok Man Cheung, as well as members of the Sassoon family and of the Keswick family of the princely *hong* Jardine Matheson.[37]

It was during his time as registrar general that Stewart Lockhart got married and raised a family. His bride, Edith Louise Rider, had been born and brought up in Hong Kong. The second daughter of Alfred Hancock, a successful bullion broker and long-time resident of the exclusive district of the Peak, she met Stewart Lockhart when her family socialized with him as part of the small Hong Kong society.[38] A rising star in the colonial administration Stewart Lockhart was an attractive prospect for a young local woman from a financially secure background. Although Edith did not share his scholarly passion for things Chinese, she revelled in playing the role of a charming hostess of a senior colonial official.

The most able of registrar generals in the nineteenth century, Stewart Lockhart substantially strengthened this office as the link between the government and the local Chinese community. His knowledge of and sympathy towards the Chinese enabled him to gain the confidence of the latter even 'with matters connected with Chinese family morals and business ethics'.[39] It was during his long tenure that the Chinese community started to look beyond their own local leaders, such as directors of the Tung Wah Hospital, to the registrar general for guidance in 'matters concerning missing wives, children, and young girls, even domestic and business disputes'.[40] Always cool, rational and constructive, Stewart Lockhart entrenched the two most important institutions for the Chinese community in urban Hong Kong. They were the Tung Wah Hospital and the District Watch Committee.

Although Tung Wah came into existence in 1872 and soon took on the role of a medium between the local Chinese community and the government,[41] it was Stewart Lockhart who 'helped to reorganize the Tung Wah Hospital to save it from abolition'.[42] This happened when Hong Kong suffered from the bubonic plague, which spread to local Chinese who had been infected by people travelling to the colony from Canton in 1895.[43] Caught up between what the local Chinese saw as draconian preventive measures imposed by the colonial administration and what the government and expatriates saw as irresponsible behaviour by the Chinese, the Tung Wah Hospital came under threat.[44] It became the focus of hostility from all sides who

James Stewart Lockhart with directors of Tung Wah and Po Leung Kuk after the opening of a new hospital (1900). Standing on Stewart Lockhart's right was Ho Kai.

blamed it for not delivering what each saw as essential from their own particular perspectives.

As registrar general Stewart Lockhart was able to act as a bridge between the Tung Wah board of directors and Governor Sir William Robinson who found each other intransigent and uncooperative. Above all, he succeeded in fending off the vociferous attack that Legislative Councillor T. H. Whitehead launched against it while a member of a commission to enquire into the work of the Tung Wah Hospital after the plague.[45] Stewart Lockhart's success in preventing a complete rupture of relations between the government and Tung Wah and in neutralizing Whitehead's attack saved the Tung Wah Hospital as a key institutional link between the colonial administration and the local Chinese community.

In the 1890s Stewart Lockhart also significantly reformed and strengthened another major institutional link between the government and the local Chinese, the District Watch Committee. Required to work with the registrar general this committee of prominent local Chinese was set up to oversee the District Watch Force, which was created in 1866.

It came into existence because local Chinese merchants were

frustrated by the failure of what in those days were the corrupt and ineffective colonial police. With the blessings of the colonial administration, they organized a local force of Cantonese speaking Chinese constables, recruited, controlled and paid for by themselves for the protection of their businesses, properties and persons.[46] Until its dissolution in the early postwar period it was a special police force for the Chinese community that ran parallel with the colonial police. As it was put under the registrar general's control it also became his main instrument for dealing with the local Chinese on a daily basis. Its constables, called district watchmen, generally served as runners for the registrar general, police guards, detectives and census enumerators. They also traced runaway girls and intercepted young women brought into Hong Kong for prostitution while its senior officers mediated local disputes within the Chinese community.[47]

What Stewart Lockhart did was to treat the District Watch Committee as the colonial government's highest advisory body on the Chinese community. This increased the prestige of being a member of the committee and turned it into a further progression in social standing from directorships of Tung Wah among the local Chinese.[48] By so doing, he entrenched the District Watch Committee as a valuable link between the colonial administration and the local Chinese.

Stewart Lockhart again proved his worth and left his mark when he was called to give advice on and then oversee the incorporation of the New Territories after the British government decided to lease it from China in 1898.[49] At first he lobbied for himself to be appointed British resident for this new dependency of Hong Kong. He proposed the head of the administration there should be styled 'a Commissioner, subordinate to the Governor of Hong Kong, but in all other respects independent'.[50] His wish was not granted because it went against Secretary of State Joseph Chamberlain's decision that the New Territories should be treated as 'an integral part of the Colony of Hong Kong'.[51]

Stewart Lockhart nevertheless devoted himself to setting up a government that would suit the settled rural character of this new acquisition and the limited human resources the colonial administration could deploy for its governance. This demanded a different approach from that practised by the colonial administration in Victoria. It was in the New Territories that Stewart Lockhart combined the experience of British district officers elsewhere in the

British Empire with the Chinese concept of *fumuguan* in governance. He borrowed in particular from the experience his colleagues gained in Ceylon on the one hand, and made the most of the existing structure of authority in the local communities in the New Territories on the other.[52]

In this endeavour Stewart Lockhart had a free hand because the government was administered not by a career colonial administrator but by Wilsone Black, the general officer commanding the troops in Hong Kong, who filled in between Sir William Robinson's handover of the governorship to Sir Henry Blake. The end product was a hybrid. It was one that embodied the British approach to governance and retained many existing Chinese practices. The objective was to uphold British standards and yet minimize the impact this transfer of power and sovereignty would have on the local people. After Stewart Lockhart finished establishing the administration in the New Territories:

> In the villages, elders continued to hold sway. However, instead of a Chinese Magistrate ruling over them, British District Officers ... now fulfilled that function. The only additional layer of power which immediately affected the populace was the police force, stationed at strategic points throughout the territory to maintain law and order. One suspects that, after the initial disturbances in April, the inhabitants of the New Territories were aware of little noticeable changes in their lives following the assumption of British rule.[53]

In the long term, the hybrid nature of his creation brought the local people tangible benefits in terms of governance. The most notable was the elimination of the key bane of the traditional Chinese approach to local government, namely the systemic corruption inherent in inadequate funding of the magistrate's office known as the ugly practice. Fully aware of this problem, Stewart Lockhart was determined to remove this ill while he preserved local institutions and practices.[54] The British administration in the New Territories was put on a sound financial footing from the beginning and this removed any need for the ugly practice to be tolerated, even though corruption at the local level was not eliminated.

The system of governance in the New Territories ended up providing the local people with honest experimental implementation of the Chinese concept of the *fumuguan*, albeit by British rather than Chinese officials. This achievement can justifiably be attributed to Stewart Lockhart because a commissioner unfamiliar with Chinese history would have been less sensitive to Chinese customs. The system of administration in the New Territories survived long after Stewart Lockhart moved on and, indeed, into the postwar period.

As an ambitious man frustrated by the lack of further promotion after his career reached a plateau at the level of colonial secretary in Hong Kong, Stewart Lockhart looked beyond Hong Kong after he had laid the foundation of the New Territories administration. Instead of waiting for an opportunity for promotion to a governorship elsewhere, he actively prepared and nominated himself as a candidate to take charge of the leased territory of Weihaiwei in the Shandong province of China.[55] Weihaiwei was leased at about the same time as the New Territories was secured, for parallel imperial concerns.[56] Since it was taken to balance the Russian acquisition of the southern Manchurian seaports of Lushun and Dalian, Weihaiwei was put under military administration after its lease. Stewart Lockhart saw that the time for its transfer to civil rule was getting near and offered himself as its first civilian commissioner. He was duly appointed and left Hong Kong to take up this new office in 1902.

In his 23 years of service in Hong Kong, Stewart Lockhart demonstrated how much scope there was for a particularly able cadet to make an impact on the colonial administration in the nineteenth century. He was in an important sense a transitional figure among the earlier cadets. During his time there was still scope for some of the more senior and able cadets to leave their mark on the offices they held. By and large the scope for individual cadets to do so in a similar way ended after his time.

By the start of the twentieth century, the colonial administration in Hong Kong had already fully settled into a set of established routines, procedures and even codes of conduct among senior officials. The opportunity for a senior administrator to leave his mark as presented by the acquisition of the New Territories was one that did not come up again until after the Pacific War. Even then it happened only during the period of the British military administration (1945–46), when the civil administration was in the hands of a particularly open minded, pragmatic and sensible cadet, Brigadier

David MacDougall, who served as chief civil affairs officer under Rear Admiral Cecil Harcourt.

Stewart Lockhart's most remarkable impact on the administration was how he enhanced the registrar general's office. Unlike the special commissioner post created for him in the New Territories, this was one of the oldest established senior positions in the colonial administration. He was able to make an impact on it partly because his knowledge of the Chinese and great rapport with the leaders of the Chinese community put him in a position to see how this office could function more effectively. Holding the office of colonial secretary concurrently and for three years after he gave up the registrar general post also gave him leave and allowed him to preserve his mark on the office of registrar general. As colonial secretary, Stewart Lockhart was head of the civil service in Hong Kong and this made it difficult if not impossible to reverse or abandon the enhanced role of the registrar general he himself had initiated. As Hong Kong entered the twentieth century, institutionalization in the civil service meant that established procedures increasingly limited the scope for individual officials, including cadets, to make the kind of impact on an office that Stewart Lockhart was able to do.

**The making of an elite**
Despite their small numbers cadets quickly emerged as the elite of the colonial administration. By the 1880s they were already sufficiently well established to be given preference in filling a wide range of senior offices within the administration. These included the offices of assistant colonial secretary, chief clerk at the secretariat, treasurer, clerk of councils, postmaster general, assistant postmaster general, registrar general, first clerk at the registrar general's office, captain superintendent of police, deputy registrars of the supreme court, police magistrates, inspector of schools, and superintendent of the gaol.[57] The only top level office to which cadets were eligible but not given a preference for appointment was that of colonial secretary. This was because it was, as a general principle, deemed 'desirable that the Colonial Secretary should be selected from among able and experienced members of the Civil Service in other Colonies'.[58] This was seen as particularly relevant in a small colony like Hong Kong, for it was important for such a high office to be filled by someone 'unconnected with any of the parties and cliques' that might exist

locally.[59] The career of Stewart Lockhart has, however, illustrated that this consideration did not stop him, the seventh cadet, from filling this office before the turn of the century. Nor did this principle handicap Francis Henry May, an intake of 1881, from succeeding him as colonial secretary from 1902 to 1910. In career terms May was even more successful because he returned to Hong Kong in 1912 as governor – the first cadet to do so.

The increasing institutionalization of the colonial administration as Hong Kong entered the twentieth century in fact entrenched the cadets' elite status. Having been recruited and promoted on the basis of merit they formed a meritocracy and occupied a special place in the administration as generalists who were also professional administrators with a reputation for competence.

The specialists, who were recruited in steadily rising numbers in the twentieth century, did not challenge their place in the government. The professional engineers, lawyers, medical personnel, teachers and policemen who joined the colonial administration were employed as specialist officers in positions that required their specialist knowledge. They were not professional administrators with wide exposure to different aspects of work in the colonial administration. That they too were recruited and promoted on the basis of merit was not enough to enable them to challenge the elite status of the cadets.

Indeed, as cadets were deployed to fill in different offices as and when needed from the start of their bureaucratic careers, they built up a reputation as able officials who had the capacity to hold down a large variety of senior posts with little or no prior training. This gave them an advantage over specialist officers in the government's service with respect to promotion as heads of departments. Consequently, cadets even headed specialist departments like education, the post office and police, though in the case of the police only up to the 1930s.[60]

With the cadets an identifiable group of officials groomed for high office, they were well placed to form an elite within the colonial administration. A corollary of this development was the emergence of an *esprit de corps*. Cadets formed such a close-knit group that even though, strictly speaking, there never was such a thing as a cadet service of Hong Kong, to all intents and purposes they behaved as if there were one.

The Colonial Office's attempt at the turn of the century to combine the cadetships of Hong Kong, the Straits Settlements and the Federated Malay States did not change this. Although they had by then become Eastern cadets 'liable to be transferred at any time from one [Eastern Colony] to another, at the discretion of the Secretary of State, without being given compensation for any special local privileges or allowances', they remained first and foremost Hong Kong cadets.[61] This situation continued even after the creation of a unified colonial administrative service in 1932, to which Hong Kong cadets were given membership.[62] Hong Kong cadets were so sure they were the best in the government service that there were hardly any senior offices, including non-administrative ones like the office of chief justice and of attorney general, they did not think they could fill competently.[63]

The assertiveness of the cadets in expanding their reach within the colonial government was in an important sense a manifestation of the *esprit de corps*. The same is true of the cadets' occasional efforts to ensure a good promotion prospect for themselves by petitioning the secretary of state that they had 'a preferential claim' to senior offices that became vacant to officers transferred from outside Hong Kong.[64] As with their claim to be given preference for appointment to senior legal and judicial offices, the Colonial Office rejected this preferential claim.[65] Notwithstanding the Colonial Office's robust rebuttal the cadets never gave up their efforts to carve out a special position for themselves in the Hong Kong government.

Their efforts reflected their self-image. The high esteem with which they held themselves provoked members of the Colonial Office to take swipes at them occasionally, remarking for example that the Hong Kong cadets were 'capable of advancing "claims" to act for the Almighty'.[66] If their behaviour could be seen as arrogant and pompous, it also reflected their confidence as individual officers and their collective pride as Hong Kong cadets. This strong sense of *esprit de corps* asserting themselves as the elite was in itself highly conducive to sustaining such a status within the colonial administration.

The assertiveness of cadets at the beginning of the twentieth century in seeking to ensure rapid promotion was also a reflection of how rapidly advancement had come to their predecessors or senior colleagues. By the calculation of the Colonial Office, at the turn of the century Hong Kong cadets reached top posts much faster than their colleagues in Ceylon or the Straits Settlements. In the case of appointment to the office of colonial treasurer, it took a Hong Kong cadet 11 years, whereas it took 27 years for his colleague in Ceylon and 22 years in the Straits Settlements.[67] As to the top office in the administration, a high flying Hong Kong cadet took 11 years to rise to the office of colonial secretary.[68] His opposite number in Ceylon had to put in 19 years of service while that for the Straits Settlements had to serve 16 years. It should be noted that neither of the latter were cadets of their respective colonies.

In their efforts to improve their career prospects, the younger or junior Hong Kong cadets enjoyed the support and patronage of their senior colleagues who had reached the top. Their turn of the century appeal was, for example, strongly endorsed by Colonial Secretary Francis May.[69] Likewise, another effort a decade later was, from the perspective of the Colonial Office, pushed excessively hard because Hong Kong's colonial secretary at the time, Cecil Clementi, was another cadet.[70] The remarkable career trajectory of the early Hong Kong cadets and the patronage of senior colleagues therefore encouraged younger recruits to adopt a go getting attitude, which, in turn, reinforced their *esprit de corps*.

The entrenchment of cadets as the elite in the Hong Kong government paralleled developments elsewhere in what were known within the British Empire as the Eastern colonies. The more important of them included Ceylon, the Straits Settlements and Malaya, in addition to Hong Kong.

At the turn of the century, a review of the administrative officers in the dependent empire as a whole revealed how far the Eastern cadets had gone in building a reputation for themselves. It started with an instruction from Secretary of State for the Colonies Joseph Chamberlain to review recruitment of administrators for all colonial territories, including the self-governing settlement colonies, with a view to assess the prospect of integrating them into a common 'Colonial Service'.[71] It should be noted that in the nomenclature of British imperial administration in the late Victorian era India was an empire distinct from the rest of the colonial empire. The Indian Civil Service was also a separate and distinct one. Neither came under the jurisdiction of the Colonial Office or the secretary of state for the colonies. The diversities in the rest of the British Empire and the difficulties involved in creating a common service were so great that a unified service could not in fact come about for another three decades, despite Chamberlain's advocacy. Nevertheless, the unpublished report presented by parliamentary under-secretary Lord Selborne highlighted that the Eastern cadets, who numbered about 100, already enjoyed an elite status among the 434 higher colonial administrators in the empire.[72]

While there was a wish that they would provide a pool of high quality administrators for appointment as colonial governors elsewhere, they were deemed 'not generally available'. It was because the Eastern cadet services 'offered within themselves so attractive a career that it would ordinarily have required more inducement than the smaller administrations [or poorer African colonies] could offer to tempt their members away.'[73]

Although Chamberlain's attempt to create a unified colonial administrative service did not materialize, the need for the British Empire to have a better system to recruit, deploy, manage and remunerate its colonial administrators did not disappear. Indeed, with new demands created by modernity and by the First World War, the need to modernize the way the Colonial Office managed the empire through colonial administrators became more acute. A new review was commissioned in April 1929. The head of the home civil service Sir Warren Fisher led a committee and spent a year studying the issues before he made a full report. It advocated the creation of a single colonial service.[74]

The Fisher Committee recognized that the 'Colonial empire has become a problem' as 'the duties of government have been increased in number and immeasurably increased in complexity'. It saw Britain as responsible for establishing 'a regime which seeks to preserve what is best in the traditional native culture, rather than to provide a cleared ground for the establishment of a ready-made alien polity'. It was a demand that required 'a high degree of knowledge and understanding on the part of the administrators'.[75] This perceived need for good governance and acceptance of a moral responsibility to the imperial subjects meant professional administrators with proven records and wide exposure were highly valued. They happened to be the qualities experienced cadets, who were appointed and promoted on the basis of examination and performance and not patronage, had to offer.

Indeed, when Britain was finally ready in 1932 to introduce a unified colonial administrative service, it was built on the findings and recommendations of the Fisher Committee. It was based on the idea of a meritocracy inherent in the Eastern cadetships even though it also abolished recruitment by examination for Hong Kong and other Eastern cadets, who had become members of the new colonial administrative service. In place of the old examination was to be 'a single method of entry: selection by the Secretary of State, on the advice of the Colonial Service Appointments Board'.[76] This was to apply to all administrative officers across the dependent empire, under which all were liable to be transferred for service in another colony, provided the terms of service and value of the work involved would not be diminished as a result.

The introduction of the colonial administrative service should be seen as a superimposition of a common identity to colonial administrators in the dependent empire. It did not involve or lead to the end of Hong Kong cadets. Henceforth, administrative officers for Hong Kong were recruited on the new basis, in line with their colleagues elsewhere in the empire. But those selected for service in Hong Kong continued to be appointed by the governor as cadets and posted to specific offices in the colony as the governor saw fit. The elite status of the cadets in Hong Kong or, for that matter, within the colonial administrative service was not diminished as a result.

While the cadets continued to play a key role in keeping the colonial administration on an even keel through the turbulence of the first half of the twentieth century, they also suffered from getting stale. Hong Kong was a small colony and the eastern most outpost of a worldwide empire. The high standing Hong Kong cadets enjoyed within the colonial administrative service did not, however, make them humble civic servants in their colony, populated mainly by a people not accepted by members of the service as their equal.

With a few notable exceptions, the majority of cadets did not empathize with the local Chinese population sufficiently to know their concerns beyond making a living or their views towards the colonial government. Nor did they manage to acquire real insights into the driving forces that were changing the international situation in East Asia as the 1930s unfolded. Few demonstrated real understanding of and sympathy for Chinese leaders who were struggling to build a nation in neighbouring China, against domestic challenges from warlords and the communists as well as Japanese imperialism externally.[77]

As long as war and disorder were confined to neighbouring China and the rising Japanese imperialists and militarists bided their time without revealing their true intentions towards this British imperial outpost, the cadets collectively managed Hong Kong comfortably. Although it had only an establishment of 35 officers, which meant only 26 were in fact available for duties at any time once language training and absence on leave were taken into account, their small number was no excuse for the complacent attitude they had over events unfolding in the vicinity of the colony. Instead of looking ahead to anticipate new challenges and threats that could confront Hong Kong, most cadets preferred to bask blissfully in the warm glow inherent in the serenity of the empire where the sun never set.[78]

It was the inward looking disposition of the colonial government dominated at the policy level by the cadets that let Hong Kong down when the first challenge to the survival of this crown colony came. In the cold assessment of an unusually forward-looking cadet, David MacDougall, who was seconded to the British government working on wartime propaganda in Hong Kong shortly before the war, 'the local authorities' were 'a lot of pig headed provincials'.[79] This critical but fair assessment was made by MacDougall to his wife in private and not publicized. Only after the Japanese attacked Hong Kong in December 1941 were the inadequacies of the colonial government and its elite revealed and recognized.[80]

Although Hong Kong had no chance of successfully defending itself against the superior Japanese invaders, the colonial government was caught by surprise by the audacity and capabilities of the Japanese, whose abilities it did not hold in high regard.[81] Above all, in the year when the colonial administrators were preparing to celebrate the centenary of British rule, the failure of the cadets and the government more generally to win over the support of the local Chinese was dazzling. Except for a small number of local Chinese who joined the Hong Kong Regiment or were employed in essential services, the local government had neither the imagination nor the capacity to mobilize the local Chinese to assist in the defence of their homes.[82] Cadets could not but take the lion's share of the blame for the colonial government's failure to win over the loyalty of the local Chinese, just as they readily took credit for providing nearly a century of stability, order, prosperity and good government.

As Hong Kong fell, the majority of the cadets obeyed Governor

*Governing Hong Kong*

David MacDougall with his mainly local staff, 1930s.

Young's surrender order and were subsequently held captive in the Stanley internment camp. Those who fought as members of the Hong Kong Regiment were treated as prisoners of war by the Japanese, and most of them were held in a prisoner of war camp in Hong Kong though a few were shipped to Japan before the war ended.

An exception was G. S. Kennedy-Skipton, who was the only cadet to evade captivity and who stayed in occupied Hong Kong. Being Irish he claimed to be a national of neutral Ireland and served under the Japanese. His conduct deeply distracted his fellow cadets. When the war ended they disowned him. There were also two cadets on secondment to the British government and engaged in special operations in Hong Kong who refused to surrender and successfully evaded the Japanese. Ronald Holmes continued the fight by joining the British Army Aid Group in China. MacDougall eventually headed the Hong Kong planning unit in the Colonial Office after making a daring escape together with a Chinese admiral in a British torpedo boat that was sunk by Japanese gunfire.

*Chapter 4*
# EFFECTS OF THE PACIFIC WAR

The Pacific War, which started when Japan attacked Hong Kong almost simultaneously as it bombarded Pearl Harbour in Honolulu in December 1941, was a watershed in Hong Kong's political history. The Japanese invasion and occupation of Hong Kong, which lasted until September 1945, were often ignored because Hong Kong got back on its feet quickly at the end of the war and moved on to rebuild itself. However, even though the Japanese occupation did not leave a positive legacy by way of rule and policies, it left an indelible mark on the British approach to governing this outpost of the British Empire.[1]

What really made a lasting impact was the destruction of the myth about the might of the British Empire.[2] Its image of invincibility ended as Sir Mark Young became the first British governor to surrender a colony to an enemy since the end of the American War of Independence in 1783. While the Malayan campaign and surrender of Singapore overshadowed the battle of Hong Kong, the British defeat as a whole caught the imagination of the people of Asia.[3]

By their spectacular victory, the Japanese not only humiliated the British Empire but also destroyed the superiority of the white race. As a result, even longstanding advocates of British imperialism like Secretary of State for India Leo Amery lost heart. He admitted that 'we were on the eve of very great changes in the relation of Asia to Europe' and it is doubtful 'whether in the future empires like our Asiatic empire' could subsist.[4]

This turn of events had two major implications for British policy towards Hong Kong. The first concerned its future as a British colony, for it lay inside the Allied powers' China theatre, which covered the whole of China, Indo-China and Thailand.[5] This new theatre came under the authority of Supreme Commander Chiang Kai-shek, the ruler of China.[6] Although this arrangement was primarily a gesture to Chiang and whether Hong Kong, as a British territory, was within Chiang's command was not specified, Chiang was justified in considering it within his theatre.[7] A shadow was cast on its long-term future as a British territory.[8] Indeed, once the myth of British invincibility had been destroyed, the nationalistic Chiang pondered if he could use the war to end, as soon as possible, the 'unequal treaties' to which China had been subjected from the 1840s.[9] It was with this in mind that he instructed the Chinese ambassador to Britain, Wellington Koo (Gu Weijun), to see if Britain was ready to give up Hong Kong.[10]

In London, the Colonial Office quickly recognized the implications of Britain's defeat.[11] The alarm was raised powerfully within the office by David MacDougall, a Hong Kong cadet, who joined the Colonial Office after a daring escape to China on the day the colony fell.[12] He reported that all Chinese officials he met in China, up to vice-ministerial level, assumed that Hong Kong would be returned to China after the war.[13] Acting on this recognition the Colonial Office also accepted the second implication of the rapid collapse of British power, namely that 'the arrangements existing before the Japanese occupation would not be restored'.[14]

**End of the colour bar**
When the War ended in 1945, much of the pressure over the future of Hong Kong had eased, despite the great tension between Britain and China over the liberation of this British territory within the China theatre.[15] Chiang was at that time preoccupied with dealing with the Japanese surrender in China and, above all, with the challenge mounted by the Chinese Communist Party in seizing territories under Japanese occupation.[16] To him, as much as to the British, the future of Hong Kong was an issue to be decided by diplomacy after the situation in East Asia had stabilized.[17] While this did not remove the threat from Chinese irredentism to Hong Kong's long-term existence as a British colony, it gave the British a much-needed breathing space.[18]

What could not be left on the back burner was the issue of the governance of the colony. The British dealt with it on the basis of necessity and a sense of pragmatism. To deal with the shortage of

*Effects of the Pacific War*

supplies and disruption of normal shipping and other means of communication by the war, Hong Kong was put under a military administration, even though a gallant attempt to restore a civil administration had already been made before the British fleet arrived. This was made by Franklin Gimson, who took up office as colonial secretary the day before Hong Kong came under attack and was the senior British official interned by the Japanese in occupied Hong Kong.[19] Gimson acted on a signal from London delivered to him in the Stanley internment camp by a secret agent and tried to restore British jurisdiction over Hong Kong by demanding the Japanese release some of his fellow internees and set up the skeleton of a civil administration.[20]

Soon after he arrived in Hong Kong, Rear Admiral Cecil Harcourt, the senior commander who was given the task to set up a military administration, thought he could make the most of this and appointed Gimson lieutenant governor.[21] This, however, London promptly reversed because the existence of a military administration with full power alongside a civilian government created a constitutional anomaly.[22] London's insistence on having a military administration under Harcourt rather than a civil government ensured that normal bureaucratic procedures could be dispensed with and more effective governance delivered amid the chaos of the immediate postwar situation.

Although it was meant to be a military government, administration was entrusted not to a career soldier but to David MacDougall, the chief civil affairs officer. A Hong Kong cadet since 1928, MacDougall was more progressive than most of his peers and was in private critical of their provincial and inward looking attitude.[23] He made a daring escape when the colony fell, and rose to become head of the Hong Kong planning unit in the Colonial Office when the Japanese surrendered. He was given the rank of brigadier and sent to Hong Kong by the quickest available means. Despite his apprenticeship as an administrator in a period when many Hong Kong cadets were getting stale and pompous, MacDougall did not bring any prewar baggage with him.

On the contrary, MacDougall focused on the urgent and vital tasks of getting supplies to feed the local population and maintaining stability. He pressed on without regard to prewar procedures, protocols, background of individuals or other formal requirements that could cause bureaucratic delay.²⁴ To give himself enough freedom to do what was necessary to get Hong Kong back on its feet, he decided to keep the Colonial Office informed as little as possible. He thus used the pretext that telegraphic communication was difficult because it had to be sent through the Royal Navy.²⁵ He inspired his colleagues to use their initiative and to take responsibility for finding practical solutions to the pressing problems they encountered. This eight-month interlude was therefore a period marked by administrative dynamism. MacDougall's discharge of his responsibility as head of civil affairs revealed a Hong Kong cadet at his best and most versatile.

As MacDougall and his small team of civil affairs officers worked to get Hong Kong back on its feet, the British government continued to examine the question of governance once civil authority had been restored. It acted on the recognition that a return to the *status quo ante* was neither possible nor advisable.²⁶ What was seen as particularly unacceptable was the racist element in some of the government's policies and practices. Before the war racial segregation was a reality. The Peak and hills on the island of Cheung Chau were, for example, reserved for white residents. The only Chinese people given permission to live on the Peak, the ultimate reserve for Caucasians, often compared with Simla in India, were Sir Robert Hotung and Madam Chiang Kai-shek. The former was the richest man in Hong Kong, one of the very few Chinese knighted by the crown, who was in any event a Eurasian. The latter was the wife of the leader of China. The existence of segregation before the war did not cause social unrest, for the local Chinese preferred to live among themselves.²⁷ However, the destruction of British invincibility and the emergence of a sense of pride among the Chinese when China was accepted as one of the big five among world powers, changed the situation. The Chinese no longer tolerated a slap in the face as readily as they had done before the war.²⁸

It was recognition of such changes that led Sir Mark Young to arm himself with a programme of reform when he restored civil government in May 1946. Contrary to expectations in Hong Kong and even the Foreign Office, Young was not a backward looking oldtimer.²⁹ Pressure from the Foreign Office and the acceptance that Hong Kong must be given a new deal meant that he was allowed to resume his office as governor and commander in chief for only one year. In the end Young returned to restore the honour of British arms and of the empire as the prime minister overruled the objection raised by the foreign secretary.[30] On the day he returned to Hong Kong, Young declared: 'His Majesty's Government has under consideration the means by which in Hong Kong, as elsewhere in the Colonial empire, the inhabitants of the Territory can be given a fuller and more responsible share in the management of their own affairs.'[31] Within three months, his administration had removed the iniquity of segregation by introducing the Peak District (Residence) Repeal Bill as 'it would be out of harmony with the spirit of the times to retain the ordinance'.[32]

Although the original plan for constitutional reform for Hong Kong was drafted by the Hong Kong planning unit under MacDougall during the closing stage of the war, and had already been reworked within the Colonial Office after MacDougall left, Young was personally committed to reform. Having lost Hong Kong once, he was determined to do what he could to win over the loyalty of the local Chinese in the face of Chinese irredentism. This underlined his commitment to constitutional reform.[33] It also caused him to leave a mark on the cadets, which was to start the process to put an end to the colour bar for entry.

Before the war there was a formal requirement that Eastern cadets had to be 'natural born British subjects', which was introduced in 1902.[34] Although this had been the general practice since the original scheme for Hong Kong cadets was introduced four decades earlier, this change reflected the sense of superiority and confidence of the late Victorian and early Edwardian era when the might of the empire reached a high point. This requirement was later dropped for Ceylonese with British university degrees for the Ceylon service, where the colonial service took a more liberal approach. Concessions were also later made in British Malaya, as non-European members of the less prestigious Malay administrative service were allowed to gain promotion to join the Malayan civil service, its local equivalent to the cadets.

The Hong Kong establishment, however, held fast to the ethnic requirement.[35] The existence of a colour bar was never challenged, despite efforts to localize the civil service, which were introduced to reduce the cost of administration, particularly after the worldwide recession marked by the Wall Street crash of 1929.[36] Indeed, in 1936

*Governing Hong Kong*

Governor Sir Andrew Caldecott went so far as to lay down the policy that in future 'no appointment would be made in Great Britain until the qualifications of Hong Kong candidates had been first examined.'[37] But there was never any doubt that this policy of localization was not applicable to cadets.

What really changed in 1946 was Young's keen sense of the need to act in accordance with the spirit of the time. Equally important was the availability of a suitable ethnic Chinese candidate for appointment as an administrative officer. He was Paul Ka-cheung Tsui and a student at the University of Hong Kong when the Japanese attacked. He joined the British Empire's war against the Japanese in China after the colony fell.[38] His loyalty to the crown was tested under the extreme conditions of the war when he served in the British Army Aid Group (BAAG), the unit for staging clandestine operations against the Japanese from China and constituted mainly of British subjects who had escaped from Hong Kong.[39]

It was during the war that for the first time expatriate Britons and Hong Kong Chinese 'served together without a clear and unbreakable racial divide' in the BAAG.[40] Tsui became one of the first Chinese to be commissioned as an officer in the British forces not only because of his ability but also because of his personal devotion and identification with the British cause. When the war ended, Tsui had risen to the rank of captain. It was a reflection of MacDougall's pragmatism and progressive attitude that he took Tsui on as an assistant district officer in the New Territories under the military administration.[41] But that was a time when exceptional measures were taken to meet the exigencies of the immediate postwar situation. The real test came as civil government was restored. For the first time in Hong Kong's history, the ethnic background of Tsui did not prevent him from being selected to join the elite branch of the government service when the newly restored civil government sought to strengthen its administrative cadre. The restoration of civil government in 1946 resulted in, up to then, the largest recruitment of cadets in any year. Five new cadets were appointed from among ex-servicemen. They were Jack Cater, Robert Heatherington, Ian Lightbody, Terence Sorby and Alastair Todd. In addition, Paul Tsui and Michael Clinton were appointed to the colonial administrative service though they were not appointed as cadets until later. When Tsui was finally made a cadet in January 1948 he became the first

Paul Tsui in dress uniform.

local Chinese person to be admitted to this exclusive group of elite administrators.[42] All of them shared one important thing in common; they had proved themselves during the military administration. All but Tsui arrived in Hong Kong in 1945 as members of the British forces and held the military rank of either captain or major; Tsui returned to his homeland with the BAAG. What also distinguished this group of recruits from earlier cadets was that a majority of them had not completed their university education, though they had been awarded wartime degrees. This included Tsui, the first administrative officer/cadet with a degree from the University of Hong Kong. Tsui was, among other final-year students, awarded a BA in 1942 after an emergency session of the university senate following the fall of the colony to the Japanese.[43] Cater, however, never had a university education; he had come originally from the East End of London rather than the more usual middle-class background of his predecessors.

The recruitment of Tsui, an ethnic Chinese, albeit only to the colonial administrative service at first rather than as a cadet, was a fundamental break from the past. In a sense he was given an advantage over his colleagues as he was sent off to attend the year-long Devonshire course for colonial administrators at Oxford University shortly after his appointment, while his colleagues were put to work immediately. It was on his return from Oxford that he was finally made a cadet. Despite Tsui's personal qualities, it took a farsighted and courageous governor like Young to break the longstanding colour bar.

**A new outlook**

The atmosphere in Hong Kong in 1946 was indeed different from before the war. Even before civil government was restored, the need for the new administration to come with a new outlook was keenly observed and reported to London by senior British officials, particularly Harcourt and MacDougall. What they considered essential were 'better and fairer treatment of the Chinese; carefully chosen, incorruptible British officials, with some knowledge of the Chinese; free education for the children of the poor; and, most importantly, an almost complete absence of the "old gang".'[44]

This recognition was not confined to farsighted officials. John Keswick, *taipan* of the princely *hong* Jardine, Matheson & Company, for example, urged the British government to act on it. Having served as a political adviser at the British embassy in Zhongqing and in the Southeast Asia Command during the war, Keswick was fully alive to the changed political climate. Among the changes he recommended to the British government, the most important were:

- that the crown colony of Hong Kong should be renamed and 'administered as the Free Port and Municipality of Hong Kong';
- that the governor should have his title changed and 'be supported by an elected council';
- that 'there will be equal opportunity for all without discrimination between colour, race or creed'; and
- that 'genuine citizens of Hong Kong (that is to say people born and continuously resident in the municipality) should be given same privilege within the British Commonwealth'.[45]

On a different occasion Keswick also suggested a major administrative reform. It was to transform the secretary for Chinese Affairs into a new office of 'Secretary for Chinese and External Affairs'. In his conception, either the new secretary 'should be an expert on modern China with the closest liaison with HM Ambassador in China' or a new deputy to the secretary should perform this role.[46]

It was against such a background that Young returned to Hong Kong with a view to giving the local Chinese community an as yet undefined new deal and MacDougall's appointment as colonial secretary helped. Young's readiness to take on board the new outlook was partly a reaction to his wartime experience and partly rooted in having spent his formative years as a young cadet in the more progressive Ceylon service. Unlike his Hong Kong colleagues, he had a professional career that 'included working with elected representatives and guiding the relatively more civilized colonies to constitutional advancement'.[47] MacDougall, for his part, was one of the most forward looking Hong Kong cadets among the interwar-year recruits and was one of the two leading advocates of a new outlook for the new civil government. With them seeing eye to eye over the need to take Hong Kong forward in a progressive spirit, Young kept in place most of the changes MacDougall had introduced during the military administration. That many prewar officials who had left Hong Kong to recuperate from the ordeal of internment under the Japanese had not yet returned, also affected the atmosphere in Hong Kong.[48]

For several reasons the colonial government's new outlook was less strongly entrenched than one might have expected. To begin with, the situation in Hong Kong and neighbouring China changed quickly in the immediate postwar period. As victory turned to civil war between the communists and ruling Kuomintang in China, the Chinese people's newly acquired pride was quickly being eroded.[49] Hong Kong, by contrast, was immensely successful in restoring stability and in rehabilitating its economy. As a result the clock was being turned back to the prewar era as far as a key element of Hong Kong's relations with China was concerned. It was that British Hong Kong served as an island of peace, good order and opportunity in the sea of instability, chaos, poor governance and civil wars that prevailed in late imperial and early republican China. Large numbers of Chinese, both former short-term residents and new immigrants, moved to Hong Kong as the situation in China deteriorated.

With an influx of people looking for work in what were still very harsh economic conditions, the attention of the Chinese population in the colony quickly focused more on making a living than on seeing to it that the colonial government would live up to its new promises. Ironically, in this connection the credibility Young's government had secured by promptly reaffirming that most of the progressive changes introduced during the military administration would remain, encouraged the locals to leave matters to the government. Young was disappointed because he saw such an attitude in terms of apathy. He wanted to win over their loyalty to British Hong Kong in the face of Chinese irredentism, which was why he was keen to give them a genuine say in the management of their own affairs.[50] What Young did not understand was that this apparent apathy reflected the spirit of the time in the Chinese community, including its confidence in him as the head of the government. The overwhelming majority of the Chinese living in Hong Kong still approached politics in the traditional Chinese way, which saw local officials more as *fumuguan* or father and mother officials than modern civil servants.[51] Young's positive approach to reform and reassurance of his determination on the radio and in newspapers meant there was no need for the locals to push for it. The pressure on the colonial government to institutionalize the outlook of 1946 eased.

From the perspective of the local people at the time, Young's replacement by Sir Alexander Grantham in 1947 further reassured them, for they expected this 'first truly postwar governor ... to lead the colony to a very bright future'.[52] Little did they realize that while he would on balance turn out to be a great governor, Grantham did not share Young's outlook. While Grantham was not a reactionary and did not attempt to turn the clock back to before 1941, he did not see much in Young's sense of urgency for reform. He thought that Young was misguided in believing that the Chinese of Hong Kong could ever be turned into loyal British subjects.[53] Grantham was more interested in keeping Hong Kong on an even keel as the Chinese Civil War intensified than in making sure the outlook of 1946 became part of the ethos of the colonial administration.

A good portion of the former senior officials, including cadets, who returned to Hong Kong after rebuilding their health, shared Grantham's attitude. Although the departure of the 'old-timers' in 1945 impressed the local population at the time, it was a temporary development, for even MacDougall intended to ensure that positions were reserved for those who were healthy enough to return.[54] It was a matter of keeping a balance between meeting the demands for a new outlook and doing right by those who had served the crown loyally in war and during enemy internment.

Young's replacement by Grantham turned out to be far more significant than anyone expected at the time. It both applied a brake to Young's attempt at constitutional reform and changed the administration's basic outlook.[55] It took time for the British government to examine the longer-term changes that farsighted officials and individuals like MacDougall and Keswick had recommended to it during the military administration. In the meantime, the clock ticked away and in May 1947 Young retired. As Grantham saw Hong Kong, the Chinese people and the forces of Chinese politics in a fundamentally different light from Young, he took a very different approach when London consulted him about most of these proposed changes. In fact, Grantham even opposed a presentational decision like dropping the description of Hong Kong as a crown colony, arguing forcefully against a suggestion that the colony might be renamed the 'City State of Hong Kong' on the grounds that 'the people of Hong Kong would certainly misunderstand' it and 'would interpret it as a first stage in a British withdrawal from the territory.'[56]

As a graduate of Wellington College, the royal military college at Sandhurst, and Pembroke College in Cambridge, Grantham started his career as a Hong Kong cadet in 1922, after serving in the First World War. In his ten years in Hong Kong he served mainly in the Colonial Secretariat after passing his Cantonese examination. His views on the Chinese community were affected by the fact that he had limited direct dealings with Chinese people in his work and did not as a young cadet socialize with them. While he fully recognized the entrepreneurial and enterprising qualities of the local Cantonese, he saw them first and foremost as Chinese nationals who could not be transformed into anything else. This informed Grantham's view that Young was misguided in thinking that democratization could turn the local people into loyal citizens of Hong Kong or British subjects, and explained his lack of enthusiasm for Young's proposals for political reform.

To put this matter in context, it would be too simplistic to see Young as advocating reform simply because he did not understand Chinese people. Young's approach enjoyed the full support of MacDougall and MacDougall knew the Chinese much better than Grantham did. He not only dealt with them professionally as a colonial administrator for a longer period but also got to know them through his longstanding friendships with Chinese individuals and government officials.[57] The basic difference between Young and MacDougall on the one hand, and Grantham on the other, was less about how well they knew the Chinese than about whether they believed that the 'Chineseness' of the people of Hong Kong was such that they would never trade loyalty to the Chinese state, whatever its political persuasion, for a liberal way of life guaranteed by the rule of law within the British Commonwealth.

Grantham was an astute, able and ambitious cadet who was determined to rise to the top in the colonial service. He requested a transfer in 1934 not because he was unhappy in Hong Kong but to advance his promotional prospects, even though this involved a drop of about one-third in salary.[58]

During his time as a cadet in Hong Kong, the only historical event he considered sufficiently important to record in his memoirs was the strike-cum-boycott of 1925 and 1926, one of those rare occasions when Chinese nationalism made a major impact on life in Hong Kong.[59] This momentous event inspired him into thinking that the 'fundamental problem of this British Colony ... is its relations with China and not the advancement of self-government'.[60] Hence, while Grantham had no intention of restoring the prewar order, he did not see much value in involving the local Chinese community in the management of Hong Kong and in building up a sense of local identity. Instead, he believed the key was to manage properly Hong Kong's relations with China, be it the nationalistic Kuomintang government or the irredentist communist regime.[61] He was so convinced of this that he felt that Hong Kong 'should ... have been placed under the Foreign Office rather than the Colonial Office, but with staff seconded from the Colonial Service' to administer it.[62]

This basic thinking of Grantham meant that he was receptive to the idea that a career diplomat should be seconded from the British foreign service to work as a secretary for external Chinese Affairs, provided he would not 'get into the hair' of the secretary for Chinese Affairs.[63] This idea originated in the recommendation Keswick made in late 1945. When it was examined in earnest by British officials, MacDougall felt strongly that while Keswick's basic thinking was right, it 'might be unfortunate if this matter were regarded as a specialist department'.[64] He took the view that it was most desirable for 'all senior officers of the Hong Kong Government to be more closely in touch with Chinese Affairs, not least the Colonial Secretary himself'.[65]

Given the Hong Kong cadets' lack of expertise on events in China, the Foreign Office wanted one of its diplomats to fill a new post as secretary for external affairs.[66] Sharing MacDougall's basic thinking but bowing to the reality of the shortage of local talent, Young accepted a compromise. It was the secondment of a foreign-service officer 'as a temporary measure'. He nevertheless insisted that 'officers both of the Cadet Service and of other departments should be enabled and encouraged to maintain contact with Chinese Affairs'.[67] The new office created was named 'political adviser to the governor', not least to underline the intention that he was not to be head of a specialist Department of External Affairs. C. B. B. Heathcote-Smith, a diplomat with considerable experience in wartime China, was duly appointed but he only took up office after Young retired.

Once Heathcote-Smith had proved his worth in the administration, Grantham never insisted on Young's original conditions being met. This was despite the fact that Heathcote-Smith's relationship with Colonial Secretary MacDougall was 'not terribly warm'.[68] With Grantham receptive to having a foreign service man on secondment and MacDougall retired in 1949, the office of political adviser was never opened to Hong Kong cadets as Young and MacDougall had originally intended. The task of understanding developments in China thus became the specialist preserve of this new office.

This meant that the original wish of the British government to redress a key inadequacy of Hong Kong's prewar administration – its senior officials being out of touch with events in China – was left by the wayside. Grantham did not do this to restore the *status quo ante*, but to strengthen his government's direct links with the Foreign Office, which he thought was good for the colony. The outlook of 1946 changed as Grantham guided Hong Kong in a direction different from that of Young and MacDougall.

MacDougall's ability to influence the direction of development in Hong Kong also gradually diminished. This was partly because the restoration of civil government invariably meant that the 'whatever it took' approach the military administration adopted had to give way to a more systematic or bureaucratic approach. So, as civil administration was put back on track, MacDougall's practice of giving his officials as much scope as possible for initiative came to an end. The differences between him and Grantham also meant that there was less room for MacDougall to leave his mark. Most importantly, indiscretion in his private life gave rise to a quiet confrontation between the two, for MacDougall, a married man with his family in Britain, had fallen in love with someone else in Hong Kong. Grantham took the view that it was intolerable for the officer administering the government, which MacDougall was entitled to become when the governor was away, to have an extramarital affair. MacDougall put love before his career and the almost certain prospect of a governorship somewhere and, in the spring of 1949, took early retirement at the age of 45. This was highly ironic because he, one of the most dynamic, energetic and farsighted cadets from before the war, became one of the first to take advantage of the new rule he himself had introduced to enable the postwar government to get rid of dead wood.

The outlook for 1946 steadily gave way to something else. Instead of focusing on governance and relations between the government and people, it focused on two other matters. The first was relations with China. This meant how to avoid entanglement in the unfinished civil war between the remnants of the Kuomintang government in Taiwan and the communists on the mainland, and how to sustain a policy of non-provocative firmness in dealing with the new, powerful and even more irredentist communist government after 1949.[69] The second was to sustain a stable framework of government that 'maintains law and order, does not tax them too much' and ensures that ordinary people 'can get justice in the courts'.[70] This approach of Grantham's came to epitomize the government ethos until at least 1967. Under Grantham, Hong Kong became devoted to maintaining stability, good order and prosperity as it kept a delicate balance in its dealings with the two rival Chinese regimes.[71]

Hong Kong under Grantham might have lost the reforming zeal of MacDougall's civil affairs branch during the military administration, and of Young's term; Young's reform proposal had been put to bed for good when Grantham felt he could let it go without provoking a backlash when Hong Kong's economy suffered its first postwar recession in 1952.[72] Nonetheless, Grantham's administration adopted a much more progressive approach than its pre-1941 predecessors. He wanted to see Hong Kong develop into a more progressive society and get rid of the 'insularity and provincial mindedness of some of the leading businessmen, both European and Chinese'.[73] He was pleased that 'the age of the "blimps" was over', but he did not actively promote more social integration or encourage the local Chinese to take an active part in the management of their territory.

The colonial administration's position under Grantham was to build passively a constructive partnership with the local people. The government was to provide and sustain a stable political, judicial and social framework so that they and the business communities could get on with doing what they were good at. The old discriminations that had been institutionalized before the war were quietly dropped, though no proactive efforts were made to redress any social or economic inequality; it was hoped that the important changes would take place quietly. While no other local person was appointed a cadet after Paul Tsui in the 1940s, eight were recruited through public advertisement in the 1950s.[74] Where the small administration saw a need and if the resources were available, the government also sought to improve the general conditions in which local people lived. Public housing and schools for young children were built in large numbers once it became clear to the government that there was a desperate need for them and that they were within the means of the colony. Government policy essentially remained reactive rather than proactive. With fewer than 50 cadets available even by the end of the 1950s, they were constantly engaged in dealing with the problems of the day. There was little scope for forward planning.

The cadets remained at the centre of the administration that shaped the outlook and ethos of the government. Among them a divide became increasingly discernible, for the postwar recruits by and large had a different view of the British Empire and of Hong Kong from those who had joined before the war and were interned by the Japanese. This division should not, however, be overstated. There were, for example, some prewar recruits who were not only highly able but also broad-minded officers who had little difficulty discarding the prewar mentality. Particularly notable among them were Claude Burgess, Ronald Holmes and John Cowperthwaite. Burgess worked under MacDougall as head of the secretariat in the military administration after he came out of internment and then spent almost three years working at the Colonial Office before returning to Hong Kong as deputy colonial secretary.[75] Holmes and Cowperthwaite became cadets only shortly before the war started, in 1938 and 1941 respectively, and were not interned by the Japanese.

Having escaped capture by the Japanese and therefore not forced to live in a time warp in the Stanley camp, their views of the empire and its relationship with the colonial people developed as the world moved on in the course of the war.

Practically all the prewar cadets who returned to duty in fact accepted that great changes had taken place in Hong Kong and so made no attempt to turn the clock back. However, their attitude towards the local people and how the government should be run continued to be affected by their previous experience. Where an old practice worked, there was a general consensus that it should be kept. Since they occupied most of the senior positions their attitude continued to have a significant impact on policy. With Grantham's approach now superseding the 1946 position, after Young's retirement there was little pressure from the governor to force changes.

The younger cadets or postwar recruits, by contrast, tended to take a less rigid view of how the administration should be run. Prewar practices and conventions meant little to them. They were more interested in doing whatever needed to be done in the best possible way, but they were junior officers who had to defer to their seniors and until they had risen in the hierarchy their impact was small. As time went by a higher and higher percentage of the ever dwindling number of prewar officers became 'a bit out of their depth – but often didn't realize it', as many 'were unable to adjust, or adjust fast enough, to change, which was increasingly rapid'.[76] But in the wings were the younger and more energetic postwar cadets who were keen to take over and change with the times.

*Chapter 5*
# EXPANSION

Hong Kong entered a new era after the Second World War partly because forces unleashed by the war caused faster changes worldwide and partly because the closing of China to most of the outside world gave this imperial outpost a new stimulus for development. Until the communists came to power in China in 1949, and effectively closed its border with this British colony the following year, Hong Kong existed mainly as Britain's gateway to China. Its heavy reliance on the entrepôt trade between China and the rest of the world ended after the United Nations and United States imposed embargoes on China in 1951 following Chinese intervention in the Korean War in late 1950. Hong Kong had to survive in this changed world and sought to do so by rapid industrialization. With trade restrictions in place, particularly those imposed by the USA, the colonial government found itself having to certify that goods manufactured in this British capitalist enclave were neither produced on the neighbouring communist mainland nor used their raw materials. When a certificate of origin was developed to meet this requirement, it was taken very seriously because a failure to give it credibility could have derailed Hong Kong's transformation from an entrepôt to an industrial centre. Through developments like these, the scope and span of government had to expand in Hong Kong.

As its overwhelmingly Chinese population settled down and grew, roughly adding a million to the size of the population each decade, the colonial government also had to increase its size to cope with the new demands. The old prewar attitude that the Chinese could largely be left to their own devices so long as they did not break the law and upset good order had to be, and was, replaced. Following the end of the myth of the invincibility of the British Empire and the rise of Chinese irredentism during the war, the government in Hong Kong decided to set about building a constructive partnership with the local people.[1] This meant that the government had to provide and proactively maintain a legal, political and social infrastructure that could sustain economic prosperity and social stability – the substance of good governance from the perspective of the colonial administration at the time. Given the cadets' elite status and reputation as generalist officers who could deal with any issue, they remained the core of the civil service to which the government relied on to face up to the new challenges of the postwar era.

As the 1950s unfolded, the colonial government felt the need to expand to meet the new demands, but the financial restraints the colony faced limited any expansion. As a crown colony, Hong Kong could secure financial autonomy from metropolitan Britain only by persuading London it would not become a charge on the British exchequer. Because of the war and Japanese occupation Hong Kong was put back under Treasury control, which did not end until it proved it could be financially self-sustaining again in 1948.[2] As a result, the colonial government had no option but to adhere to a very prudent or conservative policy with regard to financial management. Any sign that Hong Kong could become a financial liability on Britain, particularly in the light of the severe weakness of the postwar British economy, would have caused alarm in London.[3] The Hong Kong government was fully aware of this situation and did all it could to maximize the scope of its own financial autonomy.[4] This meant any expansion of the civil service had to be fully justified and financially sustainable. The increase in cadets was consequently modest even though the span of government was already increasing steadily and quickly.

Once the tensions caused by the rise of a communist regime in China and the Korean War had eased, the 1950s saw a steady change in attitude. Practices that before the war had seemed positive and appropriate in this outpost of the colonial empire were no longer automatically embraced. Grand old institutions with quaint names that used to evoke reverence and respect were given new, modern sounding titles with clear descriptions of what particular institutions were meant to achieve. And, needless to say, the venerable title of cadets soon became a victim of this sweeping current of change.

## From cadets to administrative officers

While the colonial administration focused mainly on local issues that required immediate responses, it reviewed its own structure and effectiveness of governance in the postwar era much more frequently than it had done before the war. This was at first driven by the need to meet new challenges and expectations produced by rapid social and economic changes.

Major challenges to the government's capacity to provide good governance could also emerge suddenly. In the early 1950s the biggest such challenge came in the form of a fire that quickly went out of control in the squatter area of Shek Kip Mei. It rendered 58,000 people homeless overnight just before Christmas 1953. It turned out to be much more than the biggest disaster of its kind in Hong Kong's history,[5] for it had a much greater impact on the administration than one would have expected given that squatter fires happened regularly in those days. It not only created the need for the colonial government to mount a massive relief operation but also resulted in both immediate and sustained demands being put on the government's administrative capacity. Two recently recruited cadets, Martin Rowlands and Peter Williams, who were receiving their initial Cantonese language training, were immediately taken off such training to give administrative backup to the relief efforts.[6] This was not an isolated redeployment of human resources, for the government was short of cadets and the language training of new recruits sometimes had to be sacrificed to meet an urgent demand for cadets. Over a longer time frame, this great fire also resulted in a change in the government's policy towards housing recent immigrants and, more directly relevant to this study, the creation of the Resettlement Department in 1954.[7] The latter required the deployment of a senior cadet, Ronald Holmes, as its director and two junior cadets to provide support at the lower levels. This meant an unplanned expansion in the span of government and an additional need for three cadets on active duties on a daily basis out of an establishment of about 50 officers, including those on leave and receiving language training.

Beyond responding to new demands generated by forces outside its control, the 1950s also saw the government beginning to recognize that it should regularly review how its human resources were deployed, rewarded and managed. The need to keep modernizing the government apparatus without waiting for major upheavals or mishaps such as the Shek Kip Mei fire to force its hand meant that the government periodically had to review the structure, organization, remuneration, morale and relations between its generalist and specialist professional officers. The first such exercise in the postwar period started with the appointment of a salaries commission in 1947 and a public service commission in 1950. While the former mainly took responsibility for reviewing the remuneration package, the latter advised the governor on promotion and ensured that civil servants enjoyed the conditions of service to which they were entitled. Such exercises were repeated periodically before they became institutionalized as the 1950s progressed, and they played a significant part in introducing changes to the colonial administration.

The rise in population, public expectations and the expansion in the span and scope of government after the war also meant that an increasing degree of professionalism was expected and required within the government. This applied particularly to specialist departments responsible, for example, for providing medical and health services, education, building the infrastructure and constructing resettlement estates. The specialist departments expanded because their workloads had increased dramatically since the prewar era. By the end of the decade this general expansion in government had also resulted in an increase in the number of departments being headed by professionals rather than cadets.[8] It had the effect of removing some of the awe in which non-cadet officials had previously held cadets.[9]

However, the rise in professional officials caused some concern among those in the government who felt that professionals who headed departments should 'give more attention to the administrative problems of their departments'.[10] Cadets had a long tradition of being forthright, not only in advancing Hong Kong's interests as they saw them, but also in asserting and defending their own welfare as the elite within the government. Some senior cadets therefore expressed dissatisfaction at the emerging trend for professional officers to take on an increasing number of directorate-level appointments, and often with higher salaries than cadets holding similar positions in other departments. This happened because cadets were on a separate salary scale from the rest of the civil service, and could only reach their maximum pay through the stages of their time scale. A high-flying cadet who was appointed at a young age to serve, for example, as assistant director of a department would receive a salary according to his seniority as a cadet rather than paid a directorate level salary.[11] This usually meant taking a salary substantially lower than that available to his non cadet colleague in a different department, who would be remunerated as an assistant director. The fact that a professional officer who took on an appointment at such a level would normally be some years older than a cadet did not assuage the feeling among cadets. In the light of the tension at the higher level of the civil service and disgruntlement among cadets, the 1959 salaries commission recommended reform.[12]

To reassure the cadets of the government's willingness to look after them while seeking to improve governance, the salaries commission recommended the provision of a more structured promotional ladder for cadets. The prewar structure of having only two ascending grades, Cadet II and Cadet I had in fact already been changed earlier by the addition of the staff grade at the top. After the 1959 salaries commission review, the staff grade was divided into Staff Grade B and Staff Grade A. It did not provide a solution to some high flying cadets being disadvantaged over pay at the directorate level, but at least committed the government to finding a way of ensuring that at the directorate level cadets would not be disadvantaged in comparison with their professional colleagues discharging similar responsibilities in a different department. This anomaly was removed by the introduction of acting pay for young cadets taking on a senior position. Such a change was made easier by the replacement of the historic title of cadet by the modern sounding administrative officer after the 1959 review. The rationale was that since all government officials at the directorate level discharged administrative responsibilities, whether they had come through the cadet or the professional stream, there should be an arrangement to ensure equal pay for taking on the same administrative responsibilities.

The adoption of the new title of administrative officer in the place of cadet was most remarkable for being a 'non-event'. It proceeded so smoothly that few even noticed it. The change in title did not change the way in which new administrative officers were selected and all new recruits were inducted into the same ethos as the old cadets. Their *esprit de corps* and promotion prospects were not affected either. Nevertheless, it is remarkable that such a change met with hardly any resistance and was seldom lamented upon among cadets. The lack of serious efforts to retain their historic though somewhat archaic title reflected the spirit of the service at the time. Cadets were more concerned with getting on with the tasks in hand and gaining the due recognition and reward within the government than preserving any institution or title of historic significance for the sake of it. They were also inclined to follow the shifting current of opinions in the society at large. Changing to meet the challenges of modernity was valued more than preserving history for its sentimental or even intrinsic value. With older officers from before the war steadily being replaced by younger recruits from the postwar era, the administrative officers preferred to look forward rather than backwards in building their careers and advancing the welfare of themselves and of Hong Kong. The title of cadet was thus allowed to become a relic of history without many tears being shed over it.

### Ever expanding scope of government activities

If the 1950s was a decade of expansion in government activities at an unprecedented rate, it was overtaken as the next decade unfolded, a process that was repeated every subsequent decade until the end of British rule in 1997. The pace of change in Hong Kong continued to gather momentum as the postwar era deepened. The increasing complexity of modern living, the ever growing number of people who travel far from their places of birth for work, the explosive expansion of industrial manufacturing, the steady increase in average and national income, as well as the associated rise in public expectations that followed the introduction of mass education, all caused expansion in the span and scope of government. In this respect the growth of government in Hong Kong merely occurred parallel with the same trend in the rest of the developed and developing world. Governments all over the world simply expanded massively in their scope and span in the second half of the twentieth century.

In an important sense this phenomenon was substantially slower in Hong Kong than in many other countries, particularly in western Europe, where the advent of the welfare state had caused much more dramatic expansion.[13] In Hong Kong, the colonial administration continued to subscribe to the idea of a small government. Its basic ethos, or working definition of good governance, remained that the government should provide sound administration and the political, social and economic infrastructure necessary to enable local people to do as they wished, rather than to play a directing role. As social welfare became a catch-phrase in Europe, including metropolitan Britain, the Hong Kong government went against this current.[14] When the Labour government, which had introduced the welfare state in Britain, pushed for the establishment of an independent social welfare office in Hong Kong in 1950, the colonial government resisted strenuously. Governor Alexander Grantham, who had started his career as a Hong Kong cadet, argued forcefully that 'from a realistic and practical angle ... such a step would be a mistake, and, at the present juncture, at any rate, would not only not advance the cause of social welfare in the Colony, but would actually retard it.'[15] Grantham did not explain how he came to this conclusion, but as the man on the spot his view carried weight and the government in London did not feel it should impose a policy it had been warned would be unrealistic and counter-productive.

The Hong Kong government under Grantham had no intention, even less a policy, to introduce social welfare in the modern sense, which had become such an important new part of government in western Europe. To deal with pressure from London, Governor Grantham agreed to call one of the assistant secretaries for Chinese Affairs a social welfare officer, an arrangement he started in the second half of 1947.[16] This policy was also set firmly in the context of the government discharging its paternal responsibility towards the local Chinese population. A separate and distinct Social Welfare Department was not set up until January 1958. Although Grantham had authorized it, it did not come into existence until after he retired. Notwithstanding its refusal to introduce modern social welfare, the colonial administration in Hong Kong still expanded very fast and quietly changed its attitude towards the size of government.

Although adopting a policy to provide 'social welfare' was anathema, the colonial government significantly expanded its provision of various services to the local community, which would have been out of the question before the war. This started on a large scale when the Public Works Department started to build emergency relief housing after the Shek Kip Mei fire of Christmas 1953. When this began, it was not meant to be a housing programme but 'to house victims of squatter fires and to clear land for development'.[17] But it gradually

Head table at Cadet's farewell dinner for Governor Sir Alexander Grantham, 12 December 1957. *From left to right:* Ken Barnett, Selwyn Alleyne, Sir Alexander Grantham, Colonial Secretary E.B. David, Brian Barlow, David Baron, and Denis Bray.

developed into a massive and sustained effort to build resettlement estates and other low-cost housing for the poor, which caused a major expansion of the Public Works Department in addition to the creation of the resettlement department and a separate housing authority. Whatever its name, the government embarking on a programme to build subsidized housing that at one stage accommodated half the local population was a kind of social welfare.

The government had also by then started to provide the colony's children with primary education on a massive scale.[18] Admittedly, such a development happened with little careful long-term planning and the government soon found itself engaged in another effort to expand secondary education substantially after it realized that the intakes to its new primary schools needed secondary education.[19] This involved further expansion of the education department, which was not originally planned for when the expansion of primary education started. Similar and often unplanned expansion in government departments occurred. The medical and health department had to expand, for example, once the government started to provide modern Western medical and health services to the local Chinese community in general and to vaccinate school children in particular.

Despite its official policy, the provision of subsidized housing, schooling for children and medical services to all who needed them, with fees waived or reduced to a nominal charge, meant that the government was in fact involved in providing limited welfare to its citizens. Although they were generally provided without forward planning and happened in a haphazard manner, this expansion of government services meant that the span and scope of government in fact expanded steadily and considerably.

Equally important was a change in the attitude of the government towards its relationship with the local Chinese population. In the early postwar period government officials very slowly but gradually came to accept that they were responsible for the welfare of the local people.[20] As cadets were mostly in charge of departments that dealt with the local Chinese on a daily basis, they took the lead in seeing a need for senior officials to discharge their duties in line with the concept of the *fumuguan* (father and mother official) that was part of China's tradition in governance.

This development should be contrasted against the situation before the war, when only a small handful of individual Sinologists among the cadets, such as Stewart Lockhart or Cecil Clementi, thought they should take Confucian principles of government into account when discharging their offices. By the late 1950s and early 1960s, however, more and more cadets had gained an awareness of traditional relationships between governments and people in a Chinese community, and they increasingly saw the sense in taking the expectations of the people into account when discharging duties that had a direct impact on the local population.

**The last of the old guard**
As Hong Kong entered the 1960s, those cadets who joined before the war and were still in Hong Kong were approaching the last decade of their service, and mostly occupied senior offices. They were a diverse group and included, among the more prominent ones, Claude Burgess, John McDouall, Ronald Holmes and John Cowperthwaite. Burgess was the senior among them as he was appointed a cadet in 1932. McDouall joined in 1934 and Holmes in 1938. Cowperthwaite was the junior as he was appointed in 1941.

Pragmatic, intelligent, focused on getting the task completed in the most efficient way, devoted to Hong Kong, able and widely admired by his colleagues Burgess took early retirement as colonial secretary in 1963 at the age of 53 for personal and private reasons. Even though he was the senior administrative officer by the time he left office and was not by inclination a reformer, he was not against changes either. He did not seek to preserve the status quo for the sake of it but he was keen not to reform unless he could see how proposed changes would produce tangible improvements.[21]

Although he was incarcerated in a Japanese prisoner of war camp after the fall of Hong Kong he was less affected by this experience than many of his colleagues who were also imprisoned or interned by the Japanese. Burgess was one of the few cadets physically fit enough and mentally sufficiently well prepared to join Colonial Secretary Franklin Gimson to set up a provisional government in August 1945 after Gimson learnt of the Japanese surrender in the Stanley internment camp.[22] Gimson achieved this by asserting control over Hong Kong on behalf of the crown even though Hong Kong was still under Japanese occupation.[23] This courageous move was formalized by Gimson getting the interned chief justice to administer an oath for him to assume office as officer administering the government. Gimson and his small group, including Burgess, then proceeded to set up a skeletal British administration and required the Japanese forces to maintain order in the colony for almost two weeks.[24] Unlike most of his colleagues who had been prisoners of the Japanese, Burgess did not spend a period of recuperation in tranquil Britain immediately after almost four years of an insular existence in occupied Hong Kong. When Admiral Harcourt's naval task force steamed into Victoria Harbour in September 1945, Burgess asked to stay on in the military administration. He went to Britain in 1946, just as many of his former colleagues were starting to return to Hong Kong to restore the old civilian administration. Burgess, by contrast, worked in the Colonial Office after a period of leave and then attended the Imperial Defence College before returning to Hong Kong in 1952. Although he did not witness the dramatic changes that unfolded in the course of the war, he took an active part in dealing with changes in Africa and general security issues in the British Empire in the immediate postwar period.[25]

His wider experience at the end of the war enabled Burgess to stay broad minded and forward looking. Indeed, it was during his time as colonial secretary that he approved a proposal to appoint female administrative officers, though he did not come up with this idea himself.[26] The first female officer, Bridget O'Rorke, was appointed in

1959 and left less than two years later. She was followed by the appointment of the first Chinese female administrative officer Shuet-yeng Chau in October 1961 and two others, Anson Fang and Shiu-ching Lo in September 1962. This was a significant policy departure for the time, but Burgess handled it without fanfare. This incident illustrated his approach as an administrator. To him the focus of the administration should be that of improving efficiency of the existing machinery, making changes that maximize results where possible and reducing abuse, including corruption where it can be achieved, so long as the changes would not rock the boat.[27] In this sense he probably epitomized the general view of his more forward looking colleagues. Until his retirement in 1963 Burgess represented the best his generation of cadets still on active duty in Hong Kong had to offer as professional administrators.

Occupying the office of secretary for Chinese Affairs for almost a decade, from 1957 to 1966, John McDouall largely shaped the direction of development of this department during an important transitional period in Hong Kong's history. He had been well versed in the ways of the Chinese Affairs secretariat when he was a junior cadet before the war. From having been interned by the Japanese, he was cut off from the numerous changes that took place all over the world in the course of the war. He returned to service in Hong Kong after a period of recuperation, which was normal for those who had to suffer the great privations of the internment camps. His outlook remained essentially of the prewar period though he did not resist all changes. When he rose to become secretary for Chinese Affairs he took on the old established approach and saw himself as the protector of the local Chinese within the colonial administration.

McDouall felt that the longstanding practice of the secretary for Chinese Affairs being the channel of communication between the government and local Chinese community suited Hong Kong. He had little time for young administrative officers who challenged his authority or tried to modernize his department. McDouall thought he knew the Chinese and how best to deal with them. His idea of modernizing his department was to focus on building up and working with the traditional kaifong neighbourhood associations instead of allowing his assistant secretaries to devote a significant portion of their time settling family and other local disputes in the community.[28] McDouall saw the kaifong associations as bridges between the government and people.[29] But he strenuously refused to introduce other changes that would provide a more modern and effective means of communication between the colonial administration and the local Chinese, or to recognize the latter as the overwhelming constituent part of the people of Hong Kong.

McDouall was such a dogged defender of traditional ways of communicating and providing pastoral care for the local community that he in fact blocked Governor David Trench's attempts to introduce major reforms.[30] Although he did not start his career as a Hong Kong cadet, Trench had served as a cadet in Hong Kong for 11 years before he left upon promotion to become high commissioner for the Western Pacific in 1961. After he returned to Hong Kong as governor in 1964, Trench wanted to introduce something akin to what later became the City District Officer (CDO) scheme. He knew from his previous service as deputy colonial secretary in Hong Kong that a new approach to handle the relationship between the colonial government and the local Chinese community was due. However, he found McDouall's resistance to his ideas too strong and chose to wait for him to retire before pushing for reform.[31]

By then, the Star Ferry riots of 1966 and the more momentous Maoist-led disturbances of 1967 had intervened. When Trench finally introduced the CDO scheme, it was widely seen as a reaction to inadequacies in the channels of communication between the government and people as revealed in the riots, particularly the Star Ferry ones.[32] While 'the confrontation' of 1967 certainly had the effect of forging a consensus in Hong Kong for the introduction of the CDO scheme, the timing of its introduction had more to do with McDouall's retirement in 1966. By the 1960s McDouall had come to represent a dwindling group of prewar cadets who were in a real sense the old guard.

The man Trench picked to succeed McDouall and introduce much needed and far-reaching reforms to the way the government communicated with the people was none other than Ronald Holmes.[33] Courageous, 'an inspirational leader' to some of his junior colleagues, open-minded and well liked by his fellow administrative officers, Holmes was described by at least one of his former colleagues as the colonial secretary that Hong Kong should have had in the 1960s.[34] Holmes first took up his appointment in Hong Kong in 1938 and served as an assistant secretary for Chinese Affairs before the war. Having fought as a member of the Special Operations Executive, he escaped after Hong Kong fell. He then joined the British Army Aid Group, a unit set up and manned largely by former residents of Hong Kong. It was based in China and its main functions were to collect intelligence and help Allied prisoners of war as well as airmen shot down behind the Japanese line to escape.[35] His wartime exploits not only earned him recognition in terms of a Military Cross and the MBE but also gave him opportunities to work very closely with his ethnic Chinese colleagues as comrades in arms. After the war, Holmes joined the military administration and attended the Imperial Defence College in London, which further exposed him to the changes that were unleashed by the war.

In the 1950s and 1960s his postings took him back to the Secretariat for Chinese Affairs in various capacities, required him to set up the Resettlement Department, and put him in charge of urban services, the housing authority, the New Territories and the Commerce and Industry Department. In some of these appointments, particularly his appointment to head urban services (1954) and the New Territories (1958) he was picked as these departments faced problems that were approaching a crisis level.[36] He was put in charge of resolving the situation and with additional resources being put at his disposal he successfully pre-empted either from developing into a full-blown crisis. His work as a senior cadet had required him to deal extensively with the local community. When he took over the Secretariat for Chinese Affairs in 1966 he did not see the local Chinese in the light that McDouall saw them. It was no coincidence that Trench picked Holmes to transform the old-fashioned and in an important sense out-of-date Secretariat for Chinese Affairs into the modern Secretariat for Home Affairs.

The reforms Holmes introduced in the secretariat were real and substantial; they were not just cosmetic changes to discard the title of an important office that had become out of kilter with the times, particularly after the Cultural Revolution related riots of 1967. The CDO scheme was the flagship of the changes Holmes introduced. While Governor Trench had conceived the basic idea for it almost a decade earlier when he was deputy colonial secretary, it was Holmes who turned it into reality.

Trench pushed for such a scheme as he thought it was 'quite wrong that the only representative of Government on the streets should be the Police, or departmental officers in their own sections', while 'there was nobody who was representing Government to the people on the streets'.[37]

In his conception the CDOs were meant above all to serve as a modern and effective channel of communication between ordinary people and the government.[38] Remarkably non-pushy as governor, Trench left it to Holmes to crystallize his idea into a policy and turn it into reality. When the scheme was finally introduced, Holmes emphasized that CDOs were 'political officers'. As such they not only must 'make themselves as accessible as possible to the people in their districts' but also assess 'the overall impact of government policies' and 'explain these policies as well as the difficulties and achievements of the Government to the ordinary people'.[39] It was the CDO scheme and other associated changes that 'served as the foundation for a new basis of legitimacy for the continued existence of a colonial regime'.[40]

Sir Ronald Holmes in dress uniform.

It would be wrong to portray Holmes as the father of the CDO scheme but he was responsible for transforming an inspired idea into a coherent policy. He also made sure it was properly implemented to reform and strengthen the administrative infrastructure without provoking any controversy in the process. Holmes's strength as an administrator was not in conceiving or advocating reform, but in inspiring his junior colleagues to do the best they could to make the institution work efficiently, whether in day-to-day governance or in introducing a new policy.[41] He belonged to the small group of prewar cadets who earned the respect and admiration of the postwar recruits.

John Cowperthwaite was a member of the old guard only in the sense that he was appointed a cadet before the Pacific War started. However, the Japanese took Hong Kong before he could get there. He spent most of the war in Sierra Leone. He really started to work for Hong Kong in the last stage of the war in London. He did so as a member of the Hong Kong Planning Unit under the aegis of the Colonial Office. He arrived in Hong Kong for the first time in the autumn of 1945 and joined the civil affairs unit under David MacDougall as part of the British military administration.[42] In general outlook and past experience he was not fundamentally different from his fellow cadets appointed shortly after the war. As an administrative officer he was among the more forward looking. In the retrospective assessment of Governor Trench he was a broad-minded and far-sighted official 'who thought for the very poor and not just for the comparatively poor'.[43]

One of the most intelligent of the postwar cadets, Cowperthwaite left his mark mainly in institutionalizing the principles that governed Hong Kong's public finances during the decade when he was financial secretary (1961–71). He was a man of integrity, a Scot 'from the Adam Smith tradition' who believed 'entrepreneurial activity does good', and resisted while in office 'the temptation to spend public money to make his mark or satisfy personal vanity'.[44] As financial secretary he was determined to keep taxes down 'in order to keep public expenditure low', for he believed the private sector was 'the best judge of investment and the best creator of wealth' and the government 'mustn't meddle in the economy unless it had to'.[45] He thought successful capitalism would benefit the poor: 'fast growth would also benefit the poor by boosting demand for labour and pushing up wages.'[46]

As controller of the public purse, Cowperthwaite discharged his duties with meticulous care and conscientiousness – so much so that his colleagues often saw him as a somewhat intimidating figure. This was partly because he was unsentimental and unrelenting in confronting his colleagues over all proposed public expenditures, and partly because his sharp mind enabled him to pick holes easily in other people's arguments. He was 'also uncommonly shy, which made for communicative deficiencies with those outside his inner circle'.[47] This gave rise to the image that he was aloof and intellectually arrogant. In reality he was eminently prepared to be persuaded by sound arguments that supported a request for public spending.[48] He was not so much tight-fisted as confident in his own judgement, and was comfortable rejecting expert views if he found such views unconvincing.

Cowperthwaite's approach was revealed in handling the government's financial commitment to building the first tunnel to link the island to Kowloon under Victoria Harbour after several false starts. At first he took the position that if the private sector considered the tunnel so important, it should finance the project.[49] But it should be recognized that even if the tunnel were built entirely as a commercial venture, the government would still have to pay for the construction of road networks on both ends of the tunnel to make the project a success.[50] When the final decision had to be made after the riots of 1967, which involved a major financial commitment by the government to make it viable, he took into account also 'the damage to the standing of the territory' if the government were to let the project collapse.[51] In addition, despite the Transport Department's expert advice that Hong Kong would only require a single-tube two-lane tunnel to meet the projected traffic, Cowperthwaite recommended a two-tube four-lane tunnel to Governor Trench as he found the traffic experts' case unconvincing over the longer term.[52] When he saw something in Hong Kong's long-term interest the government could support without risking the soundness of public finance, he was prepared to commit available public money to it.

With strong backing from Trench, Cowperthwaite built on the foundation laid by his predecessor as financial secretary, Arthur Clarke, and turned the basic principles of conservative financial management into pillars that sustained sound public finance and a competitive economy.[53] Although it was Trench who first publicly articulated the concept, in terms of 'positive *laissez-faire*' to describe the government's basic policy towards the economy, Cowperthwaite was the man who enforced it for a decade, and started to do so religiously even before Trench returned to Hong Kong as governor.[54] This policy was based on the understanding that the 'government had no business, really, in meddling with the affairs of industry and commerce because we simply weren't competent to meddle with industry and commerce'.[55] The role of the government was 'to hold the ring' and to maintain 'rules and regulations which will make sure that commerce and industry operate in as fair and as public spirited a manner as possible', without 'telling them exactly what to do with their own businesses'.[56] This formed the backbone of the policy Cowperthwaite's successor, Philip Haddon-Cave, widely publicized as the policy of 'positive non-intervention' in the 1970s.

Although Cowperthwaite was one of the most able financial secretaries British Hong Kong had had and could rank among the gods in the assessment of some of his former colleagues, he was not infallible. His and the Hong Kong government's reputation suffered in late 1967 as a result of the devaluation of sterling. When the pressure on sterling eventually became unbearable, the British government panicked and only informed the Hong Kong government of its decision to devalue by 10 per cent at two or three o'clock in the morning (Hong Kong time) on the Sunday when it happened. This did not give Hong Kong enough warning to work out countermeasures in good time, though various options were discussed in Executive Council, with the result that Hong Kong lost £60 million of its reserve.[57] With the Hong Kong dollar pegged to sterling, this inability to produce simultaneous countermeasures meant an automatic and equivalent Hong Kong devaluation. 'When the implications of this for other Asian (including Chinese) currencies became sufficiently clear, the dollar was appreciated by 10 per cent from the lowered base. This was marginally lower against non-sterling currencies than previously, and caused confusion in the minds of the general public.'[58]

In handling the aftermath of the devaluation, Cowperthwaite returned to form and behaved like a 'small Hong Kong chauvinist', a description he used on himself and some of his colleagues in private.[59] Even though he was appointed by the British government, to which he was ultimately responsible, his first loyalty as a civil servant was to Hong Kong. Cowperthwaite stood shoulder to shoulder with Governor Trench when they took the matter up with the British Treasury and the Bank of England.[60] In consideration of Hong Kong's own best interest, Cowperthwaite presided over the diversification of Hong Kong's reserve holding from sterling to a basket of hard currencies.

While Cowperthwaite undoubtedly inherited sound public finance from his predecessor he 'took that process forward, and through a mix of conservative financial policies and liberal economic policies' built up a 'growth momentum' for the economy.[61] It was the sound financial management of the 1960s that laid the foundation for Hong Kong to invest massively in, among other projects, the grandiose ten-year housing scheme of Murray MacLehose who succeeded Trench as governor. Cowperthwaite also presided over a key transitional period of Hong Kong's economy, which was merely sufficient to feed a desperately poor immigrant community in the 1950s, to a period of economic takeover that brought about real prosperity in the decade following his retirement. He did not give Hong Kong prosperity, but he institutionalized the way the government managed public finance and regulated the economy. They in turn provided a robust framework for private capital to be invested efficiently and effectively to sustain rapid growth and wealth creation, as well as enable the local people to share in the prosperity created.

In an ironic way, Cowperthwaite's apparent aloofness and intellectual arrogance reinforced within the colonial administration a sense of collective humility – recognition that civil servants could not manage the economy better than the private sector. By controlling the public purse tightly, Cowperthwaite not only scared many of his colleagues away from expanding the span of government but also made them provide sound and reasonable justification before they could increase public expenditure, without which an expansion of government was impossible. He helped to maintain the ethos of keeping the government relatively small just as Hong Kong was becoming sufficiently wealthy to have the capacity to allow the government to expand exponentially.

The old guard, as it were, was a diverse group. There were indeed some prewar officers who turned out to have obstructed changes in the administration that were overdue in the 1960s. However, others were responsible for presiding over major changes and did so well when they were called upon to do so. The cadets of the prewar vintage were not on the whole reactionary, but they did, as a group, suffer from bureaucratic inertia. The old system of government was being stretched to its limits by the late 1960s. Those holding senior offices tried to do the best they could and innovate where possible, but strains were showing. Changes were needed for good governance to be sustained in Hong Kong as the 1960s drew to a close.

**Rapid growth and changes**

Much as Hong Kong continued to subscribe to the idea of a relatively small government and Cowperthwaite controlled the public purse tightly, expansion of the administration in fact gathered greater pace than ever as the 1960s drew to a close. This could not be avoided as the capacity of the government to maintain stability and good order was put to a severe test during the confrontation of 1967. Once the disturbances were over, the government had to think ahead and take into account its inherent vulnerability in the face of irredentism in a powerful China that would eventually re-emerge from the chaos of the Cultural Revolution. It recognized in full the importance of the support of the local Chinese as it sought to maintain stability and good order against the Maoist rioters. It further accepted that its long-term survival depended on consolidating the goodwill and support of the general public. This underlined the wide support within the government for the introduction of the CDO scheme, to which Holmes was entrusted. This reform required an immediate need for an additional 12 administrative officers to serve as district commissioners and city district officers. As it involved a permanent commitment, the establishment for administrative officers and their support staff had to be increased accordingly.

With the introduction of the CDO scheme and the reorganization of the Secretariat for Chinese Affairs into the Secretariat for Home Affairs, the government publicly signalled a shift in its focus and expanded the scope of what it saw as essential to good governance. The era when the colonial administration paid more attention to the tiny expatriate community than to the huge local Chinese community formally ended, though without fanfare. It did not mean the end of the largely separate and parallel coexistence of the expatriate and local Chinese communities or an abandonment of the interests of the former by the colonial administration. The small expatriate community in fact retained ready access to the administration, and its voice was heard and usually heeded when raised. What really changed was that the government now focused its attention primarily on the vastly bigger local Chinese community, particularly when planning and organizing government services.

The rally of the local Chinese to the colonial government during the confrontation marked a turning point in the community's attitude.[62] In coming out to support the government publicly, they expected it to look after their welfare. This led to a change in the relationship between the government and the people. The largely unspoken constructive partnership with the local community, which Governor Grantham started to forge, took a major step forward. The government knew that in the future it would have to do better than just maintain law and order, as it had hitherto done. To secure its own legitimacy it would need to and be seen to be responsive to the views of the local community. This accounted for the rapid spread of advisory committees, the support of which by civil servants meant increasing the span of government.

The coming of age of a new generation of young people born, brought up and educated locally, who identified with Hong Kong, ensured the top officials' recognition of a need to change.[63] The better educated among them, students at institutes of higher education, took the lead in rallying support for the government in 1967 and continued to spearhead this important transformation. With their modern education and training in the English language, as well as access to information worldwide through the modern media, this generation looked beyond their own community for ideas and inspiration to help them find and define their sense of identity. Their coming on the scene marked the rise of a genuine citizenship among residents of Hong Kong. With the younger generation leading the way, the rest of the Chinese community followed. As the 1970s dawned Hong Kong was being rapidly transformed from an imperial outpost into a city-state with a consolidating local citizenship and increasingly vibrant civil society. This meant the local Chinese were steadily raising their expectations. Improvements in the quality of life implied increasingly higher demands being put on the scope and quality of services provided by the government.

Throughout the 1970s the government strove to meet its citizens' rising demands for a better standard of governance. It therefore grew and expanded faster than ever, though retaining its resolve to remain as small as possible. This steady expansion never imposed a great strain on public resources because Hong Kong's economic takeoff produced a rapid rise in public revenue without the tax rate being increased. This made government expansion affordable. The commissioning by Governor Murray MacLehose of an international firm of consultants, McKinsey & Company, to review the government did not put a halt to the expansion in the government's scope and span. As we shall see in Chapter 8, the McKinsey reforms called for the further expansion of government in general, but particularly of administrative officers in order to improve the quality of governance. This trend of growth and expansion in public services was a regular feature in Hong Kong all the way to the end of British rule in 1997.

*Chapter 6*
# MEETING THE CHALLENGES OF A CHINESE COMMUNITY

Although the postwar expansion of the government and administrative grade eventually produced senior administrative officers who had not served in some capacity that involved dealing with the local Chinese community on a daily basis, they remained a minority. Most directly recruited administrative officers usually served either as district officers in the New Territories or assistant secretaries in the Secretariat for Chinese/Home Affairs at an early stage of their careers. This continued even after the number of administrative officers and ethnic Chinese officers had increased significantly in the 1970s. Their scope for exposure to the local community was not diluted because the introduction of the CDO scheme in the late 1960s required and provided additional opportunities for young administrative officers to take on positions that put them in daily touch with the local Chinese community.

As life changed quickly in postwar Hong Kong, be it in the New Territories or the highly urbanized parts of Hong Kong Island and Kowloon, the work of administrative officers also adjusted to meet the rapidly changing environment.

**Life and work of a modern district officer**
The life and work of a district officer in Hong Kong shortly after the Second World War shared many similarities with that of his prewar predecessor. They have been immortalized in a popular book, *Myself a mandarin: memoirs of a special magistrate*, written by former cadet Austin Coates. In his dramatized rendition of the life of an English

colonial civil servant working as a mandarin in the New Territories (NT), Coates highlights that one of the roles of a district officer at least up to the early 1950s, when he served there, was to discharge the duties of a special magistrate. Having been assigned to such a position shortly after taking up his appointment in Hong Kong, he professed that he knew 'nothing about the common law, and very little about Chinese law and custom'.[1] However, he was mindful of the prospect of appeal and thus played safe by discharging his responsibilities as a special magistrate by 'adhering strictly to Chinese law and custom' and relied heavily on good commonsense to adjudicate disputes among members of the local community.

A distinction should, however, be made between the two roles district officers played in administering the law. The first was that of the special magistrate described by Coates, but this was in fact limited to dealing with debts. A different role that required real knowledge of criminal law was to act as police court magistrate, a role required of the district officers in Tai Po and Yuen Long but not of the District Officer South who had his office in Gascoigne Road in Kowloon.[2] The picture immortalized in Coate's lucid account is therefore slightly misleading, for he in fact started as District Officer South where he did not need a decent knowledge of criminal law to perform his duties properly.[3] With a requirement to perform the role of a police court magistrate, cadets recruited after 1948 were in fact required to pass a law examination during their initial probationary period so that they were familiar with criminal law.

In discharging his multiple duties, including those of being assistant land officer, police court magistrate and special magistrate for debts, a district officer enjoyed 'legal powers to enforce judgements'. In this sense, a district officer 'was in effect the successor to a Chinese magistrate, bearing in mind that fifty years earlier the NT had been Chinese territory'.[4] But this state of affairs did not last, as the long established arrangement for the district officer to take on the roles of special magistrate and police court magistrate ended in the late 1950s, when it was accepted that magisterial responsibilities should be performed by properly qualified members of the judiciary.

Much of the work of a district officer involved dealing with the local community. Getting to know the region and local leaders was part of the job, but it involved more than just working with members of the Heung Yee Kuk. In the NT this was the people's formal advisory and representative body, but in reality it was dominated by the local elite. When James Hayes was appointed District Officer South (1957–62) he promptly visited '180 settlements, large and small' in the first few months. He would normally walk into and around various settlements 'taking down the details of each community from the village representatives, and discussing any problems with them and the other older men'.[5] Such visits gave Hayes (and his colleagues) a better understanding of the attitude of the local people and the problems they faced – crucial when discharging responsibilities as a kind of paternal official to the local people.

Hong Kong was, in any event, developing very fast in the postwar era. Urbanization and industrialization spread into the hitherto mainly rural New Territories as the local population expanded. More than ever the work of a district officer was 'related to land: applications to purchase Crown land for building or agriculture, or to convert agricultural land to building status, or annual permits to occupy Crown land for some purpose, or permits for temporary structures, or permits for forestry lots on Crown land.'[6] Much as he was devoted to his duties as a special magistrate, District Officer Coates found himself spending 'the greater part of' his time fighting 'a rearguard action against urban encroachment, and to protect agriculture and village life, wherever this was desirable and possible, in order that the country people should not suffer by too rapid social and economic changes.'[7]

Within his area of responsibility was the town of Tsuen Wan, originally 'a group of eight eighteenth-century stone-built villages, situated in a particularly fertile rice-growing area'.[8] But it also proved an attractive site for building a new town.[9] Coates saw it as his responsibility as district officer to protect the welfare of the longstanding residents, though many of them were quite willing to sell their agricultural land to developers for a good price. Coates thought that, had they been allowed to do so quickly, they 'would have ended up destitute, being people unsuited to industrial employment'. Hence, he tried to keep land for agricultural use for as long as possible in order to give the original inhabitants time 'to adapt themselves to the new environment'.[10] Coates's paternalism reflected the attitude of the senior colonial officials at the time, who were concerned that the villagers did not fully understand the implications of moving from an agrarian to an urban-based way of life.[11] However, Coates was among the last of the district officers to take such a view. Indeed, this paternal approach had to be, and was, balanced against the benefits that urbanization and industrialization brought to the region and its longstanding residents. Even Coates was torn between these two considerations, for urbanization brought with it clean water supplies, modern sewerage, medical and health services, schools and public utilities.[12]

In the end, looking after the welfare of the local residents was a matter of achieving a balance between protecting their traditional life and helping them improve their living conditions and life chances in the modern world. It was also a matter of balancing the interests of the original residents and newcomers, the refugees from China living in horrific conditions in the numerous slums that had sprung up all over Hong Kong. Building new towns like Tsuen Wan gave them opportunities for work and to make a new life for themselves. David Akers-Jones, who was the district officer responsible for Tsuen Wan in 1959, for example, looked at its urbanization and industrialization in a much more positive light. He was pleased about the role he played in facilitating the transformation of this small 'country town, a collection of shop houses serving the needs of many villages in the surrounding countryside' in less than four decades into 'a great conurbation of an unbelievable 700,000 people, with marble-entranced shopping malls, an underground railway terminus, and multi-storey buildings with factories lodged on each floor'.[13]

What also required careful balancing were the interests of the longstanding residents and the wider interests of Hong Kong as a whole. This applied when a district officer found a major development project, such as the construction of a large reservoir, taking place within his jurisdiction. Given Hong Kong's shortage of water following industrialization and its huge population expansion, building new reservoirs was vital to its survival as a modernizing, industrializing territory. As District Officer South, James Hayes found 'the most important and time-consuming part of' his responsibilities 'was the work connected with the construction of the Shek Pik Reservoir and its ancillary projects'.[14] When a development of this nature or scale happened, the district officer was generally involved in keeping the peace between local inhabitants and the contractors over all kinds of disputes, including the disruption of geomancy (*fengshui*), and resolving the more thorny issue of relocating whole villages whose ancestral lands were needed in the wider interest of developing the colony. When Hayes first found himself in such a situation, he 'sometimes felt hemmed in by the villagers on one side and by the engineers on the other'.[15] Nevertheless, by adhering to the established policy of seeking 'to achieve our objectives through agreement' by patient negotiations with all concerned and a preparedness to 'compromise in all things', including requiring the district officer to act 'in line with time-honoured Chinese notions of how to proceed' in such matters, Hayes was able to ensure that the major developments took place.[16]

The 1950s was a transitional period for district officers. It was a time when the colonial government was still relatively small and communications between central Hong Kong and the New Territories were underdeveloped. In this period, as in the prewar era, although district officers worked under the supervision of a district commissioner, they were sufficiently remote from the centre of power in the colonial government to have almost a free hand to do their jobs as they saw fit. This gave rise to a meaningful comparison between being a district officer in British Hong Kong and a county magistrate in imperial China, namely that as long as there were no disturbances or protests in the region, a district officer (or a magistrate in traditional China) was largely left to his own devices.

Although this provided tremendous scope for abuse of power by young men put in such positions of authority, there were remarkably few abuses. Young cadets appointed as district officers found it an eye-opening experience, a serious challenge and a test of what they had learnt, particularly in their public schools, about being gentlemen and leaders. They were above all affected by the *esprit de corps* of the administrative officers. The sense of superiority and confidence associated with being cadets and a realization of what was expected of them (or an exhibition of 'imperial arrogance' as seen from the perspective of the locals) instilled in them a sense of paternal responsibility towards the local Chinese. District officers were in a position that allowed them to abuse their power easily but their satisfaction came from elsewhere. The real rewards came from a job well done and in proving their own worth among people who were, in an important sense, put under their paternal charge.

Since most cadets started their service as district officers as bachelors, they often lived a somewhat lonely and isolated life. But it was also a fulfilling one in that their achievements were easy to detect. Although they were not particularly well paid compared with the commercial sector, they were sufficiently rewarded to maintain a high standard of living as bachelors, living in government quarters and looked after by cheap domestic helpers. Being located in the New Territories also meant that there were few places in which to spend their money unless they travelled to town. This reduced the temptation for individual officers to accept bribes in a working environment that could have easily bred widespread corruption.

Brian Wilson was one of the few young cadets who was married when he served as a young district officer in the early 1950s. With a family and the need to run a car and take on other expenses, he found his salary tight and had to manage his budget carefully. He nonetheless recalls his life in Tai Po Kau as 'pleasant although cut off from the mainstream of social life in the urban areas'. It would take him 'the better part of an hour to drive on the narrow winding road to Kowloon' to do his 'shopping once a week … in Nathan Road' where he found the local grocer 'cheerful, friendly, and prepared to allow credit'.[17] With a house that had a swimming pool and gardens provided with his job, he developed 'a deep interest in gardening and a love of making things grow'.

As Hong Kong entered the 1960s the still largely rural New Territories gave way to rapid urbanization at an ever increasing pace. Following the construction of new roads and other infrastructure the New Territories was being transformed. Not only did new towns like Tsuen Wan spring up, other settlements relatively close to the urban centres of Kowloon and suitable for development such as Kwun Tong became extensions of the city of Kowloon. After Governor Murray MacLehose launched the ten-year housing policy in the early 1970s, construction of new towns like Shatin or Tun Mun gathered greater momentum.[18] By the beginning of the 1980s sizeable cities in terms of population and amenities had arisen in these 'new towns' from old villages and green fields.

With the transformation of the NT the nature of the work of district officers also changed. By the mid-1960s the old fashioned paternal approach of working with village elders and protecting longstanding residents from the encroachment of urbanization immortalized by Austin Coates was giving way to a new attitude. It reflected a recognition that the NT was by then home to many times more new settlers than old residents, with the rapidly industrializing economy demanding more and more land for factories and residential blocks. District officers still strived to strike a balance between the welfare of old residents and the wider needs of Hong Kong, but the scale on which a balance was to be struck was changing. Slowly but steadily district officers accepted the need to give more weight to the wider changes that transformed Hong Kong into a rapidly expanding industrial and commercial metropolis, where the refugees of the immediate postwar era had merged into the local population. Indeed, the focus of work for district officers also changed as Hong Kong developed further. The introduction of the ten-year housing scheme in the 1970s, for example, resulted in district officers devoting more and more time and resources to dealing with matters related to land claims.[19]

As the senior political government officer with responsibility for land, a district officer usually found himself at the sharp end of a new development or public works project in the New Territories – a process that gathered momentum as the decade progressed. The larger projects often required demolishing people's homes or building on their land or, indeed, relocating whole villages. James Hayes explains what this usually entailed:

> In the removal process, the resited villagers lost most if not all of their agricultural land, and were left with only new houses and ancestral halls. In lieu of crops or rentals from land or buildings, their livelihood now came from compensation monies paid by government, income from renting out surplus floors or entire new houses, and from the regular employment of family members.[20]

Given the impact such changes had on the local population and the complexity they often involved, district officers learnt 'the need for quick decisions' and for acting consistently, sympathetically, and fairly but insistently.[21] To do his job well a district officer had to recognize that what the 'extremely complex rural society looked to' was 'the independent, fair and impartial leadership of an official to galvanize it, to intervene and solve its disputes and to make proposals for activities which simply needed a word from a non-partisan voice from outside the community as a catalyst for action.'[22]

Most district officers learnt this quickly but there were some who did not and were less effective.

The building of roads and the advent of other forms of modern communication, particularly the telephone, radio and television, also greatly reduced the insularity of the NT and its district officers. Every passing decade saw the New Territories becoming more accessible to the old urban centres and new values and ideas being shared colony wide. Although the headquarters of the district officers or NT administration remained small and did not become overly interventionist, improvements in communications since the 1960s meant that the colonial government could keep a closer eye on the NT than hitherto. This led to a corresponding reduction in the district officers' freedom to do their jobs their own way, a freedom that was further restricted when the old minor public works budget at their disposal fell in value as a result of inflation. As district officers became reliant on additional or new allocations from the government to pay for even minor public works, they become subject to greater control from, say, the financial secretary's department.[23]

The really big change in the life and work of a district officer came with the introduction of the CDO scheme in the urban areas at the end of the 1960s. Although this scheme borrowed heavily from the experience of district officers, once the former proved a great success it in turn impacted on the way district officers worked. As time went on district officers in the New Territories, particularly in the new towns, found the main focus of their work increasingly resembled that of their colleagues in Hong Kong and Kowloon. By the 1970s the main differences between the work of a district officer and a CDO were that 'the City District Officers had nothing to do with land or planning', while a district officer needed to remain more sensitive to Chinese traditions and entrenched practices in the older communities in the New Territories.[24] This meant that, in addition to discharging the usual duties of their CDO colleagues, such as devoting time to setting up new institutions for local-level consultation like mutual aid committees, a district officer would still be required to perform the traditional pastoral duties for the rural population.

**The life and work of a CDO**
While the CDO scheme was presented as a major new initiative to bridge the gaps in communication between the government and the

people, revealed in the disturbances of 1966 and 1967, there was 'more "gradualness" and evolution than' usually recognized.[25] It was indeed a major development, as it marked an acceptance by the colonial government to end its long established aloofness, and a determination to rectify a major defect in the government structure by a massive investment of human and other resources. The need for such a reform was clearly overdue. David Trench saw the need for change when he served as deputy colonial secretary, before his promotion to become high commissioner for the Western Pacific in 1961.[26] The Social Welfare Department recognized this a little bit later but its suggestion for introducing such a scheme was given 'short shrift' by Trench's successor as deputy colonial secretary.[27] Even though Trench again saw a need for it after he returned as governor in 1964 he did not push hard for it. On both occasions Trench got no satisfaction mainly because of strong resistance from the secretary for Chinese Affairs John McDouall.[28] On the one hand this reflects how an experienced and well placed senior administrative officer could still leave a major mark on the structure of the colonial government so far into the postwar period. On the other hand it reveals an inherent weakness in the colonial administration, which was a tendency to drift rather than act decisively to tackle an identifiable inadequacy in the administration until a disaster struck or the need for reform became compelling.

When Governor Trench finally put such a reform on the political agenda, the riots of 1966 and 1967, and above all McDouall's retirement, removed all resistance. Trench and those he chose to introduce his reform sang from the same hymn sheet. As secretary for Chinese Affairs, Ronald Holmes provided overall direction whereas a veteran district officer, Denis Bray, was given the task of working out the actual details.

The colonial government sought to 'take a leaf out of the District Officer book in the New Territories and set up a similar organization in the urban areas, in order to transform communication between the government and the people'.[29] It relied on this new scheme to ensure that it would not 'be caught out by growing discontent that went unreported' prior to the riots of 1966.[30] Consequently, in the early days of the scheme, the CDOs and their staff would meet early every morning to 'talk about things they had heard in the course of their dealings with the public', and send in a summary report to their superintending district commissioners and their superiors.[31] The CDOs were also meant to be 'a local manifestation of the government, accessible for complaints and enquiries and a source of information on government policies'. They 'were also actively to get to know society in the districts and understand their own particular problems'.[32] It was with this in mind that they had offices in the busiest parts of their districts and had them decorated like local shops (rather than in the intimidating layout typical of police stations – at that time the only government offices dealing with the local people regularly at the district level).

Like district officers, CDOs were first and foremost political officers. It means they must make themselves accessible to the people in their districts and keep in touch with all local organizations. The roles the government expected them to play from the very beginning are set out in the document inaugurating the scheme:

> In addition to assessing the overall impact of government policy they are required to explain these policies as well as the difficulties and the achievements of the Government to ordinary people. They do not have extensive executive functions but it is part of their duties to advise on the coordination of services. They are free to consider whether there should be any variation in emphasis in government policies in the districts and they may initiate proposals for new policies or new procedures when the need for these become apparent from the feeling of the public. They are expected to become aware of problems and conflicts and trends of public thinking before attitudes have been struck.[33]

To ensure the success of the CDO scheme, the government 'ruthlessly picked out some of the best men in the service' to fill the initial ten vacancies, as well as the two commissioners who supervised them in Kowloon and on Hong Kong Island.[34] It was not long afterwards, however, that a posting as a CDO became a crucial stage for a young administrative officer to prove himself and learn about government at the local level.

When CDOs get down to business they 'look out for trouble', and where they find 'some aspect of government policy or action ... causing irritation or distress' they often choose to raise the matter with the relevant government department to seek redress.[35] After Gareth Mulloy became CDO Wanchai in 1971, one of the first tasks he chose to do was to improve the footpaths in his district, which were in a miserable state of repair. At first he was ignored by the relevant department as 'there was no well defined system for maintaining pedestrian pavements other than those of the Central District'. His persistence finally paid off even though he then had to persuade traders running street stalls to vacate part of the road for a day for resurfacing work to be done.[36]

A CDO's efforts to redress problems reported by local residents can also meet more powerful resistance than the usual bureaucratic inertia from various government departments. This applied in particular in the early years of the CDO scheme as syndicated corruption was still entrenched in parts of the colonial administration. Among the police division in Wanchai where corruption was endemic but not at that time properly recognized within the administration, Mulloy encountered creative obstruction as he tried to take matters up on behalf of the residents. His attempts to get the police to 'take action ... to contain the problem' of prostitution before a particular neighbourhood 'became a red light district' resulted in his initial requests being ignored while his persistent follow ups only produced 'some desultory action'.[37] Likewise, his attempt to get the police to enforce the law against garages extending their workshops to pavements, which caused a nuisance to the neighbourhood, met with 'a blatant denial that any such illegal work was being undertaken'. He did eventually manage to get the police to act but only after he had asked them to send officers to an offending garage and, in the meantime, physically 'prevented the removal of evidence by standing in front of' cars that were being repaired on the pavement until the police officers arrived.[38]

Although CDOs are not concurrently land officers and do not have responsibility for land, as district officers historically did, they also had to deal with clearing shops, homes and squatters to make way for urban redevelopment, particularly in the early years of their existence. In a case of clearance in Kowloon City where 'a few ancient legal village buildings' were cleared together with squatters in illegal structures, the owners of the legal buildings found themselves compensated less generously under the Crown Lands Resumption Ordinance than the *ex gratia* payments to the squatters. The CDO concerned took up the case for the legal residents and had to refer the matter to the governor before an amicable solution was finally found.[39] This was not an isolated case. In Wanchai Mulloy found himself taking up the cause of rooftop squatters over compensation when their homes were to be demolished, but faced resistance from the Resettlement Department over compensation. The matter was also not resolved, again in favour of the squatters, until the governor took a personal interest.[40] While the involvement of the governor reveals how the top official could get distracted from major policy issues by matters of detail at the local level, it also reflects a strong commitment to making the CDO scheme work.

From the mid-1970s to the early 1980s when the government made a determined push to improve its relations with the local people, the average CDO spent most time 'forming, managing and servicing Mutual Aid Committees' (MACs). MACs are voluntary neighbourhood organizations 'formed by the CDO, to keep Hong Kong clean, and to fight violent crime'.[41] When he was CDO at Sham Shui Po, Patrick Hase made sustained efforts 'to establish MACs wherever they were feasible'.[42] This required great devotion of personal time and effort to work with local community leaders and groups. In the whole of the last year of his office in Sham Shui Po, Hase found that he only went home for five Sundays. On the other Sundays he 'was out officiating at some District function – mostly either connected with a Mutual Aid Committee or some other grassroots group'.[43] As the colonial government had by then tackled the problem of bureaucratic corruption head on, CDOs worked closely with the police and the Social Welfare Department as they set up MACs and worked with them to improve the living conditions in their districts. As a result, 'relationships between the Police and the grassroots residents did indeed improve immensely'.[44]

As the senior representative of the colonial government in a district, CDOs also had to perform ceremonial duties. This often meant having to attend banquets and make polite public speeches. They also spent much time serving the community by performing functions for free that would usually be performed by public notaries for a fee, as CDOs were authorized to deputize for the commissioner for oaths to take sworn declarations. This could be a significant call on the time of CDOs. In the 1970s when 'a lot of schools' urged 'their pupils to take their School Certificate or "A" Level results straight round to the District Office, to take out a sworn copy of them against the possibility of the original being lost', it was not unknown for 200 such statutory declarations to be made in one office in one day.[45]

Like district officers in the New Territories, CDOs also enjoyed more scope for individual initiatives than junior administrative officers working at the secretariat. Not having a specific administrative portfolio or executive power left individual CDOs with enough room to use their own imagination and take initiatives to embark on ventures they personally judged to be of particular value. Mulloy 'thought it a good idea to try to bring about a measure of closer understanding between the military and local people' in Wanchai, a major 'bar and brothel area' catering for military personnel on rest and recreation.[46] During his time in Wanchai, Mulloy persuaded the military to make the swimming pool in the Stanley Fort available to Wanchai's youngsters one afternoon a week, with transport laid on by the army. He also talked the army into building a basketball pitch 'on a piece of waste land' in his district and celebrated the completion of this project by a friendly match, in which the Irish 'Guardsmen's height was no match for the rapid darting movements of the local lads'.[47] Mulloy's personal initiative might not have been sustained, but it no doubt improved civil–military relationships, not least by removing the mystique surrounding the military among those youngsters who were exposed to such experiments. Above all, it showed how much an imaginative and enterprising CDO could do in making a personal contribution to the district. Scope to do so made the work of a CDO particularly rewarding for young administrative officers.

**Life and work at the secretariat**
At the heart of government was the Colonial Secretariat, the proverbial corridors of power. It was the command and control centre of the administration, the coordinating centre for the drafting of most government policies, as well as home to the controller of the public purse. But it had also, light-heartedly and in private, been referred to by a non-secretariat-based senior administrative officer as a place where he would 'never come … unless I have to' since it was 'too much like a hospital where nobody ever gets cured'.[48]

The fundamental difference between working at the secretariat and in a district is that a secretariat officer works for a senior officer in the same building, whereas a district officer or CDO is usually supervised loosely by the district commissioner located some distance away. It is like the difference between a staff officer working in an army headquarters and a line officer commanding a unit in an outpost without a reliable and efficient means of instantaneous communication with headquarters. In a district an administrative officer is essentially his own boss and can take initiatives as he sees fit, provided he is willing to take responsibility and work within the limits of the law and government guidelines. At the secretariat the scope for taking decisions is more restricted, despite the small size of the administration, because of the existence of a chain of command and a clear structure for supervision.

While a junior administrative officer based at the secretariat may be working at the centre of government power, he seldom finds the same level of job satisfaction as a district officer. An administrative officer in the secretariat spends most working hours writing minutes, reviewing reports and otherwise pushing paper or meeting colleagues to discuss official business. Bernard Williams's main recollection of his first posting there in the 1950s was about how 'boring' and 'frustrating' it was, as he was keen to have regular contact with members of the public, though he also found it 'fairly useful' in gaining a general view of how the government functioned.[49] Working at the secretariat made a contrast to much of the basic work of a district officer who had more opportunity to gain a sense of satisfaction by settling a dispute or otherwise helping someone in the district. It was therefore not uncommon for young administrative officers to dislike, at least initially, their first posting to the secretariat after having served as a district officer.[50]

An 'assistant secretary was only a sort of dogsbody job'. For most it meant helping professional 'departments to sort out what they really need in some order of priority, and then help them to get it through Executive Council and Finance Committee, and Establishment as necessary so that' they could 'get the resources to deal with their problems in an orderly way'.[51] An assistant secretary's job was not, however, just to help. With a financial and economic schedule, the assistant secretary was often 'the not infrequent conveyor of unwelcome responses to requests for extra funds' from directors of government departments who wished to improve the work of their departments but produced estimates that failed to persuade the financial secretary.[52] In fact, young administrative officers posted to the finance branch were seen as potential high flyers and a posting there was generally regarded as a great honour and a test for fast track promotion in the future.[53]

The one thing in common between a posting at the secretariat and in a district was that young administrative officers were usually given their 'schedule' of responsibilities with little or no induction, a practice that endured well into the 1960s if not much later. Trevor Clark, an administrative officer of over ten years standing in Nigeria before his transfer, recalls that when he took up his first appointment in Hong Kong as an assistant secretary in 1962, he found his 'predecessor's files had no handing-over notes, summarizing where we had arrived in each, and why'. This being the case he 'had to go back through them to pick up each running tale and decide without a compass what minute to write, draft to offer or reply to send'.[54] The range of subjects for which he was responsible covered 'health, education, welfare, fire brigade, post office, Secretariat for Chinese Affairs and New Territories Administration, narcotics, labour and unions, prisons, City Hall, printery and publications, information and Radio Hong Kong'. The same experience was shared by others. When David Jordan was posted to the Colonial Secretariat upon return from long leave after an initial tour of duty at the Secretariat for Chinese Affairs, he was shown an 'empty office with a pile of files on the desk' and told to get on with his equally long list of scheduled responsibilities.[55] So Jordan and his many colleagues started a 'slow process of learning' what their duties were and how they should be carried out, though often with help and friendly advice from other assistant secretaries who had had longer experience.[56]

When administrative officers eventually rise to near the top at the secretariat they become key players in the colonial government. On the one hand, heads of branches at the secretariat oversee the implementation of policies within their schedules of responsibilities. On the other hand, they lead the presentation of new policy proposals or proposed changes to policies to the colonial secretary and, where appropriate, the governor and the Executive Council. The establishment officer, the manager of the civil service, was one such senior office at the secretariat. Geoffrey Hamilton served in this capacity from 1957 to 1962. He recalls his work in the following terms:

> [I was] responsible for hiring and firing, staffing levels, pay, discipline, conditions of service, relations with staff associations, women's pay, everything like that. ... I was really responsible for all personnel matters and I would work closely with the DCS [Deputy Colonial Secretary] quite often; instead of, as before, putting up papers, I would go and discuss with him various points and get his agreement. It was a very close relationship. So later on, when I was acting as DCS, it was an easy changeover because there was a lot, as you will have seen, of 'acting' as DCS; that would be because the Governor or the CS [Colonial Secretary] or the DCS would be on leave, and when one of them was on leave the other ones would all move up and then move down again. As it was a very close relationship, and the DCS and the CS had a very close relationship, it was the least disruptive way that one could do it.[57]

The short chain of command to the top and the scope for a senior administrative officer serving as establishment officer to act for the deputy colonial secretary did not, however, make the holder of this office as powerful a figure as it may appear. Since all government activities, including staffing, require expenditure, they have to be 'filtered through the Finance Branch'.[58] Nevertheless, a senior administrative officer holding a responsible position like this had the satisfaction that one could make a difference either through the inputs one made in the policy making or in the policy implementtation process.

Another key senior position at the core of the secretariat was the deputy colonial secretary. He was in effect the head of the secretariat responsible for coordinating various departments of the colonial government. His responsibilities covered all areas excepting matters relating to defence, which came under the defence secretary, and finance, which came under the financial secretary. The deputy colonial secretary was required to use his judgement to decide what matters should be submitted to the top and what could be decided without reference to higher authorities. David Trench, who held this office from 1959 to 1961, recalled:

> The main duty ... in those days was to deal with routine matters, routine problems, coordinate the work of the

Secretariat. The Colonial Secretary, who is eventually responsible for the routine administration of government, was nearly always tied up with two or three major issues and very often spent nearly all his time on a few major issues of the moment; whereas the DCS then took everything he possibly could off his hands in the way of minor decisions and minor questions that cropped up, or not as urgent questions that cropped up, at the same time coordinating. When I was DCS I started a system of having every branch head in, in the morning, for a strictly limited period of time. ... It was quite useful because somebody dealing with a branch here could talk across the table to somebody dealing with another branch there and sort something out verbally, there and then. ... [On a matter] that obviously wanted the Governor's decision then, clearly, it went up through the CS. If it was something that he knew what the policy was and knew what the feeling of his superiors was, he would then take the decision on the basis of what he knew and what he felt and what he thought they would think. If he was wrong, then he got a rocket. ... There's a distinction between the things that you feel you ought to go up to the Governor because they are of such importance and the answer is so doubtful, and the things which, by law or regulation, or some policy decision, have to go up to the Governor, something which only he had the authority to decide.[59]

Pivotally important as this office was, the real power of a deputy colonial secretary depended ultimately on the personality of the office holder and his relationship with other heads of major departments, which could also be headed by administrative officers of the same rank. In the case of Trench, despite his obvious ability and being a high flyer, he was unable to persuade Secretary for Chinese Affairs John McDouall to introduce the CDO scheme. Here they had a basic difference over a policy matter and both felt strongly they were right. McDouall prevailed because this was a matter within his schedule of responsibilities and not that of the deputy colonial secretary.

The Trench–McDouall disagreement over the CDO scheme reflected the huge scope senior administrative officers had to shape and transform the 'style and content' of their posts. On this occasion and with the benefit of hindsight McDouall was wrong and his steadfast defence of his views delayed the introduction of a major administrative reform that would have benefited Hong Kong. But neither he nor Trench could foresee the future. For better or worse McDouall's obstinacy or gallant defence of his firm belief was one of the qualities that made good administrative officers in Hong Kong. They are not meant to be 'yes men' but to do what they thought was right for the colony and its people, but this sometimes meant that mistakes were made. Herein lies an inherent source of job satisfaction for administrative officers. Ian Lightbody summed this up succinctly in the following observation he made in a valedictory address to his colleagues: 'I'm sure many of you have had this experience, observing how a particular job is done by different individuals in succession – one stays within well-trodden boundaries while another sees and deals with new needs, or generates new approaches to familiar old problems.'[60] It was the flexibility of the system and scope for senior administrative officers to take initiatives that made working at the Colonial Secretariat rewarding.

**Life and work in departments**
Being generalist officers, administrative officers were posted wherever the colonial government found it valuable to do so, including to professional departments that had not had administrative officers previously or for a very long time. Until the early postwar decade, this generally meant an administrative officer was appointed to take over as head of department. By the 1950s this was no longer the case because administrative officers were also posted to departments at more junior levels.

One of the most challenging appointments for an administrative officer was to a professional department at a senior but not top level. The most demanding of such appointments was probably that of the first ever police administrative secretary to which Donald Luddington was posted in 1958. The police had previously been put under the command of a cadet in 1867 after two decades of dismal performance.[61] But professional police officers regained the headship in 1933 and staffed its top echelon ever since.[62] The appointment of an administrative officer at the senior level therefore provoked resentment from some police officers who saw this as a 'backward step'.[63] Others gave Luddington a sense that they suspected he might have been placed there by the secretariat to spy on them. It was therefore not a hospitable environment when Luddington, a middle ranking, very able and rapidly rising administrative officer, took up his assignment. Although it took some time, Luddington did break down the suspicion the police had of him.[64] He did so by proving that he was there to help the police deal more effectively with the secretariat and, in the words of Commissioner Henry Heath, 'did very well indeed'.[65]

Luddington translated the secretariat's instructions into words the police could understand. He removed misunderstanding between the two sides, and trained senior police officers in administrative housekeeping to enable them to discharge their managerial duties more effectively.[66] By doing his job well he helped the police put its case more successfully to the secretariat and proved that he was not the latter's mole. He bridged gaps that had long existed between the secretariat and one of the biggest and most important professional departments. In the end Luddington did well not only by the police but also by himself and the secretariat, for he demonstrated how administrative officers and professional departments could improve governance by working with and complementing each other.

Administrative officers were also deployed to set up and manage other important departments. When a new department was created, it was not unusual for a senior administrative officer to be put in charge until a suitably qualified professional head could eventually be groomed to take over. When the old labour office in the Secretariat for Chinese Affairs was upgraded to become a department in the late 1940s, Brian Hawkins was appointed the first commissioner. Within the department more junior administrative officers and specialists from the United Kingdom served together.[67] After a cadre of departmental labour officers was established, the non-directorate administrative officers were posted elsewhere and senior advisers or labour officers from the UK ceased to be recruited.

A similar development happened at the Social Welfare Department, which came into existence in 1958. When Cadet David Baron was appointed to head this new department he set out to improve its professional expertise and efficiency.[68] Under Baron's direction serving officers were selected for professional social work training. They included Thomas C. Y. Lee, who rose to become head of the department in the mid-1970s. Baron at first also relied on energetic administrative officers to put the department on a sound footing. When he found the relief section wanting, he secured the service of a newly recruited administrative officer David T. K. Wong to reorganize it. Although Wong was still on probation, he made the most of his previous experience as a journalist and of his good common sense to overhaul this section. He quickly turned it around and ensured hot food and other essential relief were delivered to victims of fires and natural disasters efficiently and effectively. As Hong Kong relied heavily on the voluntary sector to provide welfare services, the director of social welfare worked closely with the social welfare advisory committee to ensure all available expertise and resources in his area of responsibility were fully utilized.[69]

Working in a department could also offer administrative officers an opportunity to serve Hong Kong in an unexpected way. This applied in particular to those administrative officers posted to the Commerce and Industry Department. This was primarily the result of the success of Hong Kong's textile exports attracting pressure from its main markets to impose restrictions on them. It fell on the Commerce and Industry Department to represent Hong Kong in trade talks after the United States pushed in Geneva for the exclusion of cotton textiles from the normal rules of the General Agreement on Tariffs and Trade (GATT), and the British government responded to domestic lobbying and sought to require Hong Kong to restrain its export of textiles to the UK. In seeking to represent and defend Hong Kong's commercial interests, the department worked closely with the Cotton Advisory Board, formed in 1961 as the forum for consultations on the negotiations to come. However, before the deputy director of the Commerce and Industry Department became the chief trade negotiator it was John Cowperthwaite, then deputy financial secretary (economic), who took the lead in representing Hong Kong when these talks started in the early 1960s.[70]

One of the administrative officers who rendered sterling service as Hong Kong's chief trade negotiator was David Jordan when he served as deputy director at the Commerce and Industry Department at the end of this decade. In terms of intellect Jordan was probably the brightest of the administrative officers of his generation, though his penchant for debate or confrontational style meant he did not enjoy as cordial a relationship with his colleagues as most of them usually did among themselves. When he was reading Chinese as an undergraduate at Oxford University Jordan refused to learn to pronounce a word of Chinese because he was being taught classical rather than modern Chinese. He reckoned that an ability to speak classical Chinese would not enable him to communicate orally with any Chinese person he might come across and there was therefore no point in learning to speak, as distinct from read and write, the language.[71] His adamant refusal did not, however, stop him getting a first-class degree in Chinese at Oxford. This episode reveals his intellectual capacity and his personality. He had great confidence in his own judgement and a willingness to confront others regardless of rank whenever he felt he had good reasoned grounds to do so.

When appointed to the Commerce and Industry Department Jordan had no prior experience of working in trade, economic or financial matters. He readily admitted that until then he had not realized that GATT meant two things: a document known as the General Agreement on Tariffs and Trade and the organization that services the contracting parties to the agreement.[72] After failing to get anywhere in his first mission in negotiating with the Swedes and Norwegians, Jordan quickly learnt the basic rules about negotiations and how they applied to Hong Kong's trade. The first is to avoid getting 'personally involved' and 'get angry with the other chap because he's taking an unreasonable line unless you know that he's doing it off his own bat'. Usually he is merely carrying out instructions and by not personalizing the negotiations, agreements can be reached despite sharp arguments being exchanged.[73] The second is that it is ineffective and pointless to present the case as seen from one's side; one must 'present it in a way that it makes sense to the chap on the other side' in order to persuade the other side of one's case.[74] The third is to look at the long-term relationship, which requires honesty in negotiations, and refrain from seeking an advantage through deception or even omission as this will eventually be known to the other side and harden its position in subsequent negotiations. This applied particularly to Hong Kong's trade negotiations in the 1960s and 1970s as they needed to be renewed or updated regularly. The fourth is to focus on getting something valuable in return when making a concession. One must use accommodation or toughness, not for emotional reasons but as the situation requires, securing an agreement based on reasonable give and take.[75] What Jordan and other Hong Kong trade negotiators had to bear in mind all the time was the reality that Hong Kong negotiated for one purpose only and from a position of inherent weakness. It was to secure as high as possible quotas for exporting its manufactured textile goods and, in this sense, was always the supplicant in trade negotiations.

While most of the trade negotiations were tough because Hong Kong had no muscle to flex and little to offer by way of concessions that would not hurt its exports, the trickiest and most unpleasant aspect of this work involved handling relations with British colleagues based in the United Kingdom. There was a tendency for United Kingdom officials not directly responsible for Hong Kong to see the governor as just another British civil servant, and ignore the fact that he was also at the same time head of a separate government and thus responsible for the welfare of the people under his charge, albeit within the framework of a British dependent territory. While the British government could instruct the governor this was an authority that should only be exercised by the responsible secretary of state. Senior civil servants in the UK had no right or authority to instruct officials of the colonial government directly.

Within this context a case of unwarranted interference in Hong Kong's trade negotiations by UK officials occurred in the summer of 1970, when a Canadian delegation was on its way to Hong Kong to start negotiations.[76] A telegram from the Foreign and Commonwealth Office forbade Hong Kong to negotiate with the Canadians on the grounds that Hong Kong had informed London earlier. Jordan was at that time acting director for Commerce and Industry and had to fly immediately to London to find a solution. When he arrived in London he quickly ascertained that this telegram had originated from the Department of Trade and Industry for its own reasons and had been sent on to Hong Kong by the Foreign Office without ministerial approval. Armed also with knowledge of the proper constitutional relationship between the UK and Hong Kong he was able to persuade the assistant under-secretary in charge of Hong Kong affairs at the Foreign Office not to take the side of the trade department. In the end Jordan achieved a significant victory. He secured an agreement from Sir Antony Part, the permanent secretary at the Department of Trade and Industry that while Hong Kong 'should continue to keep the British Government informed, Hong Kong should be able to make its own decisions about what the negotiating instructions to its negotiators should be' in their negotiations with the Canadians.[77]

Working as Hong Kong's trade negotiators or taking on quasi-diplomatic duties representing Hong Kong's primarily economic or trade interests abroad was a dimension of work administrative officers did not have before the war. In the postwar period it started with a senior administrative officer being posted to London as Hong Kong's liaison officer in the metropolitan country, an appointment that evolved into the Hong Kong commissioner in London. It was, however, the advent of trade negotiations that required senior administrative officers to take on quasi-diplomatic duties negotiating with foreign governments. Administrative officers who were put in such appointments had generally done well and they gained much satisfaction from successfully having promoted or defended the interests of the territory.[78]

Where the negotiations were under the umbrella of the cotton textiles arrangement (from 1962) or the multi fibre arrangement (from 1973) to which Hong Kong was a signatory, they were straightforward discussions between the two sides. The task of the Hong Kong negotiator was made more complicated when the subject matter was not covered by those arrangements and GATT issues were involved. In such a situation Hong Kong had to operate under the United Kingdom umbrella, and there had been occasion when a British trade official was in the lead, with the Hong Kong representative being a member of such a delegation doing his best to ensure that Hong Kong's best interest was not undermined. In this regard the Jordan–Part understanding contributed significantly in affirming Hong Kong's right to exercise its autonomy even where a British trade official was imposed on a Hong Kong delegation to keep a watching brief.[79]

The tenacious efforts of Hong Kong trade negotiators to assert autonomy in the conduct of their commercial relations had an important unintended consequence. When Britain entered into negotiations with China over the future of Hong Kong in the early 1980s, it allowed Hong Kong to claim justifiably that it had full autonomy in the conduct of its commercial relations and be deemed a contracting party to the GATT. This was critical in that it enabled the Hong Kong Special Administrative Region to become a member of the World Trade Organization ahead of China's own accession.[80]

## Fighting corruption

With perhaps a few exceptions all through Hong Kong's history as a British colony, administrative officers did not succumb to corruption and even among the few who might have done so none had it proved in a court of law. This is remarkable since there were tremendous opportunities for administrative officers to take bribes and bureaucratic corruption was endemic within the colonial administration until the 1970s.

What insulated the administrative officers from corruption was the successful translation into reality of the original rationale for their introduction, namely to build 'a meritocracy from ... gentlemen of professional background'.[81] Indeed, the average early administrative officer came from 'a solid, though not rich, upper middle-class family, went to a public school ... and then went up to one of the older universities,' and was not brought up with expensive tastes or habits.[82] Those picked were 'not too brilliant' but were supposed to have the potential to become 'a leader ... who could safely be sent to ... wherever and could be relied upon to function with the minimum supervision, and to act sensibly and calmly in the face of the most difficult circumstances'.[83] Any temptation to stray was contained by a good remuneration package that included not only a good salary but also living quarters, long leave with pay and paid passages, health and education provisions for one's dependants, and a generous pension. Above all, from their earliest days the administrative officers built up an *esprit de corps* that instilled in new recruits a spirit that valued hard work, healthy recreations and a pride in being a member of the elite in the administration in the shape of a league of gentlemen. The recruitment of ethnic Chinese officers to their ranks did not change this at all, for no Chinese administrative officer would be promoted or would choose to stay if one could not embrace this *esprit de corps*. It implied a belief that corruption was beneath them. The other side of this much cherished pride and spirit was arrogance and aloofness, as well as detachment from the reality of government at the lower levels.

Until the case involving Police Chief Superintendent Peter Godber caught the imagination of Hong Kong in the early 1970s, most administrative officers generally felt that corruption was going on at the lower levels of the administration where petty officials accepted advantages but few took the matter sufficiently seriously to take decisive action to suppress it.[84] They should have known better but most were in fact at that time shocked by the revelation that a senior officer, albeit a police rather than administrative officer, like Godber was implicated. The way Claude Burgess, one of the most able and pragmatic of administrative officers of his generation, looked at this problem when he was colonial secretary reflected the general attitude of his colleagues. He knew there was 'corruption in the public service' and did not think it would 'ever be entirely eliminated'. While he was 'most anxious to reduce it below its present level' he felt the government was 'hampered by information without which it is virtually impossible to proceed in particular cases'.[85] There was complacency among administrative officers on the issue of corruption but it was not something they condoned. Most administrative officers were focused on doing their duties and did not look out for evidence of corruption. Some also overlooked corruption because it was dismissed as just an evil practice associated with the underlings who were poorly remunerated.

As city district officer in Wanchai when the corrupt policeman Cheng Hon-kuen was divisional superintendent, Gareth Mulloy had first-hand experience of being invited by 'CID Wanchai ... to join the Club'. Mulloy knew immediately that this was 'the plain brown envelope Club and not the Police Sports Association' but his 'first reaction nevertheless was incomprehension'.[86] As he recalls: 'It never occurred to me to accept the offer.' But he felt he needed to know more before he 'could take any definitive action to nail the putative corrupter'. The middleman on this occasion was one of his assistants in the city district office and Mulloy saw him as 'an ally' until it became clear that he was working for the corrupt police syndicate. When Mulloy realized that he could get no useful information about the syndicate, he reported the matter to his head of department, fellow administrative officer Donald Luddington. Luddington promptly informed the head of the police anti-corruption branch. The police enquiry soon ended after Mulloy's contact denied that the meeting at which he invited Mulloy ever took place. Subsequently, this middleman, an underling, was merely moved to a different post while Mulloy, the gentleman administrator, was asked by the head of the civil service 'to explain in writing why where was a delay between the first approach' and his reporting to Luddington. It was not surprising that he 'felt sullied' with this 'dispiriting outcome'.[87]

When Mulloy tried to understand why corruption was tolerated within the police, his police friends told him that in the view of many in the police 'real' crimes were murder, rape, robbery and such like. Compared with these, 'taking a backhander for turning a blind eye to a minor social crime which was going to continue to be committed anyway was acceptable', particularly since money thus acquired could be used to buy information to solve some of the 'real' crimes. Mulloy found such a justification unacceptable.[88] His view was shared by most administrative officers until the government finally made a determined effort to tackle corruption in the 1970s. What they failed to see was the commonality in the justification made by these police officers and in their own failure to face squarely up to the problem of bureaucratic corruption.

To generally incorruptible administrative officers who dedicated their working lives to becoming gentlemen-bureaucrats, 'petty corruption' by the lower orders was also implicitly dismissed as a kind of 'minor social crime which was going to continue to be committed'. They did not take on bureaucratic corruption earlier partly because it was an inherently very difficult problem to tackle within the limits imposed by the law.[89] But it was also because they did not see the real extent of the problem and its seriousness clearly enough to understand that it was a 'real' crime and a major problem undermining good governance.[90]

Much as administrative officers, collectively the guardians of good governance, should be criticized for not tackling syndicated corruption earlier, they should be given credit for ensuring the relatively quick success of the campaign against corruption once it was launched. What was involved was not so much that administrative officers headed the new Independent Commission Against Corruption (ICAC) in its formative years. After all the successful creation of the public image that administrative officer Jack Cater was 'Mr ICAC' needs to be balanced against the pivotal role that former special branch officers John Prendergast and G. A. Harknett played in ensuring that the commission delivered what it promised the general public.[91] The really important contribution of the administrative officers (and heads of professional departments including the police) was their ready cooperation with the ICAC. The non-corrupt nature of the administrative officers and other top level civil servants meant that there were no vested interests in the upper echelons of the colonial government that resisted or sabotaged the campaign to attack bureaucratic corruption.

When they finally took on corruption most administrative officers were not seeking to make amends for their earlier failure in neglecting corruption. Most did not recognize their earlier failings. They merely did what they had always done: do the right thing by the government and by the people. Corruption was repugnant to most, if not all, administrative officers and they were only too happy to play their part to get the corrupt elements removed from government service once this caught their imagination.

*Chapter 7*
# LOCALIZATION

Although the Hong Kong government formally adopted a policy of localization in 1936 this was implemented only half-heartedly before the Second World War and it did not in any event apply to cadets.[1] The first break with the long established tradition of recruiting only young men of pure European descent as cadets was made after the war when Governor Young appointed Paul Tsui as an administrative officer in 1946.[2] While Young intended to offer Hong Kong a new deal, and Tsui's appointment reflected this in part, it did not mark the beginning of a sustained new policy to recruit local talent to join the colonial government at the administrative officer level. Tsui was a special case. He had previously demonstrated his loyalty to the crown by service in the British Army Aid Group during the war and proved his suitability as an administrator in the British military administration. Compared with his immediate predecessor and successor, Governor Young was unusual in his views of Hong Kong's future and politics.[3] He believed that Hong Kong could not secure its future as a British territory without involving the local people in the management of their affairs as much as possible. But his impact was limited because he was in office for less than a year. Tsui's appointment should therefore be seen as a landmark event, but it was not the real beginning of a policy to localize at the administrative officer level. Indeed, it was not until the early 1950s that the colonial government started to advertise vacancies in Hong Kong in addition to recruiting in the UK.

The recruitment of local administrative officers had a slow start partly because the expansion of the administrative class had always been conducted at a deliberate pace, but also because it took time for suitable local candidates to see this as an attractive career opportunity. More important was the mindset of the government. For a long time there was an unspoken understanding that the bulk of administrative officers would continue to be recruited from the UK or from transfers from within the empire. It was only after the initial intake of local officers proved a success that an increasing percentage of them came to be recruited. Even then, in the 1970s, there was a feeling within the colonial administration that 'a "balance" of local-expatriate recruitment to the police inspectorate and the Administrative class' was needed 'to show both Beijing and the local community that Britain remained committed to Hong Kong'.[4] It was not until Hong Kong's future was settled in the first half of the 1980s that the recruitment of expatriate officers was eventually stopped and differential fringe benefits as part of their overall remuneration package completely removed.

'Decolonization' elsewhere in the British Empire did not provide much impetus for Hong Kong to localize faster. Unlike most other colonies, there was no expectation in Hong Kong that it was moving towards independence and there was therefore no sense of urgency in the implementation of a policy of localization. Instead, 'decolonization' elsewhere, particularly following British Prime Minister Harold Macmillan's 'wind of change' speech in South Africa in 1960, meant that experienced colonial administrative officers became readily available for Hong Kong to recruit. Their availability made a successful implementation of a localization policy less pressing. While such recruitment was seldom forced on Hong Kong it was encouraged by the British government in London because it had a moral if not actual responsibility to help colonial administrative officers find alternative employment upon the independence of a colony.[5]

Those administrative officers who had served elsewhere in the British Empire before their appointments to Hong Kong belonged, strictly speaking, to two categories. Some went to Hong Kong, often from British Malaya or Singapore, on transfer at a relatively early stage of their colonial administrative career, which meant they would keep their seniority gained elsewhere. Others left their colonies, often on independence, received a severance lump sum payment and were recruited by the Hong Kong government at the lowest administrative officer grade regardless of their previous seniority.[6] They came to be

*Governing Hong Kong*

After a game of cricket in the early 1960s. *Back Row (from left)*: Brian Hook (AO), Geoff Fawcett (EO), Harry Magihon (EO), Stan Pascoe (EO), Lawrence Mills (EO), Alan Bailey (EO), Eddie Cunningham (retired). *Front Row*: Jimmy McGregor (Trade Officer), Trevor Bedford (AO), Tony Shepherd (AO), Norman Whitely (Secretary, Education Department), Derek Readman (EO), Norman Oei (EO).

known informally as colonial 'retreads'. They were also distinct from the small but not insignificant number of individuals 'who came out from the Home Civil Service, sometimes just for a tour or two, but some then transferring in' and stayed.[7]

### Colonial 'retreads' and transferees

Unlike tyres for vehicles, colonial 'retreads' should not be dismissed as 'inferior goods' or seen as less able or loyal than administrative officers recruited originally for Hong Kong. In fact, among those who transferred to Hong Kong were very able administrative officers. Some became highly successful after their move to Hong Kong. They supplied in the postwar period not only a number of policy secretaries and heads of department but also two chief secretaries (Sir Philip Haddon-Cave and Sir David Akers-Jones) as well as a governor (Sir David Trench).[8]

In general terms one thing that usually marked an officer originally recruited for another colony out from those recruited for Hong Kong was the former's lack of training in the Cantonese language, though a few officers in the latter category also did not receive Cantonese training because the government could not spare them for such a purpose when they joined in the immediate postwar period. Most administrative officers who relocated to Hong Kong in mid-career were 'retreads'. They did so upon independence of their colonies, mainly in Africa, where they would have been trained in a native African language. A small number of colonial administrative officers also transferred to Hong Kong from elsewhere, though they usually did so relatively early in their career. Among those who came from Southeast Asia some had already learnt Chinese. Kenneth Topley, for example, joined the Malayan civil service after he graduated from the London School of Economics, and started to learn Chinese as part of his one-year preparatory course prior to taking up his appointment in Singapore. He had only served five and a half years in Singapore when he transferred to Hong Kong.[9] David Akers-Jones also started his administrative career as a member of the Malayan civil service and learnt Chinese before he moved to Hong Kong after one tour of duty in Malaya.[10] As they transferred to Hong Kong at an early stage of their career as colonial administrative officers, retained their seniority, had learnt Chinese and had had experience dealing with ethnic Chinese in a colonial context they integrated more quickly and fully into the Hong Kong service than some of the 'retreads' who had spent long service elsewhere, particularly in Africa.

Their lack of Cantonese did not make most imported officers less valuable to Hong Kong, though they would have no doubt found a knowledge of the language valuable, not least in helping them to understand the needs and mentality of the local people better. With the civil service expanding rapidly in the postwar era, there were more and more administrative positions, particularly at the Colonial Secretariat, where Chinese language was not essential for the work. Furthermore, officers brought in from other colonies took with them different experiences and perspectives from those who had always worked in Hong Kong. 'Retreads' James Sweetman and Roderick MacLean, for example, were the first to advocate the creation of a Central Provident Fund in 1972 because they had learnt about and understood the value of such a scheme when they served in Singapore.[11] Their recommendation was not taken up but Hong Kong did come to introduce a scheme based on the Singapore model three decades later, in 2000.

From the colonial government's perspective retreads and transferred officers were often good value for money. They had relevant experience and a track record before being recruited to Hong Kong.

They could be deployed immediately and at little risk that they would prove incompetent or unsuitable. The cost factor applied even more to 'retreads' as they were appointed at a rank or seniority lower than in their original colonies.[12] This meant lower salary costs for the government though it did not usually imply a reduction in remuneration for the retreads since Hong Kong salaries were considerably higher than in most other colonies. Once an officer had proved himself in Hong Kong, he could be appointed to a position of greater responsibility and seniority quickly if such a call for experienced human resources existed. Trevor Clark, for example, was appointed as a basic level administrative officer on arrival in Hong Kong though he had previously secured an accelerated promotion after a decade of service in Nigeria, but he found himself deployed to take on the responsibility of a Staff Grade C officer after only nine months.[13]

The government's efforts to secure value for money, however, caused disgruntlement and tension. To begin with it did not do much for the morale of many of the more senior or experienced retreads. In the case of Clark he felt his seniority and recognition acquired in Nigeria should have been given due credit from the beginning. Roderick MacLean was also not pleased was about being 'ranked as a timescale AO back among the beginners after ten years as a superscale officer elsewhere'.[14] Those dissatisfied usually had other reasons to be unhappy as well. To Clark the different atmosphere that prevailed in the Hong Kong service and in Nigeria was a significant factor. After his first day in Hong Kong he wondered whether he 'had made a dreadful mistake' as he 'had left an administrative service that was a family' to one 'that thought it was a corporate business'.[15] MacLean was dissatisfied as he saw his longstanding Hong Kong colleagues as narrow minded, backward looking, pompous and insufficiently driven to understand the local population. From his perspective, the 'cadre of Administrative Officers was dominated by officers who had never served anywhere else' and they too 'firmly embraced the doctrine of Saint Hong Kong, the true light and only path to redemption'.[16] Whether retreads who took this view were justified or not, their disenchantment could not have enhanced their performance as administrative officers.

The practice of importing experienced administrative officers also had a negative impact on morale among the more junior officers appointed specifically to serve in Hong Kong. From their perspective the insertion of outsiders at a point of higher seniority to them brought frustration as they could not but see their prospect of promotion being pushed back.[17] Eric Peter Ho observes that when he joined as a cadet from within the government, he was number 39 on the timescale list but when the list was next published, he found he had been pushed back to number 43, as transferees had been slotted in at higher seniority. It made him indignant: 'professional working experience in Hong Kong did not count towards seniority, but watching the Masai bleeding their cattle for a cup of blood, and contemplating the tropical sunset under a palm tree, did!'[18] Indeed, MacLean, a retread, readily expressed understanding the frustration of his more junior, and in particular local, colleagues, and he saw the recruitment of retreads as unnecessary if the government had adopted an effective localization policy earlier.[19]

The tension between retreads and administrative officers specifically recruited for Hong Kong needs to be put in context. It existed and was a source of disenchantment for some officers but it was never so strong that it created real problems for the effective organization or operation of the senior civil service. As for the locally recruited administrative officers' reduction in promotion prospects it became less and less of an issue as the number of administrative officers expanded and localization gathered pace quickly in the 1970s. The effect of any promotion prospect was also reduced as the number of colonial administrative officers available for export to Hong Kong dropped significantly – by then most British colonies had achieved their independence. On the whole the import of mid-career officers did not undermine in any meaningful way the *esprit de corps* of the administrative officers of Hong Kong.

What the government failed to do was to use the tension between the longstanding administrative officers and retreads creatively to improve governance. The critical comments retreads like MacLean and Clark made of their longstanding colleagues were not totally unfair or ungrounded. On the contrary, those shortcomings existed and they were largely overlooked by an administration that enjoyed basking in the glory of its own success. With their inadequacies being revealed through the critical eyes of newly arrived but experienced outsiders, an opportunity existed for the top echelon to redress them. If the diversity of views and differences in approach had been directed into vigorous and constructive internal debates, both sets of officers could have understood and appreciated the other's approach better. If such dynamic exchanges were harnessed constructively they would have produced synergy. The failure of the top echelon of the administration to address this issue not only allowed a good opportunity to improve governance to pass, but also revealed that one of the key advantages of importing experienced officers was squandered. This particular failing in itself vindicated the critical assessments made by retreads like MacLean and Clark.

**Obstacles to local recruitment**

After Hong Kong had been rehabilitated from the damage caused by the Pacific War and Japanese occupation, and got through the uncertainties associated with the rise of the communists to power in China, the colonial government renewed the prewar policy of localization. What this meant was that whenever a vacancy arose, it would be advertised within the government or locally in Hong Kong first. If this should fail to produce the desired results, the vacancies would be filled through recruitment in London. But the application of this policy to administrative officers and the police was limited.

The localization of the administrative class really started in 1954, when the government finally advertised for Class II cadets in Hong Kong, but, as a former establishment officer recalled, 'there had to be a certain proportion of expatriates coming in'.[20] Even after the government adopted a general policy in 1961 not to appoint expatriate officers to the permanent establishment 'unless there appears to be no possibility of Chinese with the appropriate qualifications being available in the next few years', it continued to work on the basis that half the administrative officers should be expatriate.[21] Whether this percentage should be seen as a ceiling for recruitment or a target is a moot point. The reality was that the government failed to reach this level of local recruitment into the administrative class until the beginning of the 1980s.[22]

In the entire decade of the 1950s, only eight local administrative officers were appointed. They were John Joseph Swaine, Cheng Tung-choy, Li Fook-kow, Tan Boon-cheok, Selwyn Alleyne, Ip Chi, Eric Peter Ho, and Yeung Wing-tai. They included two who left after only about three years, two others from distinguished local families, two Eurasians and a non-Chinese-speaking overseas Chinese born in Trinidad and educated at Oxford but appointed on local terms and thus officially designated a local officer.[23] Among the six who stayed on for more than ten years three were recruited from within the colonial government, where they had served in professional capacities – Tan in social welfare, Alleyne in education and Ho in inland revenue. It was not until the 1960s that local graduates started to be recruited directly in significant numbers. From 1960 to 1969 the government appointed 65 new administrative officers, including 29 local ones. Among the latter 13 were recruited in 1968 and 1969.[24] While the local intake in this decade is more than three times that of the 1950s, the figures confirm that as a policy localization did not really take off until the late 1960s.[25]

The most widely held explanation senior expatriate administrative officers shared for the slow pace of localization in the early postwar decades was that 'Hong Kong boys and girls weren't particularly interested in going into government'.[26] One highly experienced establishment officer of this period recalled that 'It was certainly very difficult to encourage them to join the Administrative Service because they didn't want to' join.[27] This sentiment was echoed by another former establishment officer who explained that the government was 'waiting for local candidates of merit to come up' as 'there weren't enough local applicants of sufficient merit to fill various vacancies'.[28] Such a view is not, however, shared by those Hong Kong citizens who joined locally in the 1950s and 1960s. In general, they found the advertised position of Cadet II or administrative officer prestigious, well paid and attractive. But they necessarily form a biased sample as they were the successful candidates.[29]

The reality was that the colonial government did try to recruit locally, but it did so gingerly. This cautious approach was in line with the practice elsewhere in the British Empire ever since Queen Victoria first proclaimed a policy of localization for India in 1858, following the successful suppression of the Indian Mutiny. In India and the colonial empire, until the prospect for independence emerged as a serious one, localization progressed slowly.[30] Since independence was never on the agenda in Hong Kong, there was no pressure for this ingrained attitude to change until the end of British sovereignty was in sight.

This does not mean that successive establishment officers were wrong to say that human resources the colonial administration deemed suitable were scarce in Hong Kong. The total number of graduates Hong Kong produced every year was fewer than 1000 in this period, for the Chinese University was not founded until 1963 and did not start to produce graduates for another four years. The small University of Hong Kong was the only source of local graduates until towards the end of the 1960s. A significant proportion of the graduates studied medicine and engineering, and were generally not interested in pursuing an administrative career. The pool of suitable graduates was indeed small.

The actual criteria that the government had for recruitment were not, in contrast, particularly high. In the words of George Rowe, who served as an establishment officer for much of the 1960s:

> The criteria were certainly an academic standard not less than a good 2nd – not necessarily a 1st, but not less than a good 2nd – a chap who could move easily amongst his peers in that sort of way; a chap who had already shown some interest outside the academic world, that he had some other activities going, some other interests going; preferably someone who'd had something involving work with the community at large, so he knew what it was to look after a community.[31]

They were not significantly different than for candidates recruited in the UK. In reality, recruitment in Hong Kong was vetted more professionally and stringently by serving administrative officers in interviews and through competitive examinations.

By comparison, recruitment in the UK up to at least the early 1970s had been based primarily on whether the graduate applicants fitted a particular model. An expatriate officer described this eccentric selection process as 'something out of an Evelyn Waugh novel: benevolent old buffers in the opulent setting of the Foreign Office making rather vague remarks and asking questions that did not seem searching at all'.[32] Indeed, in the interwar years expatriate candidates were often screened by an informal network of tutors at selected universities like Oxford and Cambridge for their suitability before they were subjected to the formal recruitment process.[33] In the postwar era, the old network and practice were gradually replaced by more modern recruitment drives. Even then what recruiters acting for the Hong Kong government in the UK looked for were graduates with a good honours degree 'who could be relied upon to have certain attributes ... [such as] a high level of self-reliance, a high degree of dedication, and an almost limitless versatility'.[34]

At the most basic level, what put local graduates at a disadvantage for recruitment as administrative officers was the requirement of a very high standard of competence in the English language. Given the pivotal importance of minutes as the basic instrument for discharging the responsibilities of an administrative officer, a good command of the English language was absolutely essential. Not being native speakers of English, a significantly higher proportion of local graduates than graduates of universities in the UK were screened out on this basic requirement alone.

More importantly, middle-class Chinese families in Hong Kong provided a different environment for their young people to grow up in compared with their counterparts in the UK. Chinese families put more emphasis on their youngsters' academic achievements than on cultivating interests outside academic learning. Even for local graduates who had developed strong extramural interests while students at local universities, few had the same kind of attributes that would enable them to, in Establishment Officer George Rowe's words, 'move easily amongst his peers in that sort of way'. This requirement, which is vague and intangible to the uninitiated but obvious to administrative officers, partly explains why so many of the postwar expatriate recruits were products of colleges at the ancient universities of Oxford and Cambridge. More of them fitted the ideal stereotype for colonial administrative officers created by Ralph Furse, who largely shaped the policy for recruitment across the British Empire from the interwar period to the immediate postwar years.[35] They also shared more closely the background and experience of the recruiters. There was a tendency for recruiters to try to maintain the standard and ethos of the service by favouring candidates who most resembled themselves.[36] It should be highlighted that even in the UK, most graduates would not fit the model Furse had of the ideal colonial administrator.[37] But more graduates of universities in the UK, particularly from Oxford and Cambridge, were brought up in ways that would make them fit this requirement better than their contemporaries in Hong Kong.

What this implied was that the recruitment of administrative officers was 'based on United Kingdom practices and reflected cultural norms specific to that society' or at least its export version.[38] This explains why such a high percentage of the earliest local recruits were either Eurasians or members of well established local families with exposure to British expatriate ways or had been educated or worked briefly in the UK.[39] Furthermore, most of the locally recruited officers were appointed at an older age than their expatriate colleagues, which reflected a need for the local officers concerned to gain the right kind of experience and exposure to enable them to 'move easily amongst his [English] peers in that sort of way'.

Before the colonial government tried to recruit on a much larger scale through a system involving a recruitment drive at the local universities in the 1970s, a major obstacle to the localization of administrative officers was the gap in what the local universities were producing and what the government expected in new recruits for administrative officers. The cultural, familial and educational environment in which local graduates grew up made it more difficult for most of them to meet the criteria laid down.

There was another and bigger obstacle to localization. It was an ingrained and largely unarticulated view that despite the policy of localization, it was imperative that the implementation of this policy should not be rushed. There was an 'inevitability of paternalism in the classic colonial situation: "we know better than you, but we will teach you so that one day you will be able to do it yourself".'[40] While successive establishment officers did try to recruit more local administrative officers, particularly since the 1960s, and they were encouraged to do so by the Public Service Commission, they consistently failed by a huge margin to use up the 50 per cent maximum unofficial allocation for local recruits. To them, as to the government or to their fellow administrative officers, there was no question of any compromise being made in order to get more local people to join. While upholding the principle of not lowering standards is inherent in a meritocracy, it is not true that compromises, even on the basic requirement of a good honours degree, had never been made. In the context of the British Empire as a whole hundreds 'whose education had been interrupted by the war were being recruited into the Colonial Service and sent straight out, degreeless, to the colonies' after the Second World War.[41] In the case of Hong Kong, some of the intakes of the immediate postwar years did not complete their university education, though they were awarded wartime degrees and subsequently vindicated their exceptional appointments.

Irrespective of whether the strict enforcement of standards on local candidates constituted 'institutional discrimination', especially since compromises were made for some expatriates, it had two distinct effects – to slow down the implementation of the localization policy and to retain a very high quality of locally recruited officers. Those who joined had to prove not only that they could discharge their responsibilities as well as their expatriate colleagues but also confirm that they could do so in the manner in which their expatriate officers performed their duties before they could gain advancement. As a result, both the standard and the *esprit de corps* of the administrative officers were maintained if not improved by the recruitment of local officers; they were certainly not diluted.

### Beyond the 'glass ceiling'

The late 1960s and early 1970s did, in an important sense, usher in a new era in Hong Kong and in its administration. Coinciding with the takeoff of the local economy was the emergence of a new generation of locally born and raised young people who identified strongly with Hong Kong.[42] There was also a change in the colonial government's approach to handling community relations after its capacity to maintain law and order was challenged by the Maoist led riots of 1967. In a report written for internal circulation just after active confrontation ceased, Deputy Colonial Secretary Geoffrey Hamilton admitted that it entered 'a new phase ... in which the communists seize on every real or invented grievance and try to exploit it to discredit the Government', which was 'a much more difficult phase to counter'.[43] This recognition underlined the need for the government to engage the local people more actively through the introduction of the CDO scheme and other initiatives.[44] Although this process started under Governor Trench it became entrenched following his succession by Sir Murray MacLehose, a career diplomat who stressed that he was not a career colonial administrator and was not bound by old practices and old attitudes.[45]

By the early 1970s local administrative officers recruited in the previous two decades had proved their worth and loyalty. They not only steadily advanced in rank but also through their own record reassured everyone in the government that the earlier tentative localization was an unqualified success. As the 1970s unfolded the two local universities also expanded quickly and produced more graduates. By contrast, the number of British colonies still gaining their independence dwindled, and the number of experienced colonial administrative officers available for import declined significantly.[46]

All these factors came together to galvanize the colonial administration to implement the localization policy more vigorously. The time had finally come for a more systematic and sustained effort to expand recruitment of suitable local people to join the government as administrative officers. This process started in the early 1970s and was meant to combine 'a vigorous recruitment and training programme'.

By then the official policy was that there should be 'no set ratio between entrants from' expatriate and local sources, but it was intended that in due course the new drive would 'shift the balance to 2 local to 1 overseas officer'.[47] Instead of relying on personal contacts with teachers at the University of Hong Kong to encourage suitable undergraduates to consider an administrative career with the colonial government, as previously, the government sent administrative officers to the local universities to encourage final year students to apply to join, and to organize large-scale open examinations as the first stage for recruitment. This had the effect of greatly increasing the number and percentage of local officers being recruited, including many graduates from very humble backgrounds.[48]

Equally importantly, the government introduced a nine-month training programme at Oxford University for new local intakes starting in 1973. The Oxford programme was 'designed to broaden the officer's experience, general knowledge and interests, and to give him an opportunity of living in another environment in order to develop perspective'.[49] This was meant to raise self-esteem among local officers and to rectify the inadequacies local candidates were known to have suffered from, which were partly responsible for their low rate of recruitment previously.

With new initiatives like these, recruitment increased dramatically, while the basic principle that standards must not be lowered was maintained. Indeed, the vigorous efforts to maintain standards when more and more locals were appointed led Ian MacPherson to conclude, in general terms, that 'the young men and women entering the service are intellectually of a higher calibre than' the expatriate officers of either his or of an earlier generation.[50]

When the government finally started to implement the policy of localization of the administrative officers earnestly there was, however, already 'a great deal of resentment, particularly among the middle class, of Government's so-called "expatriate policy".'[51] Hong Kong shared the experience of many other colonies where the local people wondered whether 'the British were reluctant to contemplate accelerated localization of the upper echelons of the civil service because it would deprive them of their jobs and terminate their career'.[52] The belief that some kind of a glass ceiling existed for local officers was widely held at the time.

In the prewar and early postwar periods, the local Chinese and expatriate communities largely lived peacefully but separately, with little mixing or interactions unless required by work. By the late 1960s and early 1970s there were sufficient local Chinese who had become successful enough to aspire to enjoy what the expatriates had long taken for granted. The basic attitude of the expatriate community as a whole had, however, not yet adjusted fully to this change, though it was moving to accommodate this trend. Whether there was a glass ceiling for the locals became an issue, whereas few locals had given this any thought previously.

The late 1960s and early 1970s was indeed an important period of transition in Hong Kong. As Trevor Clark observed, committing 'social errors' could still have an adverse effect on the career of senior administrative officers in the earlier decade. What Clark meant was that senior expatriates who married local women or Eurasians could find themselves touching a glass ceiling.[53] Clark also had in mind the case of Kenneth Barnett, a senior administrative officer Clark aptly described as 'immensely intelligent and a born scholar'. Barnett married a local woman and 'this cut him off from certain groups of society'. As she was also thought to be indiscreet, Barnett found himself 'inevitably banished ... to backwaters ... and lowly honours'.[54] Whether Clark was right or not his view was shared by many and it provided the basis for many to think that there was a glass ceiling for locally recruited officers. Indeed, its existence was privately acknowledged to at least one local officer, Eric Ho, when he was a middle ranking administrative officer.[55]

In reality, there was no evidence that locally recruited administrative officers had their promotions blocked by a glass ceiling, at least in terms of reaching the top rank as administrative officers. Among the six career cadets recruited locally up to the end of the 1950s, four of them, Paul Tsui, Li Fook-kow, Eric Ho and Selwyn Alleyne, reached the top grade as administrative officers and held offices of great importance. This compares with the general career pattern that 'the level to which an Administrative Officer can reasonably expect to reach if he gives good though not outstanding performance, is Staff Grade B, which is equivalent to Deputy Director level in a large professional department ... [whereas] some officers will reach only Staff Grade C which, however, is equivalent to Assistant Director.'[56] It is impossible, and ultimately futile, to try to assess whether the four were more able than most of their far more numerous expatriate colleagues who achieved equal rank and were given equally important responsibilities. However, their careers suggest that the glass ceiling that might have existed was allowed to be shattered by them when they proved themselves suitable for promotion to the highest rank as administrative officers. It might have taken them longer to prove themselves but they were not blocked.

That none of them reached the dizzy height of chief secretary or governor needs to be set in the context of bureaucratic appointments at these levels. Strictly speaking, these two offices, together with the offices of financial secretary and secretary for home affairs, were 'not part of the Administrative Class' though they had 'usually been filled by Administrative Officers'.[57] In general terms, few administrative officers ever reach the two top offices, which are scarce by their nature and there is always an element of having to be holding the right post at the right time for promotion to the very top. In the specific case of Hong Kong, by the time these local officers reached sufficient rank and seniority to put them near the bureaucratic zone from which they could be considered for the governorship, Hong Kong's governor was in any case no longer chosen from among colonial administrative officers. Compared with their expatriate contemporaries they did not find themselves barred from reaching the rank and holding offices that most of their best expatriate colleagues also occupied.

Given the late start of the localization policy and the deliberate pace in promotion in the civil service, by the time the first locally

*Localization*

Non-expatriate Administrative Officers on the occasion of Paul Tsui's retirement (1973). *Back Row (from left)*: Alan Leung Ching Pun, Albert Lai Kwok Ying, Jacqueline A. Willis, Jack So, Jack Kwong, Albert Lam Chi Chiu, Anthony F. Neoh, Peter Ng Kwok Tai, Haider H. T. Barma. David Tsui Kwan Ping, James So Yiu Cho, Mayer Ng Chak Lam. *Second Row (from left)*: Walter Yeung Wing Tai, Christine Chow Kwan Tai, David Lan Hsiung Tsung, Christopher Wong Kim Kum, Shelley Lee Lai Kuen, Ophelia Cheung Luk Ping, Katherine Fok Lo Shiu Ching. *Seated (from left)*: Yeung Kai Yin, Henry Ching, Selwyn Alleyne, Li Fook Kow, Helen Yu Lai Ching Ping, Paul Tsui Ka Cheung, Anson Chan Fong On Sang, Eric Peter Ho, Augustine Chui Kam, David Lai Kar Wah. *Front Row (seated on the ground)*: Canice Mak Chun Fong, Rafael Hui Si Yan, Victor Yung Chuk Hung, Donald Tsang Yam Kuen, Billy Lam Chung Lun, John Chan Cho Chak, Fred Ting Fook Cheung, Nicholas Ng Wing Fui.

recruited administrative officers reached Staff Grade A, at that time the top rank, and became available for appointment to the top offices it was the 1970s.

In fact, Paul Tsui, the first ever ethnic Chinese officer reached this grade in 1971, about two to three years later than most of his expatriate colleagues who joined between 1946 and 1948 had done.[58] While he took longer than his expatriate colleagues to gain promotion to the top rank of the administrative officers at the time he was not prevented from doing so.[59] In any event, by the 1970s Hong Kong as a whole was changing fast. 'Institutional racism as a sidekick of snobbery did not last long past the 1960s, for the obvious reason that the colony's steady growth as an industrial and financial centre, where the Chinese were making all the real running and true wealth,

*Governing Hong Kong*

Acting Governor, Anson Chan inspects the site of the Kwun Lung Lau landslide in July 1994 (The lady behind Chan is Administrative Officer Christine Chow, Director of Home Affairs).

made it as impractical as distasteful.'[60] As Hong Kong changed the colonial government could not afford to fall behind, at least not by a long way.

Within the government the ethos of the administrative officers as the elite required it to remain a meritocracy. Thus, by the time the other early local administrative officers progressed far enough for promotion to the top grade and were therefore in a position to head a major department or branch of the Colonial Secretariat, there was no question of them being denied promotion by a glass ceiling. To reach the top of the administrative class local officers had to prove their worth and gain promotion by showing that they merited the rise, just like their expatriate colleagues. But local officers had to do so in terms defined by their expatriate predecessors and their cultural norms and traditions, which were alien to the local officers. In this sense they were put at a disadvantage compared with their expatriate colleagues, but those who proved themselves did not see their advancement blocked on the basis of their ethnic background.

On the issue of advancement to the very top office available to career administrative officers, it is arguable whether a local officer could have risen to the office of chief secretary before Anson Chan did in 1993. Since this office was available for filling only twice in the previous 15 years, in 1981 and 1986, and there were few local officers in the right bureaucratic zone and with the appropriate age profile at the time, there are insufficient grounds to conclude that any local administrative officer was passed over for such a promotion. It remains, however, possible that a locally recruited administrative officer could have been promoted to take over as chief secretary a year or two before Chan was promoted. On the occasion of her promotion Governor Chris Patten had under consideration at least one, and possibly two, other local officers who were deemed to have the ability and appropriate bureaucratic profile for this office.[61] All three candidates were recruited into government service in the 1960s and Chan was among the first female administrative officers, being an entrant of 1962. While Chan's promotion did not strictly speaking imply the breaking of a glass ceiling it was a landmark event in the history of the administrative officers of Hong Kong.

More generally, the most important break in the localization of the administrative class happened after Britain and China signed an agreement over Hong Kong's future in 1984.[62] In an important sense this development required the government to set its administrative agenda against the background of a countdown to the end of British rule. As far as the development of the administrative service was concerned, Hong Kong entered the stage that other British colonies reached as independence loomed, but with one key difference. In Hong Kong the pace leading to the end of British rule was not set by the dynamics of domestic politics in the territory and its impact on the British will to stay on. On the contrary, the countdown was conducted in an orderly fashion towards a specific date 12 years ahead. It was within such a context that the government recruited only ethnic Chinese as administrative officers from 1985.[63] It also began to give preferential treatment in promotion to locally recruited administrative officers, while expatriate officers who were 'forced to retire' or were 'passed over for promotion' were given compensation.[64]

## End of the gender bar

The generous treatment of the expatriate officers where their terms of employment put them at a disadvantage in the run up to 1997 contrasts starkly with the same imposed on local and/or female officers in the past. Equal pay for equal work between local and expatriate officers on the one hand and between male and female officers on the other did not become a reality until as late as 1982, when equal fringe benefits for all administrative officers was finally introduced.[65] Even though male local administrative officers had always received the same basic salary as their expatriate colleagues, the overall remuneration package they received hitherto was in fact substantially less than that for their expatriate colleagues. One significant expatriate benefit that local officers did not receive for a long time was the six months of paid leave with generous sea passage for the family every three years, which was changed to an annual six weeks' leave when air travel became common. Other benefits included an allowance for the education of an officer's children in British public schools and up to the undergraduate level, as well as a much more generous allowance for housing than that available to local officers.[66]

If male local administrative officers were disadvantaged in their overall remuneration package, female officers suffered even more. In strict employment terms female officers were paid only 75 per cent of their male colleague's salary until the principle for equal pay was accepted in 1970. As the pay gap was only closed over a period of five years, equal salary for equal work did not in fact become the reality for officers of both genders until 1975.[67] Locally recruited female officers suffered in particular as other fringe benefits available to their locally recruited male colleagues were also denied to them until the government finally accepted the case for equal fringe benefits for all in 1982.

While the disadvantages female administrative officers had to endure in the first decade following their first recruitment reflected the gender prejudice of the time they were also institutionalized. They not only received less pay for doing the same job and had no entitlement to fringe benefits but were also required to resign on getting married and had to reapply to be appointed on a monthly basis.[68] The last requirement was not removed until the end of 1972, after considerable lobbying by senior female officers of the government.[69] This amounted to institutional discrimination even though the spirit of the time did not make it appear as objectionable as it does now. It should, however, be recognized that the discriminatory institutions and practices existed as part of longstanding legislation and conventions and were not introduced specifically to discriminate against female officers.

Although full equality in terms of employment for local female administrative officers and their expatriate male colleagues did not become a reality until as late as 1982, the gender bar for admission to the administrative service was broken not long into the postwar era. The longstanding existence of a gender bar for the colonial administrative service was not specific to Hong Kong but empire-wide. The appointment of women as colonial administrators was sanctioned only towards the end of the Second World War by way of a Whitehall circular 'Appointments of Women: Administrative Posts in the Colonies' issued in 1944. The scheme was introduced on an experimental basis. The original appointments were all posted to African colonies. In the early years of the scheme they were intended to serve as assistant secretaries in colonial secretariats and not in the field as district officers.[70]

Hong Kong appointed its first female cadet in 1959. She was Bridget O'Rorke who did not leave any discernible mark as she left within two years. This less than spectacular success did not discourage the colonial government from recruiting more female officers. It is worthy of note, however, that most of the female officers who were recruited after O'Rorke were local candidates. Indeed, three local female officers were appointed in the two years following O'Rorke's resignation. They were Audrey Chau, Anson Fang, and Katherine Lo.[71] Chau was appointed in 1961, and was one of the five successful local candidates, out of a total recruitment of 11 new administrative officers for the year. Among the nine new intakes for 1962, three were local recruits, of whom only Yeung Kai-yin was male.[72] The three female local officers were recruited as part of the localization effort. When O'Rorke was first appointed, it represented the removal of the gender bar for admission, rather than the introduction of a new policy to recruit women to join the rank of administrative officers.

After the appointment of the three female local officers, the government did make a point of giving this change publicity, but did not give the officers concerned any special training or assistance in discharging their responsibilities. In general policy terms, the female administrative officers were treated on the same basis as their male colleagues. They were required to discharge their responsibilities on the same terms. No concession was made to enable them to take on the role of mother when the time came. In terms of assessment of their performance for promotion, the government 'by and large' did not discriminate against them even though there were individual senior male officers who did.[73] However, since an administrative officer would normally work for several senior officers (who would be responsible for assessing her performance) before she faced promotion such individual discrimination would often be, at least to an extent, redressed by the unbiased assessments of other non-prejudicial seniors.[74]

Despite the existence of institutional discrimination for two decades after they were first appointed, female administrative officers have managed to make great strides remarkably quickly. An expatriate female administrative officer who continued to serve in Hong Kong after its handover to China Rachel Cartland even goes so far as to say that 'nowhere apart, perhaps from some Scandinavian countries, has there been a government so thoroughly dominated by women and ... achieved so quickly'.[75] Although she made the observation when Anson Chan was chief secretary in Hong Kong, the dominance she referred to was a wider phenomenon than having a woman chief secretary.

What Cartland refers to are the coming together of several factors that allowed able women to rise in the administrative service, as in other parts of the government and in Hong Kong more generally. The starting point was the nature of the colonial government and of the administrative service itself. Despite the existence of institutional discrimination, the colonial government did subscribe to principles of fair play and acted on logical arguments powerfully presented in internal deliberations. Thus, though it took a long time for female and local officers to secure genuine equal remuneration for equal work with their male expatriate colleagues, the government was willing to remove the unfair practices when its expatriate male dominated top echelon found the arguments compelling. Even in the 1960s, when female officers were most disadvantaged, Anson Chan recalls that those individual senior administrative officers who took a bigoted view of female officers were not necessarily the older or even prewar officers. In her experience the contrary was true, and the older officers often behaved like proper old-fashioned English gentlemen whatever their personal feelings on the subject.[76] The government's subscription to a sense of fair play and administrative officers' commitment to a meritocracy meant that women officers were given the scope to prove themselves and, where they demonstrated their ability, to gain advancement.

As Hong Kong entered the 1970s, other forces came into play as well. On the one hand the local universities were producing 'well-educated, ambitious, tough-minded women' who wanted to build up careers and prove themselves. As more female undergraduate students studied arts subjects, including English language and literature, a greater percentage of them actually mastered the language better than their male colleagues. This enabled more female applicants to meet a key requirement for being selected. On the other hand, they were enabled to perform their duties as administrative officers by the availability of a 'plentiful supply of relatively cheap domestic help' that relieved them of 'household and childcare responsibilities'.[77] Once 'a critical mass of women has arrived then not surprisingly irritants such as patronizing comments and attitude become more or less impossible'.[78] The organization of their own trade union by female officers also helped them to build up an effective body to advance their welfare collectively.

The earlier start the colonial government made in maximizing the value of female human resources was quickly surpassed by the business sector as the business environment in Hong Kong became increasingly competitive. By the late 1970s and early 1980s even venerable colonial *hong*s like the Swire group came to realize that it could ill afford to ignore the talent women could offer. The appointment, for example, of Lydia Dunn as a director of John Swire & Sons Limited in 1978, and her appointment as an unofficial member of the Legislative Council in 1976, and of the Executive Council in 1982, marked how far Hong Kong had progressed in removing barriers against women. With women making great strides in the business sector and in the community as a whole, many educated professional women now work both inside and outside the government. As barriers that previously put female administrative officers at a disadvantage came down, they competed against their male colleagues on an increasingly level playing field. The eventual appointment of Anson Chan as the first local chief secretary in 1993 was not the result of affirmative action but the selection of the most suitable officer for the job; it happened that this officer was a woman.

### British mandarins or Chinese officials

The breaking of the ethnic and gender barriers in the recruitment of administrative officers had remarkably little impact on the ethos of the service. While their inclusion unquestionably brought in fresh perspectives, based on Chinese culture, the changing society of Hong Kong and the perspective of the female gender, they did not change the *esprit de corps* of the administrative officers. The slow pace in recruiting local and female officers and their training through a process akin to osmosis meant that new recruits, be they English, Welsh, Scottish, Irish, or Chinese on the one hand, and male or female on the other, all ended up with the same bureaucratic consciousness. As administrative officers of Hong Kong they all shared the same pride, prejudices, basic outlook, dedication and commitment to serve the local community that had been the hallmark of cadets since 1862. When 'retreads' remarked critically on the narrow-minded attitude of their longstanding Hong Kong colleagues, they were also referring to a kind of 'Hong Kong chauvinism' that those always associated with the Hong Kong government would confess to proudly. The paternalism that expatriate administrative officers had long demonstrated to the local community was in fact shared by their local colleagues. They believed in Hong Kong and in themselves as the elite of the government that was responsible for maintaining stability and good order for Hong Kong to excel in whatever it dedicated itself to do.

Strictly speaking, there has never been a bureaucratic entity known as 'the Administrative Service of Hong Kong', but the men and women of all ethnic backgrounds who served as administrative officers had forged such a camaraderie that they behaved as if one existed. This reflected the successful bonding of the expatriates with the locals of both genders. Towards the end of British rule they had to all intents and purposes functioned like a common service that saw itself as the elite and backbone of the Hong Kong government. Such a development made it irrelevant to ask if a meaningful distinction could be made between the expatriates as British mandarins and locals as Chinese officials.

Instead, the question is whether the administrative officers of Hong Kong behaved more like British mandarins in the UK or Chinese officials in China. The short answer is: 'neither'.

There is no question that the administrative officers of Hong Kong shared the same basic bureaucratic tradition as their counterparts in the British civil service. Their origins as a constituent part of the Eastern cadets and their submergence into the unified colonial administrative service after the First World War assured that this happened. In the postwar period the Hong Kong service largely continued on its old trajectory and merely took on board the need to ensure it fitted and functioned effectively in the context of the local Chinese community. The civil service in the UK was modernized to deal with different pressures and challenges. As a result, even a generalist administrator came to mean something different in Hong Kong and in the UK. While Hong Kong kept much closer to the tradition of rotating its administrative officers to practically any post within the government, in the UK administrative officers by and large only did so within the department of state in Whitehall. This meant that Hong Kong administrative officers continued to be generalist administrators, whereas their UK colleagues became generalists with specialist knowledge of the responsibilities within their respective departments of work.

Hong Kong's administrative officers increasingly and consciously sought to combine the British colonial tradition with what they understood to be the best of China's bureaucratic heritage – as distinct from contemporary Chinese politics or bureaucratic norms. There was indeed an inherent compatibility between the modern British colonial administration and the ideal of the Chinese bureaucratic tradition. This the more scholarly minded of the administrators understood and articulated, most notably Kenneth Barnett, who was widely admired by his colleagues for his knowledge of Chinese culture. His view on the matter was summarized by a colleague:

> [T]he British Colonial Administrative (like the Indian Civil) Service was the nearest to the perfect form of apolitical, paternalistic government that the world had known, to wit, the Imperial Chinese Mandarin Service. Each was recruited on elitist principles and sent to the furthest ends of their empires, to administer incorruptible justice to strangers in whose personal affairs they would have no interest. Once they became too comfortable and susceptible, they would be posted elsewhere.[79]

In making this link, Barnett and his colleagues tried to instil or reinforce in fellow administrative officers an ethos that put on the shoulders of the administrative officers the responsibility of delivering the best possible government in the Chinese political tradition in

*Governing Hong Kong*

Hong Kong. When the Hong Kong government eventually delivered this in the 1980s the administrative officers had acquired for themselves collectively a character of their own.[80] They were British mandarins dedicated to serving the community of Hong Kong in a manner that the best of Chinese officials in its long history would have approved though they remained decidedly detached from contemporary Chinese politics.

*Chapter 8*
# MEETING THE CHALLENGES OF MODERNITY

Despite the colonial administration believing in the idea of a small government its span of control and general scope of responsibilities in fact expanded steadily in the postwar era. Part of this expansion was the result of the rapid growth of population. From 1950 to 1990, the local population increased by roughly a million every decade. The more dramatic increase happened in the earlier part of this period when the population doubled from two million in 1950 to four million in 1970. It meant the government had to increase in size just to keep up with discharging its established duties. Advancing modernity also required the Hong Kong government to take on new responsibilities and roles whatever its avowed policy. As Hong Kong evolved into a modern community its government had to assume more and more regulatory roles, be they over the banking and finance sectors or over conditions for workers in factories, or school curricula. Indeed, despite the government's policy of not taking responsibility for social welfare, by 1970 it had already unwittingly become not only the largest local employer but also the largest provider of subsidized health services and the biggest landlord of low cost housing.

By then the old structure of government was clearly under strain. When the government was much smaller the heavy concentration of power at the top worked well and efficiently. Top officials could keep track of most matters, both important policy issues and petty administrative ones; they made decisions quickly and acted decisively. With the huge expansion of the government machinery in the quarter century after the Second World War, including the proliferation of departments, the old system suffered severe strain as top administrators saw their responsibilities expanding exponentially. The axiom in administration that urgent matters always get attention before important ones proved only too real in Hong Kong.[1] It stretched the capacity of the old system to its limits.

By 1970 or so, it was reaching a stage when top level officials were mainly preoccupied with immediate issues and could not find time to think strategically about important policy matters or plan for a longer-term timeframe. One of the problems inherent in the system was that the principal assistant colonial secretaries at the Colonial Secretariat who on a day-to-day basis coordinated policy and administrative matters with government departments were junior in rank to heads of departments. It meant that 'when disagreements arose, Heads of departments would insist that issues be passed upwards for decision by the Colonial Secretary or the Financial Secretary or their deputies, who consequently became overloaded, often with relatively unimportant matters.'[2] Indeed, the government's capacity to pre-empt problems was shown to be woefully inadequate by the riots of a few years earlier. As a result, some kind of reform or reorganization of the administration was widely seen as desirable. The introduction of the CDO scheme, examined in Chapter 6, reflected the government's recognition and acceptance of a need for change.

**The McKinsey reforms**
A fresh approach to reforming the colonial administration to improve governance was taken after Murray MacLehose became governor in late 1971.[3] Although the idea of reform was not new, and MacLehose's predecessor, David Trench, was willing to introduce changes, it was MacLehose who brought in a new approach. Instead of appointing a high level commission of senior or recently retired civil servants and distinguished citizens in Hong Kong, or requesting London to appoint a royal commission to review governance, as would have been the more usual practice in the colonial context, MacLehose chose to engage a modern firm of management consultants, McKinsey & Company, for this purpose.

MacLehose decided to take this novel approach partly because he felt a fresh look at the administration would be good for Hong Kong, and partly because he shared the Foreign Office's basic mistrust of the colonial government, which had been nicknamed 'the republic of Hong Kong' during Trench's governorship. A successful diplomat who had already served as ambassador to two countries of medium importance, MacLehose did not expect to be offered the governorship.[4] When he accepted the appointment at the age of 52 it was not unreasonable for him to expect a senior ambassadorial appointment to crown his career after a five-year tour in Hong Kong. He was therefore keen not to be seen to have 'gone native' by his colleagues in the Foreign Office. This underlined his decision to engage a neutral and forward-looking firm of management consultants to review and improve the government machinery rather than rely on old established practices in crown colonies.

MacLehose thought it necessary to reform the government machinery not because he deemed the administrative officers or senior colonial civil servants incompetent but because he found the colonial bureaucracy an obstacle to the major changes he had in mind.[5] When he returned as governor a decade after he served there on secondment as political adviser he could not but have noticed that the structure of the administration had remained largely intact. It was a structure inherited from the Victorian era. It was not an administration 'attuned to the formulation and implementation of development policies' nor one that had 'special capability for sophisticated forward planning or for anticipating future problems'.[6] Seeing himself as a career diplomat, MacLehose had no sentimental attachment to the colonial establishment or to administrative officers. Being a forward-looking man interested in pushing through some social policies, he concluded it was time the colonial administration were modernized to improve governance and its capacity to support his vision of social development.[7] As he put it, 'some of the procedures and arrangements of work, which are the legacy of history, do seem to me ... to merit re-examination in the light of the greatly changed conditions of modern Hong Kong including, in particular, the great expansion in the role and scope of Government.'[8]

The engagement of McKinsey in 1972 at considerable public expense caused some unease among administrative officers.[9] While few failed to see the advantage inherent in having the government machinery and its procedures reviewed from a fresh perspective, most were sceptical of the employment of a firm of management consultants for this purpose. It was a break with long-established practices. The engagement of a firm of management consultants also in an important sense hurt the pride of the administrative officers. Their 'cardinal importance' and status as 'a central lynch-pin in the exercise and operation of Government' had long been accepted in Hong Kong, but this was implicitly questioned by the engagement of outsiders not renowned for their ability as government administrators even less so in a colonial context.[10] It was fundamentally different from the appointment of a high-level commission of experienced administrative officers from the UK or another commonwealth country, who would be respected for what they were and their appointment seen as intending to provide a professional review by a detached parallel service with no entrenched interest in Hong Kong. The governor's decision to engage McKinsey cast a shadow over whether the elite position of administrative officers would be sufficiently understood, respected and protected.

Whatever individual senior administrative officers might have thought of the engagement of McKinsey, they worked with the consultants to devise reforms that would improve governance without changing the nature of the political establishment. They cooperated with McKinsey not only because they were required to do so but also because they shared the desire to improve governance and wanted to have their own input,[11] which was essential also for ensuring that their elite position within the government would not be eroded.

McKinsey & Company produced recommendations focused essentially on two different dimensions of the administration. The first was on making improvements to the existing machinery to make it operate more efficiently and rationally. They included standardizing procedures and formats for various government departments to request resources from the central administration, delegating authority downward in the Colonial Secretariat and outward to departments, and extending the use of computers.[12] They did not affect the position and work of the administrative officers directly. The other dimension was about reorganizing the top echelon of the administration to ensure better use of human resources and to strengthen the capacity of the government to plan for the future. Since administrative officers formed the core of the government, particularly its higher echelons, these changes affected them directly.

The main McKinsey recommendations in this respect were directed towards reorganizing the Colonial Secretariat, creating a new structure for the secretariat to coordinate, supervising departments without overloading the few top officials, and building into the new structure the capacity for longer-term planning in both policy matters and in the allocation of resources. More specifically, the secretariat was reorganized into six policy branches and two resource branches, each headed by a secretary equal in rank to that of a head of a major government department.[13] They took over from the more junior principal assistant colonial secretaries of the old structure. In setting up the new branches the old schedules of responsibilities that former principal assistant colonial secretaries had were rationalized and redistributed to the appropriate new branches. The new policy branches were economic services, environment, home affairs, housing, security and social services, whereas the two resource branches were finance and establishment. In McKinsey's conception, the 'policy branches should delegate much of their current day-to-day administrative load to the departments, and should take on a new role of ensuring that plans are developed for the major programmes' so that they would 'take on a greater responsibility, in conjunction with departments, for policy formulation'.[14] The introduction of major policy programmes required 'the setting of overall policy objectives in major fields for 5–10 years ahead' and was meant to remove the scope for department heads in the old system to give low priority to longer term planning.[15] The introduction of annual operating plans was to improve cost effectiveness.[16] With regard to resources, formal plans were meant systematically to 'identify the requirements for key resources across the whole of Government, the means of obtaining them, and their optimum distribution'.[17]

In devising a new machinery of government, McKinsey worked closely with senior officials, mostly administrative officers. While it recommended that 'senior jobs' become open to 'all grades', including not only the promotion of specialists to head professional departments but also ending the preservation of certain top positions for administrative officers, it did not make any recommendation that challenged the administrative officers' elite position.[18] Instead, it recognized the value of administrative officers and highlighted that their shortage was an important impediment to improving the effectiveness of the government.[19] The resulting opening of the administrative grade at the middle levels to experienced officials of non-administrative officer background was done selectively and on the basis of merit. It enabled the ranks of administrative officers to be strengthened.[20] It did not reduce promotion prospects for administrative officers. On the contrary, the McKinsey reforms created more senior positions that administrative officers were best placed to fill, not least at the secretary level.[21] More generally, promotion prospects improved as the number of staff grade posts increased faster than the growth rate of administrative officers as a whole, which averaged 5 per cent per annum in the decade leading to the McKinsey reforms.[22]

The McKinsey proposals were in fact neither original nor as carefully conceived as their drafters presented them.[23] The upgrading of branches at the secretariat to oversee government departments created confusion and tension in its early days. The creation of a home affairs branch at the Colonial Secretariat while the old home affairs secretariat was reorganized into the home affairs department created 'a muddle' in the words of the first new home affairs secretary Denis Bray. He admitted that this caused problems as the new director of home affairs Eric Ho 'naturally wanted to behave like a head of department and saw no need for the Secretary to peer over his shoulder all the time'.[24] In Bray's own recollection, 'fortunately he was a man I liked, and thought highly of, so we managed affairs without rancour or poaching on each other's territory'.[25]

The 'most contentious' McKinsey proposal involving 'the reorganization of the Secretariat' was developed into its final form after Governor MacLehose expressed 'a positive and dynamic interest' and 'asked the Consultants to develop' it further than their original suggestions.[26] The creation of the new secretary positions amounted to little more than upgrading the former principal assistant colonial secretary posts to near the top rank in the civil service and giving them more resources with which to discharge their responsibilities, which former principal assistant colonial secretaries had not had the rank or resources to accomplish hitherto.[27]

By giving the new secretaries a 'policy formulation' role, McKinsey reflected a failure to understand the proper constitutional position of senior secretariat offices. Strictly speaking, in the crown colony system that existed in Hong Kong, policy making was the prerogative of the governor in council, and the secretariat staffs were there only to assist and advise the governor in council, and to see that its policies were implemented appropriately.[28] They were staff rather than line officers, though they were regularly involved in deliberations leading to the writing of policy papers that would be submitted to the governor in council for policy decisions. In other words, senior administrative officers had long been part of the policy-making process but they were not strictly speaking policy makers. To accomplish what McKinsey proposed to do in giving the new secretaries the power to make policy, they would have to be made members of the Executive Council and, as such, be given departmental portfolios to superintend in a manner similar to that in a cabinet system. In reality, only a selected few of the new secretaries were appointed to the Executive Council and they merely took over those seats previously allocated to heads of major government departments. Neither the Executive Council nor the secretaries collectively functioned like a cabinet in the normal sense of the word. Some of the McKinsey reforms thus resulted in staff officers being given line responsibilities on dubious constitutional grounds.

Another notable problem created by the McKinsey proposals regards the legal authority of newly created policy secretaries. Until various laws were changed, heads of major government departments, not the new secretaries, were the statutory authorities that represented the government in specific matters. This legal position was not changed by the government's adoption of the McKinsey recommendations and the transformation of them into government policy. David Jordan, the director for commerce and industry, was for example mindful that it was his office that was the statutory authority under the imports and exports ordinance. This meant it was he who would be held accountable for what his department did, not the secretary for economic services, who was given the responsibility over the department.[29] Likewise, as head of department he was the budget holder for his department and it was strictly speaking he, not the 'superintending' secretary, who was accountable to the Treasury and the Legislative Council for the use of public funds in his department.[30] Since he was equal in rank to the new secretaries and he believed some of the changes McKinsey proposed were problematic on constitutional grounds, he refused to accept any direction from the secretary for economic services though he continued to accept it from the financial secretary, an ex-offico member of the Executive Council.[31] Since commerce and industry was one of the key departments in the government this did not make for an easy and straightforward implementation of the McKinsey reforms.[32]

The personal disapproval of individual senior administrative officers like Jordan and financial secretary Philip Haddon-Cave did not, however, lead to a failure of the McKinsey reforms. Most other administrative officers and heads of department were either unaware of the constitutional issues involved or willing to proceed on the basis that implementing the McKinsey reforms was government policy and *ipso facto* appropriate. After the teething problems such as those outlined above were resolved or fudged and secretaries elevated to a rank senior to heads of major departments, the McKinsey reforms were made to work.

This happened partly because senior administrative officers just got on with filling the gaps the McKinsey consultants left behind. A prime example was the lack of any provision in the McKinsey scheme to include 'a more rational system for determining spending priorities'.[33] What eventually made the reforms work was the powerful finance branch 'buying into the reform agenda itself', which made 'medium-term planning both possible and necessary, and thereby making the very necessary medium-term management of the budget possible'.[34] This started with the introduction by the deputy financial secretary, Henry Ching, 'of a resource allocation system which dovetailed well with the policy Secretaries' medium term programme plans.'[35] Indeed, despite his personal feelings about the McKinsey reforms, Haddon-Cave gave his blessings to Ching's initiative. With the chief secretary presiding over debates on the relative priorities of different programme areas and the finance branch 'keeping a tight rein over total forecast public sector expenditure' they modernized and rationalized the administrative structure of the government.[36] This also coincided with a period of rapid growth in government revenue, as Hong Kong's economy truly took off. It meant putting at the disposal of the administration significantly more new resources for meeting the new demands the old structure simply found itself too strained to meet. It ought to be recognized that the McKinsey review did not really change the way the government operated. In an effort to accommodate 'the conservatism of the civil service and the negative tenor of most public comments' the McKinsey recommendations were in fact diluted as they were implemented.[37] The dilution and adaptations were essential to the successful modernization of the government apparatus.

*Meeting the challenges of modernity*

The most important achievement of McKinsey's review was to start modernizing and upgrading the government machinery to enable it to take on new social and developmental dimensions of government, for which planning ahead and additional resources were essential. Opening up top positions in the administration to officials of the right calibre rather than the desired career background did not harm administrative officers' careers, for they formed a meritocracy and the changes coincided with a dramatic increase in senior posts. Promotion prospects for the most able administrative officers were in fact improved rather than harmed by the McKinsey reforms. They remained 'the dominant force in [assisting] policy-making'.[38]

**Accountability without democracy**
An unintended but nevertheless no less important consequence of the McKinsey reforms was the creation of an additional layer of senior positions mostly occupied by top administrative officers. This is often seen as having facilitated 'the evolution of a cabinet of some kind – made up of "political" administrative officers', who were 'increasingly expected to act and operate as ministers and ministerial staff and to be politically more sensitive and responsive to external political challenges and turbulences'.[39] While such an observation rightly highlights the rising need for top civil servants holding the office of secretary to play increasingly important political roles, it is also misleading. It reflects a misunderstanding of what the office of secretary created by the McKinsey reforms was meant to be. It was not intended to be the equivalent of a cabinet minister in the Westminster model, who is expected and required to take political responsibilities. Instead, the secretaries established after the McKinsey review were experienced administrators (though not necessarily administrative officers) who were expected to relieve the colonial secretary, the financial secretary and their deputies from coordinating and supervising the work of departments so that they could engage in strategic planning. McKinsey and the colonial government never intended the newly created office of secretary to be held politically accountable. This issue simply did not come up in the review. Secretaries created as a result of the McKinsey reforms remained civil servants and were treated by the government as such.

'Adding' political roles to secretaries came a decade after the McKinsey reforms when the community of Hong Kong had changed so much that the issue of government accountability had become a real one. However, it should be recognized that administrative officers performing line duties had always functioned as political officers. It is therefore incorrect to describe secretary-level administrative officers as having acquired new political roles in the 1980s. What was new was that the general public expected to see the government being held accountable, and it saw secretaries as the top officials responsible for the policy programmes associated with their branches.[40]

The anomaly that senior civil servants, usually holding office as secretaries, were deemed accountable for government policies by the general public did not in fact mean they were actually held responsible for policy failures by the colonial government. What was being developed in Hong Kong was fundamentally different from what happened in other British dependent territories when they transformed their crown colony system into a progressively more representative form of government. When the general public agitated for government accountability in British colonies in the latter part of the twentieth century, the British usually responded by granting self-government steadily with a view to eventual independence. The key initial change in this process generally involved the adoption of a 'member system'. This meant selected members of the Legislative Council would be asked to look after departmental portfolios and represent them in the legislature and become quasi-ministers. This marked the introduction of political responsibility to the crown colony system, and would be followed by further moves towards developing a full ministerial government – a development normally paralleled by the advent of political parties and competitive elections. Full self-government and eventual independence would come in due course. This direction of development was not attempted in Hong Kong.[41] Its secretaries were not government ministers and were not required to take ministerial responsibilities.

What was being developed in Hong Kong under MacLehose and his immediate successor Sir Edward Youde (who was governor from 1982 to 1987) was a system that gave the general public a sense that the government was accountable and responsive to its views without making any individual who served in the colonial government personally responsible. In this system there was no question that a secretary, a mere civil servant, should be asked or expected to resign even if a policy integral to the portfolio under his or her remit should turn out to be a major mistake and need to be retracted.[42]

The most spectacular example happened in 1984 when the government's decision to introduce new licensing requirements for taxis caused civil disobedience by taxi drivers and a major riot, which forced the government to retract the new policy. The transport secretary Alan Scott did attract 'the brunt of a loud and specific criticism' and was deemed responsible for this policy by the general public.[43] However, the government did not hold him politically responsible for the policy backfiring, for the governor in council made the policy and Scott was merely the most senior civil servant tasked to advise the governor in council, prepare the paperwork, advocate it on behalf of the government in public and see to its implementation. The retraction from this initiative was also not based on a decision by Scott but on a decision by the government. While it has been suggested that Scott was forced out of office because of the public outcry he was not in fact punished for the blunder over the taxi licensing requirements and the subsequent disturbances.[44] What did happen was that Scott's colleagues came to see him as either 'damaged goods' or 'accident prone',[45] which no doubt contributed to his decision to move on as governor of the Cayman Islands in 1987. Whatever his colleagues thought of him, Scott remained secretary for transport in Hong Kong until the following year and was made deputy chief secretary in June 1985 after an interval of a month as secretary (special duties) – hardly evidence of a demotion or punishment.[46]

The issue here is not one of Scott getting away with it because of patronage by the governor or British government in London. It is that in the system that prevailed he, a civil servant, was not politically responsible for the policy blunder and it would have been unfair for him to have had to pay the price for the failure of the policy. The colonial government's steadfast protection of its top civil servants might have displeased the general public, but not requiring top civil servants to take political responsibility or be used as political scapegoats was vital in maintaining their morale and loyalty. It reassured them, mostly but not exclusively administrative officers, that as long as they performed their duties to the utmost of their abilities and in good conscience the government would not allow their professional careers and reputations to be destroyed for short-term political considerations, though demonstrated incompetence or failings could and did damage the personal reputation of those concerned.

The confusing roles and positions of secretaries arose because the people and society of Hong Kong came of age and demanded government accountability but the British government decided that the usual response in other British colonies – democratization leading to eventual independence – was not an option in Hong Kong. Unlike previous generations of Chinese residents of Hong Kong, who were sojourners in an outpost of an alien empire, an increasing percentage of Hong Kong's residents in the 1970s were born and brought up in Hong Kong. By the 1980s they had formed a majority of the local population. Unlike their immigrant parents, they developed a sense of identity, received a modern education that exposed them to modern Western concepts, and developed stable and relatively prosperous careers that allowed them the material comfort, leisure and intellectual capacity to assert their rights as modern citizens.[47] They formed an ever expanding modern middle class that was gaining in civic consciousness. They might remain hesitant about 'rocking the boat' because they could see that the existence of a communist regime in China could result in the extinction of their cherished way of life, but since the 1970s they increasingly wanted their voices to be heard and to hold the government accountable for its policies and their consequences.[48] To accommodate their legitimate desires, which were expressed in civil actions that were spreading, particularly among the younger and better educated, the colonial government tried to be as responsive to public views and criticisms as possible. The adaptation of the secretary system so that top-level officials would be seen as responding to public opinion and looking after public interests, among other institutional changes, was therefore put into effect.

The role secretaries were thus required to take on *vis-à-vis* the general public was that of a political officer in the traditional sense in a colonial context, not of a minister in a democratic system. A sponsor of new social and development policies Governor MacLehose was conscious of the need to respond adroitly to public opinion and to appear to take into account views of the lower social strata, for the success of such policies needed the general public to embrace them. He 'changed the nature of the Legislative Council' when he increased the number of its unofficial members and in 1976

*Meeting the challenges of modernity*

HM Queen Elizabeth II on tour with Secretary of Housing Ian Lightbody during her first visit to Hong Kong (1975). Behind the Queen is Governor MacLehose.

appointed individuals 'from areas in society that had never been considered before'.[49] With individuals like Wong Lam, a highly public-spirited citizen and former bus driver, serving as unofficial members at the Legislative Council, it had the effect that they, in the view of a former administrative officer, would 'bring us down to earth when discussions were straying too far into imagination'.[50] The introduction of lower-middle-class nominees to the Legislative Council might not have changed the fundamentals in the working of the Legislative Council,[51] but it started a process that required secretary level officials to pay heed to the views of the community at large.

In the late 1970s MacLehose even briefly considered introducing a 'member system', but dropped it in favour of asking secretaries and, where appropriate, other senior officials to discharge their role as political officers more sensitively and effectively. The result was the hybrid that took shape in Hong Kong at the beginning of the 1980s.

The increasing importance of the traditional political officer element of the work of secretaries meant that most secretary positions ended up being filled by administrative officers. This was because, with most administrative officers having served as political officers sometime in their careers – as district officers, city district officers, or assistant secretaries in the Secretariat for Home (previously Chinese) Affairs – they had an advantage over their colleagues from a professional or specialist background. Also, being generalists rather than specialists, they were more comfortable taking on the political role expected of secretaries than their colleagues from a professional or specialist background. Furthermore, it has long been part of the administrative officers' ethos to take on whatever new responsibility may be required of them in good spirit. They also welcomed knowing that, while accountable for their personal failings, their senior colleagues in the administration, mostly fellow administrative officers, would never make a scapegoat of them should a government policy fail or backfire.

**Preparing for the end of empire**

The need for secretaries to perform their political roles well became more acute as the future of Hong Kong was settled and political reforms introduced in the middle of the 1980s. The addition of indirectly elected members to the Legislative Council came about in 1985.[52] This had 'become desirable and politically necessary' to ensure the British House of Commons would support 'overwhelmingly the 1984 Sino–British agreement' on the future of Hong Kong.[53] Indeed, this agreement 'required the Hong Kong legislature to be constituted by election by 1997 at the latest, which could not be achieved without reform since all members of the then existing [Legislative] Council were appointed, not elected'.[54] Following the reform of 1985, the new Legislative Council consisted of 57 members, of whom 12 unofficial members were elected by an electoral college, another 12 by functional constituencies, and 22 appointed by the governor. There were also ten official members while the governor presided.[55] Even though the elective elements introduced were not returned through direct elections on the basis of universal franchise, they nevertheless behaved differently from 'the great and the good' that used to be appointed as unofficial members, who were deemed 'docile and subservient to the British colonial authority'.[56] This changed the dynamics in the Legislative Council and the 'once staid assembly did get a lot livelier'.[57]

With indirectly elected unofficial members having a need to answer to their constituencies they demanded greater accountability from their official colleagues in the Legislative Council. With both the unofficial and official members working together, they also started to hold the meetings of the finance committee and the public accounts committee in public. As a result, secretaries who were also members of the Legislative Council found they had almost completely lost the 'protection of anonymity, as they are pushed into a limelight they never sought and were not trained to cope with' in their civil service careers.[58] Nevertheless, secretaries, particularly those who were administrative officers, were determined to rise to this new challenge. By and large they felt that this was just another new demand put on them and faced it confidently, for they believed they had in any event always been accountable – in the sense that they had habitually borne in mind and acted in the best interest of the community.[59]

The changes unleashed by the reform of the Legislative Council in 1985 were, however, only the beginning. Further developments in increasing the democratic elements in the old colonial system of government progressively demanded the executive branch to be answerable to them over government policy. For the rest of the 1980s administrative officers continued to work on preparing for the progressive expansion of democratic self-government, which culminated in the publication of a government consultation paper on the further development in representative government in May 1987.[60] However, their efforts did not produce much result because the Chinese government's resistance to democratization in Hong Kong forced the Hong Kong government to slow down for the rest of the decade.[61]

The next and more significant change happened in 1991, when the number of elected members in the Legislative Council was raised to 39 (including 19 directly elected members) out of a council of 60. This followed heightened public demand for a faster pace of democratization in response to the Tiananmen Square massacre of 1989.[62] The Legislative Council became a body that increasingly sought to hold the government to account in public.

This development was given a further and major impetus after former British cabinet minister Chris Patten became governor in 1992. Even though most of his reform package, outlined in his policy address of October that year, was not implemented until 1995, he ended dual membership of non-officials in the Executive and Legislative Councils, and introduced governor's question time to the Legislative Council without delay.[63] They marked a basic change in

Just retired Hong Kong Commissioner greeting Prime Minister Thatcher at the Hong Kong Society dinner on 8 June 1989. Others in the picture are Woodrow Wyatt (far left) and Henry Keswick (middle).

the relations between its executive and legislative branches. This was that while the government should remain an executive led one, the executive branch should be seen to be held accountable to the legislative branch in public on a routine basis.[64]

What this career politician governor introduced was not designed to impose political responsibility on top civil servants. It was meant above all to enable the colonial government to find an elegant way out of the political predicament inherent in Hong Kong's transition from a British crown colony to a Chinese Special Administrative Region. By then the people of Hong Kong clearly wanted a faster pace of democratization, but any such development was fundamentally constrained by the policy of the Chinese government to contain democratization as codified in the basic law for the post-1997 Hong Kong SAR. With his hands thus tied, Patten had to introduce some changes quickly, as distinct from his main reform package, which was open to discussions with the Chinese.

In Patten's conception, the separation of membership between the Executive and Legislative Councils was meant to give him justifiable grounds to claim that he had made a significant step forward in democratization, and to remove the public expectation that leading

Democratic Party legislative councillors be appointed to the Executive Council.[65] He thus promptly introduced a change that would enable him to assert that he had turned the Executive Council into something akin to the US cabinet and made it accountable to the legislature.[66] The introduction of the governor's question time, modelled after the prime minister's question time in the House of Commons, was intended to showcase a flagship democratic institution of the British parliamentary system. With both in place Patten could justifiably claim to have advanced democracy in colonial Hong Kong. Although Patten handled governor's question time himself, the general atmosphere in the Legislative Council changed. For the remaining five years of British rule, legislative councillors demanded and expected secretaries to be held publicly accountable in the legislative chamber. Furthermore, as the administration could no longer take it for granted that bills endorsed by the Executive Council would normally be passed in the Legislative Council, policy secretaries 'had to lobby Legco members to get' government policies under their bailiwick approved.[67] While there had previously been occasions when the colonial administration had to lobby a sceptical Legislative Council to pass a bill about which it was doubtful, lobbying had by the 1990s became almost a regular practice.

This development reached a high point after the implementation in 1995 of Patten's 1992 package for reforming the Legislative Council, which finally eliminated all appointed members. Although the council no longer had official or ex-officio members, secretaries were invited to appear in council to introduce, explain and defend government policies. When they thus appeared they were questioned and deliberately embarrassed in ways that were unthinkable a decade earlier.[68] The proceedings of a council meeting on a randomly selected day in the middle of 1996 when there was no major political controversy raging produced, for example, the following exchange, as the secretary for security Carrie Yau tried to answer a question from Councillor Howard Young, on the visa requirements for Chinese citizens visiting Hong Kong.

> SECRETARY FOR SECURITY (in Cantonese): Mr President, with effect from 1 August 1993, PRC nationals transiting through Hong Kong to or from overseas countries are allowed a visa-free stay of up to seven days as visitors provided that they

have valid passports, confirmed airline bookings and valid visas for their overseas destinations. The purpose of this arrangement is to facilitate their overseas travel by connecting flights in Hong Kong or stopping over here before returning to China. This transit facility is however not allowed for journeys from China to Macau since PRC nationals in China can go to Macau direct. ...

At present, we have no plan to relax the visa-free arrangement to allow PRC nationals to transit through Hong Kong to Macau. Such a relaxation will invite abuses to bypass the existing schemes controlling PRC nationals visiting Hong Kong.[69]

MR JAMES TO (in Cantonese): Mr President, the first paragraph of the Secretary's main reply is in fact logically refutable because if we say they can go to Macau from China directly, they can also go to Thailand or any other places in the world from China directly, and do not have to go through the Hong Kong Airport. Therefore, there is a logical contradiction in this concept. Nevertheless, my question is on the point in the last paragraph of the main reply where the Secretary said that in so doing, the system would be abused. However, if they only go to Macau for one or two days during that period and then come back to Hong Kong and they can produce proof that they will go back to China, I wonder what security significance is there that the authorities have to refuse their entry to Hong Kong or put them under close scrutiny. Mr President, my question is on security significance.[70]

With the political system changed into one in which the political future of members of the Legislative Council may be affected by their apparent success or failure to hold the administration or its top officials to account, the balance of responsibilities for secretary level officials shifted.

Despite these changes one thing remained fundamentally the same. Secretaries and top administrative officers continued as politically neutral civil servants though they now had to be publicly answerable to directly or indirectly elected legislative councillors. The increased demand on them to perform their political duties did not in fact make them politically responsible in the sense that ministers are in a parliamentary system. The increasing requirement to discharge their political duties effectively might have meant administrative ability alone would no longer suffice for able administrative officers to discharge their responsibilities at the top. However, the political element of their duties remained fundamentally that of a political officer role in the colonial context.

The political neutrality of the civil service and its senior administrative officers was maintained partly because of bureaucratic inertia and entrenched practices. But it was above all because it was essential to ensure a smooth transition of Hong Kong from a crown colony to a Chinese SAR. It was intended to enable the civil service as a whole to continue to serve Hong Kong to its best ability regardless of the impending change of sovereignty.

To enable a seamless transfer of power to happen in 1997, the colonial government swiftly moved to reassure the civil service and prepare it for the eventual handover of sovereignty, after Britain reached an agreement with the Chinese over the future of Hong Kong in 1984. Since the Sino–British agreement in fact committed Hong Kong to accept fundamental changes in 13 years' time, a basic consideration for the colonial administration was to ensure stability, order, prosperity and predictability in the transitional period. For the British government there was an 'over-riding fear ... that the [colonial] administration might collapse before 1997', which made it very keen to keep the expatriate officers on board while it prepared for localization.[71] Indeed, as 'in other British colonies in the days before independence', the civil service was deemed 'the bulwark of stability in uncertain times, the repository of fairness, justice, and the continued observance of long-established rules.'[72] The colonial government therefore promptly set out to assure members of the civil service that their future would be secure. On the day after the Sino–British agreement was initialled, chief secretary and head of the civil service Philip Haddon-Cave wrote to all members of the civil service in the following terms: 'Appointments and promotions will be based on qualifications, experience and ability as at present. Matters such as recruitment, discipline, training and management of the public service will continue to be dealt with in accordance with existing principles and practices. The present practice of restricting certain posts to British nationals will be discontinued.'[73] Apart from reassuring the civil servants and maintaining their morale, the government decided to accelerate the process of localization so that the civil service would be in a form suitable to continue to serve Hong Kong after the transfer of sovereignty in 1997.[74]

The government's overt commitment notwithstanding, localization of the administrative officers continued to proceed at a deliberate pace at first, even though the government ended the recruitment of expatriate administrative officers after the Sino–British agreement was signed in December 1984.[75] The longstanding commitment to a meritocracy meant that while more and more top posts were increasingly made available to local officers they were still promoted on the same basis as before without accelerated promotion. Two years after the agreement was reached, of 197 directorate level administrative officers (or those of Staff Grade C and above), fewer than half or merely 93 were local officers.[76] At the very top, only three of the 14 secretaries and four of the 11 Staff Grade A officers were local. In the light of the age profile of the senior administrative officers in the mid-1980s, when the handover was scheduled to take place in 1997, top positions in the government, which had to held by local officers, would be filled mainly by the approximately 40 local administrative officers holding the rank of Staff Grades B and C in the mid-1980s.[77] This meant in general terms that more than half of them could expect to rise to the top. It provided a powerful incentive to the senior local administrative officers to stay and do their best.

As the colonial administration started to plan and prepare for the eventual transfer of sovereignty it needed to think not only about having suitably qualified and experienced local officers to take the helm in due course, but to consider the welfare and future of expatriate officers whose promotion to the top would be blocked in the run up to 1997. It was a delicate balance because maintaining the effectiveness and efficiency of the government required sustaining the morale and team spirit of all administrative officers, be they expatriate or local. When a policy for localization in the light of the handover was being worked out in the latter half of the 1980s, expatriate administrative officers still dominated the top echelon of the administration. The balance they struck was to provide scope for accelerated promotion for the most able local officers closer to the handover date and to provide a generous package to compensate those expatriate officers whose career prospects suffered as a result.[78]

*Meeting the challenges of modernity*

In addition, they also introduced changes to ensure that the provision of a pension to retired local and expatriate officers would be protected despite a change of sovereignty in 1997.

The decision to promote local officers in preference to expatriate officers started in 1987 and, as a result, ten senior expatriate civil servants lost their jobs to local officers in the first three years of this arrangement, with the expatriate officers concerned being paid HK$ 10 million in compensation.[79] Also in 1987, for the first time the number of local officers exceeded that of expatriates at the directorate level, with the percentage shifting in favour of local officers at a faster rate in the early 1990s.

Localization entered its final stage in 1993 as Governor Patten appointed Anson Chan the first local and female chief secretary, and Donald Tsang the first local financial secretary. From this point on, in the retrospective assessment of Patten, they 'led a mainly Chinese civil service, which withstood the political buffetings of the following years with character and confidence.'[80] Although Patten was right to pay tribute to the local administrative officers and other members of the civil service as they loyally served Hong Kong and the British crown right until the handover, this should not be taken to mean that racial prejudice had completely disappeared from the colonial establishment. Leo Goodstadt, who served as the head of the government think tank, the Central Policy Unit, in this period recalls that after Chan's appointment as chief secretary 'it was suggested that her access to official documents should be limited on the grounds that she did not have formal Positive Vetting clearance.'[81] This was despite one of her recent predecessors, Philip Haddon-Cave, having refused to be positively vetted yet nonetheless been 'given unrestricted access to official files'.[82]

In the final years of British rule, top Hong Kong officials, by now dominated by locally recruited administrative officers adhered to the ethos of the service to provide an administrative framework to ensure stability and good order so that the private sector could continue to generate prosperity. With the support of British diplomats and the confidence given to them by Governor Patten, they resolved numerous issues with their Chinese colleagues that could have hindered a smooth transfer of sovereignty. Compared with the period when Sir David Wilson was governor (1987–92), when an annual average of almost 40 working agreements were reached between Hong Kong and the Chinese authorities, nearly 100 was reached every year under Patten until the last.[83] Goodstadt attributed this success to the fact that the local 'Hong Kong officials faced no language or cultural barriers in addressing either the community or their Chinese counterparts, which made it increasingly difficult to challenge their right to argue Hong Kong's case,' and because they proceeded on the basis of 'clear policies that reflected the community's own preference and priorities'.[84]

As a result, when the end finally came the Hong Kong government and its administrative officers were as well prepared as they could have been for the transfer of sovereignty. Admittedly, they did not pass on a form of government most suited to the people of Hong Kong at the end of the twentieth century. However, they did bequeath a well structured and administered civil service headed by a professional cadre of administrators committed to performing their duties to the best of their ability as politically neutral civil servants in order to further the interests of Hong Kong. It should be recognized that the colonial government had no master plan for the transfer of power, though more planning was put into preparing for it than for almost any other policy in a century and a half of colonial rule. Despite having put extra resources into preparing for the transfer of sovereignty, the colonial government handled the matter largely as it had always done, namely to adapt to changing situations and perceived needs and do what its top administrators saw as essential and appropriate. It worked because the long-established structure and procedures in the administration ensured that senior officials were given the scope to discharge their responsibility as best they could. For better or for worse, administrative officers formed the core of the colonial administration and should take the lion's share of the responsibility for its success or failure.

*Chapter 9*
# AN ELITE WITHIN THE GOVERNMENT

From the outset when the cadet scheme was introduced in the 1860s, administrative officers were intended to be the elite within the colonial government.[1] Whatever flaws they might have suffered collectively, they did not fail to live up to this expectation. Right up until the end of the British period, administrative officers played the leading role in seeking to improve governance in Hong Kong. This is not to imply that other constituent parts of the civil service, particularly professional officers serving in various departments, did not make major contributions. They did, but their specialist qualifications and orientation meant that most of their contributions were towards improving the quality of professional services and performing specialized duties.

Administrative officers, by contrast, served first and foremost as generalist officers deployed to perform a wide range of duties. What ensured cohesion and a strong team spirit among the administrative officers, despite the non-existence of a formal corporate organization called an administrative service, was the existence of a strong *esprit de corps*.

**Esprit de corps**
The *esprit de corps* of the administrative officers at the end of the British period was not fundamentally different from that created shortly after the first cadets were appointed over a century earlier. It is based on the fact that they were, in the words of former cadet and

Governor David Trench, 'all very highly educated, fairly highly motivated people ... chosen for their apparent qualities of character' to improve the standard of governance.[2]

While a good public school and university education made the early cadets in general terms the best educated officials in Hong Kong in the middle of the nineteenth century, the same educational attainment towards the last decade of British rule could no longer be deemed 'very highly educated'. In Hong Kong, as in modern Western countries and Japan, the educational standards of civil servants had improved exponentially in this century and a half. Towards the end of the twentieth century most civil servants in Hong Kong above the clerical and menial grades, be they specialists in professional departments or locally recruited executive officers, usually had received a university education. In terms of educational achievement, administrative officers were merely above average among the graduate intakes of civil servants.[3] What marked them apart from most of their graduate colleagues, however, was their strong sense of motivation and 'their apparent qualities of character'. Towards the end of the British period what really made the administrative officers of Hong Kong the elite within the government was not so much superior education but the spirit instilled in them by their senior colleagues.

The 'qualities of character' to which Trench refers are by nature intangible and difficult to define. For most of the British period they were perpetuated in the first instance by serving administrative officers seeking to recruit people like themselves. These qualities were then shaped and reinforced among new recruits by the strong *esprit de corps* inherited from senior administrative officers. By the 1990s this came to be done more professionally and was institutionalized in the recruitment process. By then successful applicants would need to be graduates who showed 'integrity and powers of analysis who can assume the role of arbitrator of different interests in policy formulation', and have a 'broad outlook' as well as the 'ability to work with a wide spectrum of personalities'.[4] These qualities encourage and enable administrative officers to behave with great confidence and take initiatives.

These qualities also implied a willingness on the part of administrative officers to take on the role of guardian of the public interest. This does not always mean defending existing bureaucratic practices, even though administrative officers collectively dominated the upper echelons of the bureaucracy and were never reticent about claiming their turf. On the contrary, it means that administrative officers believed that upholding the public interest required them not only to defend established bureaucratic practices where appropriate but also to break rules or to advocate ending practices where necessary. Choosing one or the other was a matter of judgement – whether the protection or enhancement of the public interest would justify or even demand either course of action.

Administrative officers accepted that their judgements and therefore their actions might turn out to be misguided but they believed they must act according to their conscience and do the best they could. This reflected in part the confidence they enjoyed as a long-established elite within the colonial government. Being part of the policy-making establishment made them feel more a part of the administration than most of their colleagues in the civil service – except for the small number of professional officers who rose to the top and became part of the policy-making machinery.

It also reflects the reality, highlighted in Chapter 8, that even top administrative officers were not held politically responsible for policy failures in the sense that elected politicians are in the British parliamentary system. In general terms, they could perform their duties to protect the public interest knowing full well that this would not put their careers and livelihoods at risk. To administrative officers, being politically neutral meant above all acting according to their conscience as civil servants and in the best interest of Hong Kong as they saw it, regardless of party political concerns or the politics of the impending transfer of sovereignty towards the end of the British period.

A corollary of the administrative officers' tremendous self-confidence is their willingness to be highly flexible. The ethos of the administrative officers was built on the tradition of the early cadets, who proudly served as gentlemen administrators ready to take on any task assigned to them with no notice, let alone prior training. They were the embodiment of the best and the worst of the British amateur administrator tradition.

With few exceptions administrative officers in colonial Hong Kong generally had a very wide range of postings in their careers. Ian Lightbody, for example, joined as a cadet after having served in the military administration (1945–46) at the end of the Pacific War. He

Assistant Colonial Secretary (Lands) Ian Lightbody visiting a Buddhist Temple.

was immediately deployed as an assistant secretary for Chinese Affairs, required to act as social welfare officer less than three years later, and moved to serve as assistant director for commerce and industry and then as an assistant secretary at the Colonial Secretariat even before he was given a chance to study Cantonese.[5]

As soon as he completed his language training, and as a cadet of only a few years' standing, he was dealing with 'enormous complexities of airline cabotage, as well as becoming acquainted with the ins and outs of British nationality and naturalization' when he was clerk of councils in 1953. He was then tasked to take over running civil defence, and was subsequently required to handle relations with

*An elite within the government*

Housing Department Office Party 1973. Secretary for Housing Ian Lightbody chopping the suckling pig on the occasion of the Housing Department Office party in 1973.

the British garrison at the defence branch before being made responsible for land policy and administration in 1956. Two years later he ran the establishment branch, and then took charge of the Transport Department, organized the Festival of Hong Kong and served as commissioner for resettlement.

He eventually rose to become secretary for housing, served as secretary for administration and then as chairman of the Public Service Commission before retiring in 1980. The only post in which he served for a sustained period of four years was when he was secretary for housing (1973–77). In all his postings he never received 'any detailed induction' even though 'considerable familiarization' was required to discharge well his various responsibilities in every posting.[6] Apart from being deployed before receiving Chinese language training, his experience was not exceptional. The willingness of administrative officers to take on any job was a great strength and was an important part of their ethos. This exposed them to a wide range of government activities and prepared the more successful of them to take on top level positions later in their careers. Above all, it enabled them to flourish in positions of authority even at a very young age, for they believed in themselves, both individually and collectively, as administrative officers, and demonstrated their confidence that they could handle whatever problems they might be asked to tackle.

This very strength also, however, carries weaknesses. The belief that administrative officers could just 'hit the ground running' was such that until towards the last two to three decades of the British era when an administrative officer left for a new posting he would not, as a matter of general practice, leave 'handing over notes, summarizing where' the office 'had arrived in each, and why' to his successor.[7] While most administrative officers clearly did hit the ground running it was less certain that they were always running in the direction that would bring the best results when they hit the ground. The cavalier attitude towards preparing handing over notes as a matter of good routine practice could not but have reduced efficiency for the government as a whole. As the world got increasingly complex and problems government must tackle got highly technical and specialized in the latter part of the twentieth century, it became doubtful if these 'gifted amateur administrators' always had a good understanding and grip of all the issues involved as they functioned as key players in the policy-making process.[8] Such shortcomings never deterred administrative officers from seeking to take charge of the situation and find solutions to whatever problems they might face. The capacity of senior administrative officers to act decisively compensated to an extent for any lack of expert knowledge as a decision at the right moment at the top would set the bureaucratic wheel in motion, and it would in any event have benefited from the expert knowledge of professional colleagues who contributed their views and recommendation in the paper trail of minutes leading up to the officer in charge for a decision.

The aggressive expression of individual and collective confidence and pride in the service also implied arrogance in attitude. There is little doubt that this caused resentment from some of their non-administrative officer colleagues. However, their sense of superiority also underpinned the integrity of the administrative officers as a whole. What appeared as arrogance to others was also a source of pride and self-esteem as the elite of the Hong Kong government. It instilled in the minds of most (if not all) administrative officers that corruption was beneath them – it was a vice to which underlings and perhaps the like of policemen and sanitary inspectors would succumb but it was one that no administrative officer would contemplate.[9] As explained in Chapter 6, while their good remuneration package unquestionably helped them to resist the temptation of bribes, the ultimate guarantor of the integrity of administrative officers was their high *esprit de corps*.

### Relations with non-administrative officers

As highlighted in the examination of administrative officers' work in departments in Chapter 5, there was tension between administrative officers and their professional colleagues and it got worse in the early postwar era compared with the situation before the Pacific War. Michael Wright, a professional architect who eventually rose to become director of public works and the first head of Hong Kong's representative office in London from a non-administrative officer background, recalls the early postwar period as a watershed. He remembers a view 'prevalent before the war' still being articulated as late as the late 1940s: 'the Cadets were the thoroughbreds, the racehorses, of the Colonial Service' while 'the professional officers were the cart horses'.[10] But tolerance of this view soon ended as professional departments expanded fast to meet the needs of a rapidly expanding and increasingly more sophisticated population. They 'spawned an increasing number of senior officers who met the Administrative Officers, especially those in the Secretariat, on equal terms which usually resulted in mutual respect and understanding' though it also 'led to the loss of much of the mystique that had surrounded the Cadets in the prewar years'.[11] With the end of the mystique their willingness to accept the privileged position of the administrative officers was eroded.

The large increase in the number of professional officers at the directorate level in the postwar era meant that more and more professional officers were dealing on a daily basis with administrative officers not as subordinates but as equals, or more often as superiors. Since the overwhelming majority of them served in departments that provided services, their dealings with administrative officers at the secretariat generally involved securing resources and blessings so that their respective departments could increase and improve the services they provided. By contrast, administrative officers at the secretariat, particularly at the finance branch, were responsible for scrutinizing all requests for public expenditure and coordinating government activities across departments. In practice, it meant that directorate level professional officers regularly had to deal with junior administrative officers who served as assistant secretaries at the secretariat. Many 'resented having to submit a case for a new school, hospital or road and were even more resentful if the request was not approved'.[12] This resentment would intensify 'if they thought that their "professional judgement" was questioned' by generalist administrative officers who did not understand the issues involved.[13]

This tension reflected more than resentment on the part of professional officers towards the longstanding sense of superiority of the administrative officers. It was also based on the difference in general terms between the kinds of tasks these two categories of officers performed. The duties that most professional officers in a service department had to perform were those of a specialist line officer. By contrast, most tasks administrative officers had to perform below the top managerial level or at the frontline as a district officer were those of a generalist staff officer. The inherent tension between line and staff officers applied in Hong Kong as it did elsewhere. This was intensified by the elitist position administrative officers enjoyed over professional officers who found themselves in the frontline performing line duties that, from their perspective, the staff administrative officers did not understand. This, combined with the special position administrative officers enjoyed within the government, led many professionals and departmental officers to believe 'that their career prospects are adversely affected by the privileged access of administrative officers to the directorate, and who feel a sense of relative deprivation as a consequence'.[14] This source of tension was not removed by the fact that administrative officers did not form a closed group and had since the 1970s recruited a significant percentage from among other civil servants. In the mid-1980s, for example, '20 per cent of all administrative officers had more than five years' service in other government departments before becoming administrative officers'.[15]

Tension between professional officers in departments and administrative officers at the secretariat was also caused, particularly in the 1960s when John Cowperthwaite was financial secretary, by his resistance to 'any forward planning which might be used to justify long-term financial commitment'.[16] The professionals at the Public Works Department, for example, were frustrated over feasibility studies for major new projects such as the mass transit railway or major new road projects to improve communication with new towns that were being constructed. The power of the financial secretary 'to exercise a veto on any project was open to question' and caused frustration and sullenness.[17] This applied in the case of some professional officers in the Public Works Department, though its director, Michael Wright enjoyed 'a very good working relationship' with Cowperthwaite and the two had mutual respect for each other. Cowperthwaite's strict control of the public purse in fact provoked antipathy not only from his professional colleagues but from administrative officers running departments and responsible for seeking resources from the government. Cowperthwaite treated them equally and merely set a very high standard for releasing public funds in order to ensure proposed public projects were carefully thought through and their costs properly assessed before public resources were committed. His approach reinforced in the minds of many senior professional officers the old stereotype of administrative officers behaving like God's gift and this caused resentment.

The deployment of administrative officers to departments could have the opposite effect, even though tension between administrative officers and professionals in specialist departments was not completely eliminated as a result. A senior administrative officer handling personnel issues generally enjoyed a key advantage over a professional colleague doing the same job. Anson Chan recalls from the time she worked at the directorate level at the Social Welfare Department that there was a tendency for senior departmental officers to hesitate to take effective action against a professional colleague who failed to measure up because they formed a tight-knit group and taking action that might ruin the career prospects of a fellow social worker was frowned upon. As a senior administrative officer, Chan was not susceptible to such peer pressure and never hesitated to take what she deemed the best course of action for the department, even if it should damage the career prospects of individual officers.[18] While this kind of action generally had a long-term positive impact on the department and would eventually earn the senior administrative officer respect, in the short term it caused resentment among the professionals. Indeed, there were also occasions when posting administrative officers to directorate level posts in professional departments simply 'generated more heat than light' as this practice was seen as 'poaching' by departmental officers and 'was bitterly resented'.[19]

Where administrative officers did help to reduce negative feelings against them was when they were posted to a professsional department that retained a career professional officer as head of department. Donald Luddington's experience as the first administrative secretary of the police, highlighted in Chapter 6, was no exception. His successor Peter Williams also earned the respect of his senior police colleagues.[20] Like Luddington, Administrative Officer Williams deployed his full skills and knowledge of the inner workings of the administration to help the police service secure 'the funds from the Finance Committee of the Legislative Council' so that it could pursue its plans for expansion, training and the acquisition of modern communications equipment.[21] This was the case of an imported staff officer contributing positively by getting more resources to the line officers and thus enabling the latter to perform their duties more effectively. The then commissioner of police Henry Heath thought highly of Luddington and Williams because they acted for the police. In Heath's words, 'they were useful in telling you how far you can get with the Secretariat' and 'they invariably presented a case which was (a) done with ability, and (b) which they knew would be acceptable to the Secretariat'.[22] Administrative officers who played a senior staff role in professional departments earned the respect of their professional colleagues as they were more effective in securing the Secretariat's blessings for departmental agendas and, from the view of the department concerned, 'turned out to be on our side, they were working for us and they did very well indeed for us'.[23]

**Relations with London**
Until the greater part of Britain's overseas empire had been given independence, Hong Kong occupied a special place in its relations with London. It was a significant imperial possession at the periphery of the British Empire about which few in the Colonial Office knew very much. Consequently, the Colonial Office and British government relied more than was usual on the judgements of successive governors of Hong Kong. This does not, of course, mean

*An elite within the government*

Secretary for Municipal Services Augustine Chui presents film star Jackie Chan to HM Queen Elizabeth II during her visit in 1986.

that London was any less inclined to advance its interests in Hong Kong than in other colonies. The dynamics in the relationship between the colony and metropolitan Britain depended, however, also on how the colonial administration saw and handled its relations with London and pressure from the United Kingdom government.

Although they formed the core of the British ruling elite in Hong Kong, it did not follow that administrative officers were the main means through which the British government in London ensured that colonial Hong Kong advanced UK interests. Admittedly, administrative officers were more likely than professional officers to be occupying positions that required them to deal with their UK colleagues, and they routinely defended British interests, but they would uphold the interests of British Hong Kong rather than advance those of the UK at the expense of Hong Kong. The way most administrative officers looked at this issue was summed up by David Jordan, who negotiated on Hong Kong's behalf over trade in the late 1960s and early 1970s and, on various occasions, had to defend Hong Kong's interests against those of his UK colleagues:

> I always felt that we should, so far as possible, and it was generally possible, try to compromise between the interests of the United Kingdom and those of Hong Kong. The trouble was that under short-term pressure from industries, from back benchers, from political organizations, the TUC, or whatever, under these short-term pressures a British Government would often seek to take action damaging to Hong Kong that was not in the long-term interests of the United Kingdom either. I frequently used this argument that we will not, we never do, oppose what you can clearly show, and consequently what we will accept, is in the long-term interest of the United Kingdom. When we're talking about long-term interests we must try to achieve a compromise between your views and ours; that's the only way we can proceed. We can't afford, neither of us can afford, to have a succession of serious confrontations between the United Kingdom Government and the Hong Kong Government. It would be a disastrous way to proceed, but we never really had any serious difficulty in avoiding such confrontation over trade, in time. It was always these short-term things that caused the trouble.[24]

In general, Jordan was right. Administrative officers, like the colonial government, on the whole advanced British interests without having to divide their loyalty between Hong Kong and the UK since the interests of the two mostly coincided. However, there were occasions when they differed and even conflicted with each other. In such circumstances, administrative officers invariably chose to defend Hong Kong's interests against those of the UK in the postwar era, though with varying degrees of success.

One of the very few occasions when Hong Kong's basic interest clashed with that of the UK happened shortly after the People's Republic of China came into existence. For Hong Kong, this involved the delicate but vital issue of handling Hong Kong's relations with the new Chinese regime, which had just forced Chiang Kai-shek and the remnants of his Kuomintang government to take refuge in Taiwan. For its part, the UK found its fragile state of economic rehabilitation being put at risk by an American threat to cut off Marshall aid if Hong Kong failed to comply with an American request.

What was at issue was the disposal of 71 aircraft owned by the China National Aviation Corporation (CNAC), a Chinese state-owned company with 20 per cent of its shares held by Pan American Airways and the Central Air Transport Corporation (CATC), an agency of the Chinese government.[25] The aircraft 'were of American lend-lease origins and were physically grounded in Hong Kong' when Mao Zedong proclaimed the People's Republic of China (PRC) in October 1949. Needless to say, they became a bone of contention.[26] Once Britain recognized the PRC in January 1950, under Hong Kong law these aircraft belonged to the PRC because the latter had replaced the Republic of China as China under British law. While Governor Alexander Grantham, who started his career as a cadet, could see that it was in Britain's strategic interest in the cold war not to allow the aircraft to fall into the hands of the Chinese communists, he was more concerned that Hong Kong should not be dragged into a dispute over the ownership of these aircraft and antagonize the new Chinese regime as a result.[27]

In principle, Britain shared Hong Kong's view and interest over this matter. Had the fate of the planes and their spare parts not become the subject of a major diplomatic issue, London would have supported Grantham and allowed the courts in Hong Kong to settle the contested claim, which was put forward by the PRC government and the new American owner of the aircraft. The latter was Central Air Transport (CAT), a company set up by General Claire Chennault, head of the American Flying Tigers in China during the Pacific War, which enjoyed the service of General William (Wild Bill) Donovan, head of the American wartime Office of Strategic Services, the precursor to the Central Intelligence Agency. CAT was able to purchase the planes cheaply and quickly after raising the issue directly with Chiang Kai-shek in Taipei shortly before Britain recognized the PRC as Chiang was keen to prevent these planes from falling into communist hands.[28] Chennault and Donovan then mobilized considerable support in Washington. As a result the US government applied tremendous pressure on Britain to deny the aircraft to the PRC and by implication to deliver them to CAT.

On this occasion the basic conflict of interest between Hong Kong and the UK lay in that it was in Hong Kong's interest to let the law run its course and to avoid taking action deemed hostile by the PRC whereas it was, on balance, in the UK's interest that Hong Kong should do the opposite. This was because the USA threatened the UK that handing the aircraft to the PRC 'might seriously endanger the continuation of Marshall aid and of the Military Assistance Programme'.[29] Given the state of the UK economy at the time, the maintenance of economic assistance under the Marshall Plan was critical and the British government therefore had no choice but to yield to American pressure, though this was seen by some as repugnant within the Cabinet.[30] For a matter of such importance to the UK and under huge pressure from London, the Hong Kong government eventually acted as it was required by a royal Order in Council, 'which overrode the law as it stood and in effect made a new law, which would inevitably pass the planes to the Americans'.[31]

What is pertinent and important was the way Grantham handled the matter. For a few months he argued forcefully against the instructions he was receiving from London, for example, by stressing that 'the strength of our position in Hong Kong' required his government to treat 'both [the Kuomintang] and the Communists exactly similar and absolutely according to law'.[32] By putting up a powerful case that on this occasion it was against Hong Kong's basic interest to defer to the UK's need to accommodate the USA, Grantham and his staff were able to ensure Foreign Secretary Ernest Bevin's support that London should take responsibility for this matter and Hong Kong should not be made to pay the price where avoidable.[33] The Hong Kong government's insistence on not violating the law also won the sympathy of the British attorney-general Sir Hartley Shawcross. Without key ministerial support it is doubtful that Hong Kong could have minimized potential damages to itself by ensuring that the UK would make clear this policy was made in London and that Hong Kong had no choice but to implement it.[34] It was with this in mind that a royal Order in Council was chosen as the instrument to resolve the matter in May 1950. This was meant to minimize the amount of wrath the PRC might direct against Hong Kong when the aircraft and their spare parts, Chinese state property before Hong Kong's law was changed, were eventually given to the Americans. Grantham could not defend Hong Kong's basic interest at the expense of that of the UK, but his steadfast stand reduced the cost to Hong Kong. Above all, he did not hesitate to defend Hong Kong's interest even on an occasion when the UK's own economic wellbeing was at stake.

Perhaps more revealing was that Grantham was economical with his knowledge when London and Hong Kong came under unrelenting American pressure to detain those planes in Hong Kong before the law was changed under the authority of the royal Order in Council. As British policy makers in London frantically sought a credible legal basis for the Hong Kong government to keep the aircraft there before the British cabinet discussed the matter for the first time in early April, Grantham did not inform or remind London of all the powers at his disposal. It is impossible that he and his advisers were not aware of the new powers he had acquired under the Emergency (Control of Ships and Aircraft) Regulations 1949, as it was passed only on 21 October, just three weeks before the aircraft dispute came to the fore. Under this set of regulations the governor could lawfully detain the aircraft.[35] Instead, he allowed his London colleagues to find a solution on their own.[36] They could only come up with a highly unsatisfactory alternative. It was to apply Article 60 of the Colonial Air Regulations Order to prevent the aircraft from flying. The desperation of the UK government was revealed in the cabinet meeting in which the British attorney general stated that such an application 'would be something of a subterfuge, since the primary object of this power was to ensure the safety of aircraft in the air' and 'the use of the Order could only afford a period of delay'.[37] This is because application of this Order could not prevent the Chinese from proceeding 'to remove the aircraft over land'.[38]

Grantham did not inform London of the powers at his disposal to detain the aircraft and their spare parts until after the British cabinet had made a policy on this matter. Significantly, when he was instructed to resort to the Colonial Air Regulations Order after the cabinet had met he was also told that there were 'doubts whether your powers' would go so far.[39] Only then did he mention that there were two other legal instruments, the Importation and Exportation Ordinance no. 32 of 1915 and Emergency Regulations of 1949, which would be more effective and appropriate, though he continued to express strong opposition to resorting to them.[40] By the time Grantham gave the game away the British cabinet had already decided to yield to American pressure and it was only a matter of how best to proceed. There was no longer any chance that Hong Kong could avoid detaining the aircraft and their spare parts until a solution that would be acceptable to the Americans and least damaging to the other interests of the UK and Hong Kong could be found. The planes were eventually handed over to the Americans in 1952 after lengthy legal proceedings. Significantly, Hong Kong did not have to pay a price for this affair as the PRC did not try to punish it by, for example, organizing unrest or demonstrations within Hong Kong or heightening tension at the borders.

What happened in 1950 was an extraordinary case. UK and Hong Kong interests did not clash with such intensity in the rest of the British period. However, even in less exciting times there remained occasions when Britain's own interests conflicted with those of Hong Kong to varying degrees. In addition to trade negotiations already highlighted earlier, these included air transport agreements, the implications of the British nationality acts for Hong Kong, defence cost agreements, and specific issues over the future of Hong Kong during the Sino–British negotiations of the 1980s.[41] Conflicts came up even more frequently in the late 1980s and early 1990s in the run-up to the transfer of Hong Kong's sovereignty to China in 1997. Simon Vickers, a middle-ranking administrative officer in this period recalls:

> There were a number of major issues where HK was openly opposed to the UK. Immigration and trade were the main area with the right to UK passports being the biggest immigration issue after [the] Tiananmen Square [incident of 1989]. AOs fought strongly for all groups, Indians and Eurasians for full passports because they could not expect to be incorporated as Chinese citizens, HK Chinese for an emergency bolthole, as many as possible with full residency right passports at once, all with the possibility of asylum if everything went wrong. The relatively right-wing Home Ministers of John Major's government were taken on without fear: in response to a statement by [Charles] Wardle that HK Chinese did not need an assurance of asylum because they would be Chinese citizens 'with all that goes with the status of citizenship' the PAS put out a Line to Take to all overseas offices, i.e. in full sight of the British diplomats and using their communication channels, saying 'People may point out that the worst case being assured against will be caused by China, so telling them that they are alright because they have right of abode in China and consular protection by

China is hardly an honourable position for the British to take'. So AOs were quite happy to call their British 'bosses' 'dishonourable' — hardly either classic Whitehall or classic colonial behaviour.[42]

The willingness of administrative officers to argue against London's expressed wishes was not a new development as transfer of Hong Kong's sovereignty to China came up on the horizon. Even before the British Empire was largely wound up in the 1960s, when a unified colonial administrative service still existed, as David Trench explained, individual administrative officers 'didn't think of ourselves as UK civil servants'; instead they considered themselves 'civil servants of whichever territory was paying us, we [were] working for.'[43] Hong Kong's administrative officers simply 'did not start from the position that they could not question or even change British positions and practice, even go against British interests where HK interests were different'.[44]

The preparedness of administrative officers to stand up to London on behalf of Hong Kong should not be interpreted as implying that anyone took pleasure in confronting London or picking fights with it unless it were unavoidable. In the postwar period when administrative officers and other senior Hong Kong officials were required to choose to defend Hong Kong's interest against the preference of the UK government, they merely displayed a 'lack of loyalty to London'.[45] In so doing, administrative officers were not always just defending Hong Kong's interests; they could also be defending a preference of the Hong Kong government and its people against that of the UK government.

Their willingness to stand up to London should not be equated with their or the Hong Kong government's successful defence of Hong Kong's interests or its preferences. There were indeed major policy issues over which Hong Kong's preference differed from that of the UK and the latter prevailed. The best known examples were disagreements over the end of capital punishment and the treatment of Vietnamese boat people. On both matters London took a more liberal view at Hong Kong's expense, preferring to end capital punishment and insist on a more humane treatment of the Vietnamese boat people.[46] It is doubtful if the administrative officers or colonial government could have achieved more than securing significant concessions from London, such as keeping capital punishment in name but ending its enforcement in practice. But any assessment of this issue needed to take into account the factor that most administrative officers were more worldly and 'more liberal than HK people generally' on such moral issues and were therefore not minded to fight as hard as when defending Hong Kong's straightforward interests.[47]

Governments of different political persuasions and individual ministers in London also differed in how far and how often they leant on colonial Hong Kong. Ironically, it was the more left-wing governments formed by the Labour Party that tended to put more pressure on Hong Kong.[48] Administrative Officer Kenneth Topley recalls that the main issues over which London would lean on Hong Kong to follow Britain's lead were mostly from the Labour Party agenda. They were matters like promoting trade unions, introducing a minimum wage and nationalizing the docks.[49] A British minister that administrative officers particularly remembered for his proclivity to put pressure on Hong Kong was Lord Goronwy Roberts, who wanted to 'send a senior Whitehall official to the secretariat in HK as an "enforcer" of HMG's will'.[50] While this was successfully resisted, it did not stop him from pushing 'for more investment in sterling from HK', though this was met with 'a furious reaction from FS [Financial Secretary] Philip Haddon-Cave'.[51] By contrast, Michael Wright warmly remembers Conservative minister Anthony Royle in the early 1970s for his initiative to enable Wright, Hong Kong's representative in London, to mix in diplomatic circles despite Foreign Office officials' routine efforts to put him down. It was Royle who broke with previous practice by instructing that Hong Kong's representative in London should be taken to the ambassador's waiting room when invited to meet him in the Foreign Office, and be invited to a luncheon he hosted for a retiring ambassador.[52]

Most of the time when administrative officers found themselves defending Hong Kong's interests against pressure from the UK they did so against UK officials at the working level rather at the 'Hong Kong versus UK' level. British officials at the Department of Trade and at the Foreign Office, as distinct from the Colonial Office before it was subsumed into the Commonwealth and then the Foreign and Commonwealth Office, in particular could be even more aggressive than ministers in trying to subjugate Hong Kong's interest to that of the UK. Denis Bray, recalling his experience while serving as Hong Kong's commissioner in London, noted that 'in some quarters, there really was a belief that it was the job of the colonial government to promote the interests of the UK, even when these conflicted with those of the colony.'[53]

A particularly bad case of this nature was touched on in passing in Chapter 6, in connection with David Jordan's work as acting director of commerce and industry in 1970. Essentially, it was a matter of some British officials in the Department of Trade getting the Foreign Office to send a telegram to Hong Kong forbidding it to negotiate with Canada over some trade issues on the grounds that it would violate British policy, even though the Canadian negotiating team was already on its way to Hong Kong. Jordan flew to London and quickly ascertained that the UK officials involved had acted without ministerial approval, and the telegraphic instructions therefore did not represent British government policy. He also knew from previous experience and accumulated knowledge that the UK government had not yet decided on a policy on this matter. Armed with such information he took the matter up first with the assistant under-secretary at the Foreign Office and then the permanent secretary at the trade department. He argued forcefully that 'you are telling us that what we propose to do is contrary to British policy' when Britain had not yet made a policy on this, which amounted to forcing Hong Kong 'to conform to a policy you haven't even decided on yet'. He added that it was not 'very reasonable to ask that Hong Kong should prejudice its trading interests in order merely to leave your options open as to what this policy decision shall be'.[54] He then pushed his argument to its logical conclusion: 'You are asking us to do something in the interests of British policy which we believe to be contrary to Hong Kong's trading interests. If we do as you say and the result is, as we believe it will be, to damage our trade, are you going to compensate us, and if so, how?'[55] Having won the argument Jordan then secured an agreement with permanent secretary Sir Antony Part of the Department of Trade by which the Hong Kong government could proceed to issue its own instructions to its negotiators meeting up with their Canadian colleagues.[56]

The colonial government's defence of Hong Kong's interests against pressure from the UK was of course not a preserve of administrative officers. Others were known to have done so, though to varying degrees of steadfastness: they included professional officers put in a similar situation such as architect Michael Wright when he was administrative commissioner in London, as well as diplomatic service governors. The first career diplomat to be appointed governor in the twentieth century, Murray MacLehose, was deemed by at least one administrative officer as 'more ambivalent' than his predecessors and 'backed down too early' on specific issues, and his appointment was seen by another as an attempt by the Foreign Office to put in place someone with 'build-in political direction'.[57] Indeed, when he first took up his appointment he told senior administrative officer Denis Bray that 'he could not understand why we always seemed to be in battle with the Foreign Office'. However, 'not long afterwards' he said to Bray: 'I cannot understand those people in the Foreign Office – they seem to regard me as a cross between Makarios and a bandit chief.'[58] MacLehose's successor as governor, former British ambassador to China Edward Youde, underwent a similar conversion. Senior Administrative Officer Robert Upton recalls: 'I find it poignant that Teddy Youde, whose very face lit up when he entered the Foreign Office, should have been in outright disagreement with FCO [Foreign and Commonwealth Office] policy at the time of his premature death' in office.[59] As Bray rightly reminded MacLehose: 'that is par for the course for a colonial governor'.[60] The same applied to being administrative officers, the cream of the Hong Kong government, although the occasions when they had to stand up to London were the exceptions rather than the rule.

*Chapter 10*
# INHIBITED ELITISM

When the British flag was finally hauled down in Hong Kong in 1997, the administrative officers remained the political elite and continued to take the lead in providing good governance despite momentous political changes. The existence of a politically neutral professional civil service, the most important element of which was the administrative officers, was one of the greatest legacies the British left for the people of Hong Kong. Much of this was of course due to the high degree of institutionalization in colonial Hong Kong. In this context, administrative officers performed no better or worse than any other constituent parts of the civil service. However, the local community and the civil service as a whole had long looked up to administrative officers to take the lead in ensuring a high standard of governance. Administrative officers were also the political officers of the colonial administration and were therefore politically engaged with the affairs and people of Hong Kong. They thus occupied a place in Hong Kong's governance that no other collective group of civil servants could rival. It raises two interesting and important questions: What enabled administrative officers collectively to play such a positive role in delivering good governance? What are the wider implications of their experience?

There are two aspects to the successful search for good governance by the administrative officers of Hong Kong. Both are ironic if not somewhat paradoxical. The first is the very nature of the people selected and the ethos developed. The other concerns the acceptance by administrative officers that the span and scope of government should be limited despite the intoxication of power and status brought about by being the unquestioned elite of the government and society for over a century.

**Intellectual brilliance versus good governance**
Their unrivalled status in the colonial government should not be taken to imply that administrative officers were mostly individuals who were so brilliant or thoughtful that they had or should have earned a double first or a first-class degree from the top British universities. They were not. On the contrary, their experience shows that good governance can be delivered by a civil service staffed not by the brightest and most academically able graduates. As a matter of fact, the top scoring British graduates who sought a career in the civil service did not usually choose to go to Hong Kong. In order of preference these graduates generally picked the British Treasury, followed by the British diplomatic service and the Indian Civil Service while it existed before considering the Eastern cadetship or colonial administrative service. Admittedly, some of those who chose to work overseas might not have wanted to join the home civil service in Britain. The fact remains that Hong Kong's administrative service was not filled with the brightest graduates that the best British universities produced, though they were mostly staffed by very good and able graduates from some of Britain's finest universities.

The great majority of administrative officers from 1862 onwards were not first-rate thinkers or intellectually exceptional, though among them were individuals who were brilliant or so intellectually gifted that they were scholars in their own right despite pursuing a non-academic career. Among the better known postwar administrative officers, John Cowperthwaite and David Jordan were brilliant, while the scholarship of James Hayes earns and deserves general respect and high regard from the scholarly community.[1] The overwhelming majority of administrative officers, however, were more akin to today's graduates from an established British university with a good upper second-class honours degree. They were highly able, well educated and hardworking individuals dedicated to serving Hong Kong proudly in their collective identity as cadets or administrative officers. They might not have been the most intellectually stimulating and imaginative individuals but it was they who collectively played the greatest part in ensuring that, on balance, the colonial government delivered good governance within the context of the times over the course of a century.

The most important factor to underpin the success of the administrative officers as a whole was the strong *esprit de corps* they forged together. The qualities in which successive generations of administrative officers took pride were 'fair-mindedness, even-handedness, integrity, consistency, determination, flexibility and a will to meet and overcome challenges of all sorts'.[2] Ever since the first cadets were appointed, most administrative officers worked together with 'a strong sense of collegiate purpose and commitment'.[3] This was what enabled them to produce synergy and achieve collectively substantially more than adding up the achievements of individual officers would have suggested.

The positive value of their cohesion and of their *esprit de corps* should not be underestimated. Because the administrative officers came from very similar educational, cultural and class backgrounds, particularly in the first century of their existence, they understood each other and could easily develop a rapport. Once the *esprit de corps* was created it was transmitted to successive generations of new recruits by a process akin to osmosis. It also worked because most of the recruits fitted in well with the ethos of the service. Until the latter part of the twentieth century, the procedures by which they were recruited may seem amateurish and unprofessional by modern standards, but the right people were usually spotted for the purposes for which they were intended. An officer recruited because he 'could move easily amongst his peers in that sort of way' was one who would willingly accept induction into this elite group and embrace its *esprit de corps* without question.[4]

Part of this *esprit de corps* was the idea that administrative officers should focus on doing their jobs well, for which they could expect their colleagues to give support where required and to offer recognition when due. It was not by accident that administrative officers received the bulk of senior honours bestowed by the crown on the citizens of Hong Kong. The idea that loyalties to Hong Kong and to fellow administrative officers were complementary to each other was cultivated from the beginning.

By implication, engaging in debates for the sake of intellectual discourse or advancing in general terms the understanding of abstract matter was frowned upon as a distraction. Satisfying one's intellectual curiosity was not deemed sufficient grounds for upsetting the applecart of good governance, though challenging existing practices or procedures in order to improve governance was acceptable behaviour for an administrative officer.

While the ethos of the administrative officers would and did galvanize highly competent, dedicated and focused civil servants to do their best and work together, it was not one that would easily satisfy the most intellectually brilliant, imaginative or creative individuals. Administrative officers in Hong Kong worked well and effectively together as they were first and foremost team players focused on delivering good governance rather than brilliant individuals devoted to the quest of knowledge or satisfying themselves that the best policy was devised and delivered under their personal charge.

Indeed, among administrative officers, the truly intellectually brilliant few were often seen as loners, mavericks, or intimidating figures rather than good team players by their colleagues, even though they were no less dedicated to the wider interests of the community and the government. David Jordan, for example, was an extremely able administrative officer with a first-class mind that enabled him to analyse and understand highly complex issues and then explain what the crux of the matter was in a clear and well structured manner. He enjoyed vigorous debates and was devoted to Hong Kong and to improving governance. He was also ready and willing to concede he was wrong if a colleague (or, for that matter, anyone) could put forward a better explanation or argument than he managed to produce. He loved winning arguments but was even more pleased when someone could beat him in a well-reasoned debate and come forward with a better solution to a problem. However, as he usually put up a better case and revelled in his intellectual superiority, he was also arrogant and many of his colleagues looked upon him as a megalomaniac, too full of himself, wild or a non-team player.

In the end, for true team work and synergy to occur the personal ability of the brightest officers like Jordan mattered less than how they were seen by their peers. Unless they could work together effectively in a collegial and complementary manner they could not add up to more than the sum total of the individuals.

Had individuals of Jordan's intellectual calibre been the rule rather than the exception among administrative officers they would no doubt have produced clearer, more rational and better thought out policies through vigorous debates in the policy-making process. Would they have ended up devoting much more of their time, precious resources for the colonial administration given the small number of administrative officers in service until the 1970s, to policy debates and unwittingly reduced the quality of governance by significantly delaying the implementation of policies? There is no straightforward answer to such a question. On occasions the avoidance of a poorly conceived policy would more than compensate for delay in having a policy in place. On other occasions the reverse would be true, and the prompt implementation of a reasonably devised policy would be more beneficial than the delay involved in working out a better one.

In reality, whether the administrative service would on balance have provided better governance had its officers been cleverer remains doubtful. One must bear in mind that good governance requires decisions to be taken 'quickly and firmly when necessary' and this 'can be affected if an "intellectually brilliant mind" sees too many options and spends prolonged periods weighing all possible pros and cons'.[5] It is also by no means certain that such officers would be equally willing to embrace the *esprit de corps* of the administrative officers and hold it as if sacrosanct. It is more likely that they would challenge it with a view to improving it but may end up repeating an inherently endless process rather than focusing on delivering good governance quickly. As it happened, administrative officers preferred to act defensively about their privileged standing within the government to debating among themselves about how they could improve their *esprit de corps*, and in so doing they sought to justify their privileged position by demonstrating their contribution towards improving governance.

Indeed, a key strength of the Hong Kong administration was its ability to make prompt decisions and implement them quickly rather than try to formulate the most appropriate policy over the long term. The need to balance working out the most appropriate policy involving protracted debates against reaching a decision quickly after some debates to enable the bureaucratic wheel to be set in motion is a somewhat ironical one. If one puts aside the moral preference that one must always strive for the best and focus on efficacy instead, one cannot deny that probability implies that if a decision on even the most complex and complicated matter is made by tossing a coin, 50 per cent of the time the decision will be the right one.

Given that policies in Hong Kong were made through a process of careful deliberation involving a string of professional administrators adding their views in minutes (which often did involve debates) without regard to party politics before a policy paper was finalized and put to the governor and Executive Council, even if a policy were then adopted without further critical examination, it had a substantially better chance of working well than tossing a coin. In such a context, procrastination, even for the laudable purpose of seeking the most suitable policy, is often the worst enemy of good governance because it will produce no result and let opportunities slip. Thus, the capacity of the government to act promptly on the whole outweighs the advantages that more thorough and spirited debates would bring in pre-empting some of the negative side effects. After all, even the most vigorous debates by the brightest individuals do not necessarily produce the most suitable policy.

What Hong Kong had among its administrative officers was, with the benefit of hindsight, a fortunate compromise. It recruited and groomed a civil service elite that prized collegiality and pragmatism above all but also included a small number of brilliant individuals. This was an accident of history rather than the product of a deliberate policy. But the existence of a small number of brilliant officers who occasionally raised awkward questions or challenged the appropriateness of specific policies or practices forced the service and the government to reflect periodically on what they said. They might prove an irritant to most administrative officers some of the time but they also reduced the risk of allowing the service as a whole to get too complacent. In a different way, the appointment of administrative officers on transfer from other colonies in the postwar period also had a similar effect. Some of them had served under local ministers in their former territories prior to their independence, and such experience gave them a wider outlook and led them to question some of the practices prevailing in Hong Kong.[6]

An elite that is not periodically challenged is more prone to be intoxicated by its power and status – as indeed happened to administrative officers in the interwar decades. Apart from Governor Clementi Smith, hardly any cadet during this period exhibited sufficient intellectual prowess and standing to challenge the complacency of the others.⁷ The administrative officers, and the top echelon of the colonial government as a whole, thus fell prey to complacency and basked too readily in the warm glow of Britain's imperial serenity in East Asia. The result was the government's complete lack of capacity and preparation to mobilize the local Chinese community to face up to the steadily rising threat from the emerging Japanese empire.

For most of the postwar period, with Hong Kong caught between the warring sides of the Chinese Civil War on the one hand and the Chinese communist government and capitalist West in the cold war on the other, the environment for governance within the colony was quite benign.⁸ Despite the massive increase in population, mainly through the influx of refugees and economic migrants in the late 1940s, or a few notable social disturbances, there was no movement to flout the authority of the colonial government, even less an anti-colonial insurgency.⁹ As a challenge to the capacity of governance even the Maoist inspired and directed confrontation of 1967 was fundamentally different in nature and extent from the strike-cum-boycott of 1925-26, not to say the Japanese attack of 1941.¹⁰

Indeed, despite the presence of an irredentist Chinese government in Beijing since 1949, it did not organize and sustain a movement to challenge British colonial authority. The success of the administrative officers and the colonial government as a whole should be set in a wider context that takes into account this benign environment. However, it should also be recognized that the basic approach and attitude of the colonial administration in the postwar period helped create or reinforce this environment. Its existence was in part attributable to its administrative service being dominated not by brilliant individuals confident that they could take on everything but by a small dedicated group of able officers narrowly focused on getting the immediate tasks done as well as they could. Beijing could bide its time over the status of Hong Kong because the colonial administration did not embark on any ambitious plan that required it to respond by raising the issue of Hong Kong's future until the beginning of the 1980s.

In terms of what constituted 'good governance' in the two decades or so after the war, public expectations were still limited. At first they amounted to little more than expecting the colonial government to provide a stable political and social environment to enable them to get on with their lives. As time went on, the local people looked increasingly to the government for help at times of natural disasters and in providing health and educational services, but the standards of government services the general public expected were still low by modern measures. The colonial government's delivery of 'good governance', the meaning of which changed over time, should therefore be understood in this context. 'Good governance' was judged to have been delivered if the government on balance managed to meet the expectations of the general public. Until towards the end of British colonial rule, the local people's expectation of good governance amounted to a government that was basically efficient, fair, honest, paternalistic and yet non-intrusive in the lives of ordinary people.[11]

**An inhibited political centre**
Although the crown colony system of government in principle vested near dictatorial power in the office of governor and his advisers, subject only to regulation by the British government and parliament in London, in general terms the colonial administration did not in practice exercise such power, particularly in the postwar period. The existence of the rule of law meant a strong judicial infrastructure and a law abiding attitude governed the conduct of its officials.[12] The relative lack of abuse of authority was also to a large extent because administrative officers, focusing almost solely on matters of governance, dominated the administration. They were primarily interested in making 'policies on the basis of what' they believed to be 'the best interest of the Colony'.[13] They were not intellectually imaginative or arrogant enough to want either to challenge or to justify the assumptions behind the existing political system, or to seek to remove the gap between the constitutional provisions and the political reality in the exercise of power, or to change society in line with any intellectual or ideological belief.

While the colonial administration had from its inception as part of its ethos a commitment not to abuse its power, it was substantially less inhibited from doing so in the prewar period than in the postwar era. In the first century of British rule, the administration imposed summary measures against the local Chinese community that would be considered abusive and offensive by the standards of the twenty-first century. They included criminalizing some of the everyday activities of certain sectors of the local Chinese community in the nineteenth century and restricting where the Chinese could reside.[14] They were imposed, in the context of the time, not so much to put the Chinese at a disadvantage as to make life more comfortable for the small and privileged expatriate community. The colonial government and its administrative service simply ignored the repugnant nature of some of these measures to the local Chinese community. On balance, the prewar colonial administration was still a benign one and governance in Hong Kong compared well with what existed in southern China, but this was not so much because the colonial government was inhibited from being abusive as because it saw no reason or need to do so more often than it did.

The real break happened after 1945 as the colonial government started to remove discriminatory practices, albeit slowly. While this partly reflected general changes in colonial policy brought about by the Second World War, it was above all a response to the new reality as the government in China under Chiang Kai-shek adopted an irredentist agenda towards Hong Kong.[15] This new factor meant that the colonial government realized it must maintain social cohesion, stability, good order and economic growth to pre-empt a Chinese demand for retrocession. This underlay the colonial government's acceptance that a new outlook was needed, which, in turn, led to the emergence of an inhibited political centre. This concept can in its simplest terms be defined as 'institutions and people who allocate and exercise power but who, for various reasons, feel the need to exert considerable self-restraint in the exercise of such power'.[16] Its existence was reinforced by two developments:

> To begin with, the world turned against colonialism after the war and the British Empire was largely dissolved by the 1960s. The abandonment of democratic reform in 1952 meant a Crown colony system would have to be continued in Hong Kong amidst a world hostile to its continuation. More importantly, this happened as a powerful and nationalistic regime was emerging in the PRC, which did not disguise its intention to secure the retrocession of Hong Kong from Britain.[17]

They meant that 'if the postwar Hong Kong Government had provoked a domestic crisis because of irresponsible policies or because of incompetence, it would risk its own very existence.'[18] This was a powerful incentive for the colonial government to act on the inhibited political centre effect and encouraged the introduction of some of the key administrative reforms, such as the CDO scheme.

Notwithstanding this, the dominance of administrative officers made the acceptance of this effect a straightforward one in Hong Kong. Their commitment to fair-mindedness, even-handedness, and integrity as part of their *esprit de corps* made 'the need to exert considerable self-restraint in the exercise' of power unobjectionable once the need was recognized. In time, the need to work within the political constraints was elevated to a principle. Administrative officers came to accept that the legitimacy of the colonial government had to be 'justified against the requirements of the two great canonical principles, social cohesion and economic stability.'[19] As one of them recalls: 'We didn't do something if it was assessed as likely to upset them – we did do something if we thought they required it. Maintaining them was the only thing we could do, but had to do, to fulfil our legitimating task of keeping Hong Kong out of Chinese Communist clutches.'[20]

The fact that the overwhelming majority of administrative officers consisted of highly able but not brilliant individuals also made it easier for the colonial government to adhere to the principle of keeping the scope and span of government small. Administrative officers believed in excellence, but their commitment to excellence was limited. It was to deliver the best possible governance within the scope of responsibilities they were assigned.

Not staffed largely by the most brilliant, ambitious and imaginative individuals whose inflated egos could stoke each other and promote over-confidence, Hong Kong's administrative officers did not suffer badly from grossly inflated assessments of their abilities. Instead, they put their elitism within the colony in perspective. They did not make the assumption that they were better than almost everyone else in everything, and should therefore expand the scope of government as they could do better in regulating different aspects of social and economic life. In reality, they readily accepted that they 'had no business, really, in meddling with the affairs of industry and commerce because' they 'simply weren't competent to meddle with industry and commerce'.[21] Nor did they develop a desire to tell ordinary people how to live their lives or deliver social justice by weaving a complex web of the tax system to ensure the poor received the 'right' kind of benefits. It was recognition of their limitations that underlined the colonial government's commitment to keeping the span and scope of government small. Such recognition came more easily to the highly competent but not the brightest than to the most brilliant individuals. A humble genius is an oxymoron.

**Wider implications**
The first key lesson one can draw from the administrative officers' search for good governance is the somewhat ironic one that one does not need the intellectually brightest individuals to provide good governance. Indeed, the Hong Kong experience points in the other direction. On its own it is insufficient to provide grounds for generalization. Nevertheless, it is a case study that should not be ignored by those interested in public administration. Hong Kong's case should make an interesting contrast with the experience elsewhere, not least in the performance of the Treasury in the UK and in that of the old Indian Civil Service, both staffed in general terms with officials of higher intellectual calibre than Hong Kong's administrative officers. In the end the Hong Kong officials did at least as well if not better than their colleagues in the other two services, which recruited from the same general source.

Another lesson is that despite its colonial character Hong Kong's administration 'reached the standard of "as good a government as practicable" in the traditional expectation of the Chinese' by the early 1980s.[22] Although the highest standard of good governance in traditional China did not require the existence of a democratic government, the achievement of such a standard without democratic checks and balances in colonial Hong Kong was no less remarkable. In the absence of democratic politics the top echelon of the colonial government's successful resistance of the corrosive effect of power corruption was largely attributable to the administrative officers and their *esprit de corps*.

It was an ethos that embodied a collective and continuous quest for good governance as the mission of the administrative officers. It cultivated among generations of administrative officers that they were the elite in the government but one with a limited and highly focused objective. It ensured that they devoted their energies to running the administration and providing public services as efficiently as they could. It helped all but possibly a handful of administrative officers to desist from accepting bribes, though their good remuneration package was unquestionably important in sustaining honesty. It also allowed the inhibited political centre effect to work in the absence of democratic checks and balances.

The existence of the inhibited political centre played a critical part in steering the colonial government towards abandoning its inherently racist past. Since the late 1960s it has also increasingly helped it to acquire a proactive attitude towards removing abuse of power and enabled it to focus on delivering good governance to the local Chinese population. This was in sharp contrast to what prevailed in the prewar century when the benefits of good governance were meant first and foremost not for the vast local Chinese community but for the tiny expatriate community. This change was more the result of a steady shift than the product of a change of governor at the top, though Governor MacLehose's emphasis on public relations unquestionably accelerated the process. Nor was it a direct response to the challenges of the 1967 disturbances. This change started with the advent of the 1946 outlook that Governor Mark Young acted upon after the eviction of the Japanese occupiers. It became clearly discernible during David Trench's tenure as governor. While forward looking governors took the lead, it was administrative officers who were largely responsible for turning this shift in attitude into practical policies, not least by jettisoning the prejudice of the old time and adopting a more progressive outlook in their own generational succession.

The largely expatriate British composition of the administrative officers until the last two decades of British rule had the ironic effect of reinforcing the inhibited political centre in the absence of democratic checks and balances. With the very future of Hong Kong being put on the political agenda and then settled, the colonial government took on the character of a caretaker administration as the year 1997 got nearer and nearer. Increasingly, it became difficult and awkward for the British government in London or the expatriate elements in the Hong Kong government to take bold initiatives unless they were embraced by the local population. Governor Patten could introduce a political reform package as late as 1992 and claim it to represent major political advancement because by then the general public in Hong Kong was keen to see progress in this direction. It might have provoked strong negative reactions from some of the leading businessmen in Hong Kong and vociferous responses from the Chinese government, but it did not represent a lessening of the inhibited political centre effect. On the contrary, it revealed its effectiveness by requiring the last governor to act in accordance with the public wish. After all, a middle class had by then arisen in Hong Kong and it not only engaged in such issues but also 'required paternalism to be reinterpreted in relation to their concerns and aspirations'.[23]

In such a context the administrative officers, both expatriates and locals, continued to play their long-established role and maintain their elitist position within the government. It remained the leading force within the administration that searched for and delivered good governance while trying to avoid where possible being ensnared in daily politics. They could do so because they remained politically neutral. Political neutrality in the Hong Kong context was not a matter of not advancing the interests of a political master in the shape of a political party that has won power through electoral politics. Right up until the end of British rule in 1997, Hong Kong never developed into an electoral democracy. Admittedly, the top echelons of the administration, which administrative officers dominated, were more comfortable dealing with leading business people than with members of the general public. However, to them, political neutrality meant not serving the political interests of anyone, including metropolitan Britain or the business tycoons, but doing what administrative officers considered to be in the best interests of the Hong Kong community. The administrative officers' long-standing credibility was what ensured that the general public retained confidence in them and in the government as a whole until and, indeed, beyond the handover of sovereignty in 1997.

As the sun finally set in this last major imperial outpost of the British Empire, the total of more than 500 now predominantly local administrative officers became one of the most valuable legacies of imperial rule. However, despite Britain and China's shared wish to maintain the status quo in Hong Kong, the transfer of sovereignty implied wider changes of considerable significance, the most important being the removal of the two key circumstantial drivers behind the existence of an inhibited political centre – the colonial nature of the government in a world hostile to colonialism; and a threat to the existence of colonial Hong Kong in the presence of the irredentist PRC.

This was a basic change because the existence of an inhibited political centre was crucial for maintaining the ethos of the government and its administrative service, including a sense of humility and acceptance that the business community and free market could manage the economy better than the government could. That this change had indeed occurred became evident when the Hong Kong Special Administrative Region tackled the challenges posed by the Asian financial crisis of 1997/8 when the Hong Kong dollar and its stock market came under tremendous pressure from speculators. The SAR government boldly committed 10 per cent of its reserve to ward off the speculators. It was a gamble that paid off handsomely in retrospect, but it was a huge gamble that, had it occurred during the colonial period, would have caused much soul-searching had it not simply been resisted on the grounds of being reckless. The old factor that inhibited the colonial government from taking risks had been replaced by local officials behaving like masters of their own territory. The inhibitions at the political centre had just melted away when Hong Kong ceased to be a British colony.[24]

What should be recognized is that if administrative officers are to continue to make the same basic contribution as before the transfer of sovereignty, the general conditions that underlined the success of the old political structure would need to be sustained. This does not necessarily imply keeping the old order, for important changes had occurred and they called for fresh ideas in response. Nevertheless, the conditions that ensured the old *esprit de corps* of the administrative officers and that allowed the inhibited political centre to work so well need to be retained or, more appropriately, recreated in a different way.

One has to accept that the SAR cannot be insulated from the developments and politics of China in the same way as the old crown colony was protected from the political vicissitudes of metropolitan Britain on the other side of the world.[25] The regimes in London and Beijing are fundamentally different in nature and they see their relationship with Hong Kong through different prisms. As a result, the very concept of maintaining a politically neutral civil service in Hong Kong has undergone a basic change since 1997. To ensure that administrative officers can continue to play the successful and positive role they had in the colonial period, they need to be insulated from domestic strife and from the politics of dealing with mother China.

This insulation of the senior career civil servants from the vicissitudes of everyday politics and handling the inherently delicate relations with China usually calls for the introduction of a class of career politicians to serve as government ministers above the politically neutral civil servants or administrative officers. This applies particularly to a political system whose internal logic for modern development is to evolve towards a Westminster model. For a ministerial level of government in such a context to have the desired effect it must command credibility among the local people and be seen as responsible to them. This means that they must not be appointees, for as such they would have no claim of legitimacy and credibility in the twenty-first century, and no means of showing that they had earned a mandate from the general public. For a ministerial system to work in general, and to work hand in glove with the administrative officers in particular, there is no alternative but to hold open and fair elections to be contested regularly by well-organized political parties. It is only when ministers are drawn from the ranks of elected politicians and are thus accepted as publicly accountable to the local people that they can gain sufficient credibility to take over the political direction of the government. In such a system the inhibited political centre will be replaced by a subordinated centre. In other words, the self-restraint of those in power in an authoritarian system will be replaced by checks and balances in a democratic one. Such a development will allow the administrative officers to focus on delivering good governance.

# NOTES

## Chapter 1. Governance in a colonial society

1. *Hong Kong Register* (Hong Kong), 11 August 1846, p. 127.
2. *The Times* (London), 15 March 1859.
3. Carroll 1999, pp. 16–20.
4. Carroll 2005, p. 18.
5. Sayer 1980, p. 154.
6. Endacott 1964a, p. 43.
7. Public Record Office (Kew), Colonial Office archives, CO129/13, Enclosure to Davis to Stanley dispatch 114, 20 August 1845.
8. CO129/13, Gladstone to Davis, dispatch 32, 7 March 1846.
9. *China Mail* (Hong Kong) 23 June 1859.
10. Endacott 1964b, p. 63.
11. Ibid., p. 61.
12. Ibid., pp. 61–4.
13. For a detailed analysis of the Caldwell affair and the events leading to both him and Anstey leaving office, see Munn 2001a, pp. 307–21. See also Chapter 2.
14. Munn 2001b, p. 23.
15. Christopher Munn 2001a, p. 212.
16. Endacott 1964b, p. 122.
17. Sayer 1980, appendix II.
18. Ibid., appendix X.
19. Endacott 1964b, p. 125.
20. For the class and racial divide in early Hong Kong, see Tsang 2003a, pp. 62–6.
21. Munn 2001a, p. 113.
22. Ibid., pp. 147–50.
23. CO129/6, enclosure to Davis to Stanley 21, 18 June 1844 (Ordinance 13).
24. Ting 1990 pp. 154–5; Endacott 1964a, pp. 37–8.
25. Carroll 2005, pp. 28–32.
26. The classic on this subject is Ping-te Ho 1962.
27. This was also helped by Loo acquiring an official rank from the Chinese government in the course of the second Anglo–Chinese War in the late 1850s (Smith 1985, p. 109).
28. Carroll 1999, p. 23.
29. Eitel 1983, p. 282.
30. Tsang 1995, p. 5.

31. Hobsbawn 2000, p. 96.
32. Finer 1999, p. 1616.
33. Tsang 2003a, p. 54.
34. Quoted in Endacott 1964b, p. 95.
35. CO129/82, minutes by CZg commenting on Robinson to Newcastle, dispatch 160 of 25 September 1861.
36. *British Parliamentary Papers: China 25 (Hong Kong, 1862–1881)* (Shannon: Irish University Press, 1971), p. 5 (Robinson to Newcastle, dispatch 220, 16 December 1861).
37. Endacott 1964b, p. 95.

## Chapter 2. The cadet scheme

1. Tsang 2003a, p. 35.
2. Tsang 1995, p. 144.
3. Feuchtwanger 1975, p. 91.
4. Chapman 2004, p. 11.
5. Clarke 1962, p. 220.
6. Chapman 2004, p. 16.
7. Beales 1969, pp. 186–7.
8. Chapman 2004, p. 12.
9. Compton 1968, p. 265.
10. Feuchtwanger 1975, 92.
11. CO129/80, Robinson to Newcastle, dispatch 39, 23 March 1861.
12. Sayer 1980, p. 221.
13. Cameron 1991, p. 85.
14. Collins 1952, p. 96.
15. *British Parliamentary Papers: China 25,* 20 (Robinson to Newcastle, dispatch 220, 16 December 1861).
16. CO129/80, Robinson to Newcastle, dispatch 39, 23 March 1861.
17. Eitel 1983, p. 364.
18. CO129/80, Robinson to Newcastle, dispatch 39, 23 March 1861.
19. Compton 1968, p. 266.
20. CO129/80, 'Sketch of a scheme for the establishment of Hong Kong cadetships', undated, c.March 1861.
21. CO129/80, Rogers to Hamilton, letter of 7 July 1861.
22. CO129/80, 'Interpreter pupils – Hong Kong', undated, c.June 1861.
23. Lethbridge 1978, p. 36.
24. For a critical analysis of the Chinese system, see Ichisada Miyazaki 1976, pp. 111–29.
25. CO129/80, 'Subjects for nomination for Hong Kong cadetships', 29 June 1861.
26. Dewey 1973, p. 274.
27. CO129/312, 'Hong Kong, Straits Settlements, and Federated Malay States cadetships', December 1902.
28. Dewey 1973, p. 267.
29. Jeffries 1938, p. 7.
30. Collins 1952, p. 107.
31. CO129/80, 'Sketch of a scheme for the establishment of Hong Kong cadetships', undated, c.March 1861. This proposal was accepted almost *in toto* apart from the

*Governing Hong Kong*

age of recruitment, which was raised slightly. For an approved version of this scheme, see Tsang 1995, pp. 149–50.
32. Cameron 1991, p. 92.
33. Collins 1952, p. 104.
34. Ibid., p. 110.
35. Hamilton 1969 p. 18.
36. Lethbridge 1978, p. 3.
37. Collins 1952, p. 110.
38. Ireland 1905, p. 34.
39. Hong Kong Government, Sessional Papers 1893: Commission Report on Working of Treasury Department, p. 3.
40. Lethbridge 1978, pp. 41–2.
41. Lethbridge 1978, p. 40.
42. Perham 1960, p. 302.
43. CO129/120, MacDonnell to Carnarvon, dispatch 183, 7 January 1867.
44. CO129/126, MacDonnell to Buckingham, dispatch 416, 14 December 1867.
45. The only exception happened between late 1891 and early 1893, when Major General A. H. A. Gordon served as captain superintendent.
46. Tsang 1995, p. 167.
47. Observation of E. J. Eitel, cited in Lethbridge 1978, p. 40.
48. Eitel 1983, pp. 526–7.

## Chapter 3. Benevolent paternalism

1. Woodhouse 1997, p. 27.
2. Qian Mu 2002, pp. 174–5.
3. Chu 1962, pp. 22–31.
4. Ping-ti Ho 1962, pp. 48–9.
5. Grantham 1965, p. 6.
6. Airlie 1989, pp. 11–4.
7. Part of Cadet F. H. May's experience as recorded in his diary was published in the Sunday edition of the *South China Morning Post*, 10 October 1980.
8. Lethbridge 1978, p. 37.
9. Wilson 2000, p. 6.
10. Grantham 1965, p. 7.
11. Ibid., p. 6.
12. Airlie 1989, p. 18.
13. Lu Xun n.d., p. 6.
14. Endacott 1964b, p. 276.
15. Hong Kong Sessional Papers 1912, 'Report on New Territories, 1899–1912' by G. N. Orme, 9 June 1912. District Officer South was previously known as Assistant District Officer South and before that, Assistant Land Officer (South).
16. Tsang 1995, p. 39.
17. Collins 1952, p. 137.
18. Chu 1962, p. 2.
19. Smith 1983, p. 45.
20. Chu 1962, p. 16.
21. One of the more serious incidents of resistance, which involved the burning down of a police mat-shed in the market town of Taipo on 3 April 1899 and called for

*Notes*

the immediate dispatch of the Royal Welsh Fusiliers to relieve Captain Superintendent of Police Francis May (a cadet), whose party came under attack from a hail of broken bricks, had more to do with *feng-shui* than governance. For May's account of the event, see CO882/5, May to Colonial Secretary, 4 April 1899. This incident was a prelude to the most serious resistance to the British takeover, when the hoisting of the British flag was challenged, eventually by a force of 2600 later in the month. The Chinese challenge was overcome by two companies of the Hong Kong Regiment with ease in the vicinity of Kam Tin. A summary report on Chinese resistance efforts can be found in ibid., Blake to Chamberlain, dispatch 107, 28 April 1899.

22. CO882/5, Stewart Lockhart to Colonial Office, dispatch 38, 8 October 1898.
23. Hong Kong Sessional Papers 1912, 'Report on the New Territories 1899–1912'.
24. The papers left by Stewart Lockhart are available at George Watson's College, the National Library of Scotland and the Stewart Society, all in Edinburgh.
25. Cadets were strictly speaking not available for deployment in Hong Kong when they were under language training or on leave or on secondment to the Colonial Office or elsewhere. When there was a serious shortage, it was not unknown for cadets receiving language training to be deployed.
26. Cadet positions were not open to women before the Second World War.
27. He was born James Haldane Lockhart but incorporated into his own surname the name of his mother's family, Stewart of Lorne, when he married in 1889. For consistency, he is referred to by his preferred name of James Stewart Lockhart in this volume.
28. Airlie 1989, pp. 3–11.
29. CO129/80, 'Hong Kong cadetship', paper submitted to Sir T. Roger, 2 July 1861.
30. CO129/220, Bowen to Derby 89, 23 February 1885.
31. Tsai 1993, pp. 127–44.
32. Airlie 1989, p. 37.
33. CO129/220, Bowen to Derby 89, 23 February 1885. For an assessment of why Bowen might have misunderstood the nature of this incident, see Tsang 2003a, pp. 90–1.
34. CO129/232, Bowen to Herbert, 3 May 1887.
35. Airlie 1989, p. 40.
36. Ibid., p. 51.
37. Ibid., p. 57.
38. Ibid., p. 54.
39. Sinn 1989, p. 156.
40. Ibid. Sinn's book provides a detailed account of how the Tung Wah Hospital played a key role in the local Chinese community in the nineteenth century.
41. Tsang 2003a, p. 69.
42. Sinn 1989, p. 156.
43. Ibid., pp. 156–83.
44. *Hong Kong Sessional Papers 1894*, 'Governor's dispatch to the secretary of state with reference to the plague', 20 June 1894.
45. On Whitehead's attack, see *Sessional Papers 1896*, 'Report on Tung Wah Hospital by the Honourable T. H. Whitehead', 17 October 1896, pp. 1–15.
46. Lethbridge 1978, pp. 106–7.
47. Chan 1991, p. 82.

48. Tsang 2003a, p. 70.
49. On the leasing of the New Territories, see Tsang 1997a, pp. 1–12; and Wesley-Smith 1983.
50. CO882/5, Report by Stewart Lockhart on the extension of the Colony of Hong Kong, 8 October 1898, ff13.
51. CO882/5, Chamberlain to Blake, confidential dispatch, 6 January 1899.
52. CO882/5, Report by Stewart Lockhart on the extension of the Colony of Hong Kong, 8 October 1898, pp. 13–15.
53. Airlie 1989, p. 102.
54. CO882/5, Report by Stewart Lockhart on the extension of the Colony of Hong Kong, 8 October 1898, pp. 15–16.
55. Airlie 1989, p. 108.
56. Atwell 1985, pp. 6–11.
57. Cadets were encouraged to gain a legal qualification, which would then make them eligible for appointment as police magistrates or deputy registrars of the Supreme Court. The registrar of the Supreme Court was a position that could only be filled by a qualified barrister. New offices were periodically added to this list subsequently.
58. CO129/209, Bowen to Derby 84, 23 May 1883.
59. Ibid.
60. Grantham 1965, p. 14.
61. CO129/312, Hong Kong, Straits Settlements and Federated Malay States cadetships, December 1902.
62. See below for the unification of the colonial administrative service.
63. CO129/376, Lugard to Harcourt, dispatch 145, 20 April 1911.
64. CO129/313, Enclosure 1 to Blake to Chamberlain, dispatch 534, 10 December 1902 (letter from nine cadets to Chamberlain, 21 November 1902).
65. CO129/376, Harcourt to Lugard, dispatch 193, 15 June 1911; and CO129/313, Chamberlain to Blake, dispatch of 13 February 1903.
66. CO129/376, Stubbs's minutes to Collins, 1 June 1911.
67. CO129/313, Chamberlain to Blake, dispatch of 13 February 1903.
68. Ibid. The basis of this calculation is not clear and may be dubious, as the first cadet to make colonial secretary, Stewart Lockhart, took 16 years from the date he joined to the date he was promoted colonial secretary. It would be 13 years from when he became a passed cadet.
69. CO129/313, May to Blake, minutes of 3 December 1902.
70. CO129/376, Stubbs's minutes for Collins, 1 June 1911. Clementi's recommendations can be found in ibid., Colonial Secretary to Governor, 30 March 1911.
71. Jeffries 1938, pp. 8–9
72. They exclude members of the Indian Civil Service.
73. Jeffries 1938, p. 10. For the purpose of making a general comparison, among the 30 dependencies whose governorship was open to members of the colonial administrative service in the 1930s, only six (Nigeria, Kenya, Trinidad and Tobago, Jamaica, Ceylon, and the Straits Settlements) offered a higher salary to its governor than Hong Kong. This provides an indication of the rough disparity in remuneration for administrative officers. Two of these six were in fact Eastern colonies with their own cadets.

74. Jeffries 1938, p. 62.
75. Warren report, quoted in ibid., p. 59.
76. Jeffries 1938, p. 74.
77. CO129/525/6, Memorandum from Swire and Sons Ltd to the Colonial Office, 20 February 1930.
78. Miners 1987, pp. 88–9.
79. MacDougall to his wife, letter of 27 February 1941, *MacDougall Papers*, Rhodes House Library, Oxford University. MacDougall's role after 1941 is examined in Chapter 4.
80. CO825/35/55104, Extract from minutes of 35th meeting of the Colonial Office Committee on postwar problems, 2 April 1942.
81. Whitfield 2001, pp. 8–10.
82. Bertram, p. 120. For the view of a Western educated Hong Kong Chinese person, see CO129/590/25, letter to Churchill from a Hong Kong born Chinese sent from Kweilin, 28 September 1942.

## Chapter 4. Effects of the Pacific War

1. For the Japanese occupation, see Endacott and Birch 1978; and Snow 2003.
2. Jeffery 1999, p. 319.
3. Elsbree 1953, p. 163.
4. Quoted in Thorne 1978, p. 157.
5. Waijiaobu, *Zhanshi Waijiao*, vol. 3, agreement between Chiang Kai-shek and Mountbatten, October 1943.
6. Ibid., Roosevelt to Chiang, telegram of 31 December 1941.
7. Academia Historica (Taipei), *Papers of Chiang Kai-shek: Dejiao Dangan*, 080103–058, 08A–01322, Chiang's draft message to Churchill, 1943.
8. Tsang 2003a, p. 124.
9. For Chiang's thinking, see Tsang 1997a, pp. 28–9.
10. Gu Weijun (1987) *Gu Weijun Huiyilu*, vol. 5, Beijing: Zhonghua Shudian, pp. 14–15.
11. CO825/42/55104/2, Gent's minutes, 14 February 1942.
12. MacDougall had made a vivid account of his escape in a letter to his wife dated 17 January 1942, which is being added to the *MacDougall Papers*, at the Rhodes House Library, Oxford University.
13. CO825/35/55104, Secret note by MacDougall, March 1942.
14. CO825/35/55104, Minutes of 35th meeting of the committee on postwar problems, 2 April 1942.
15. Tsang 2003a, pp. 133–8.
16. Zhou Hongtao 2003, p. 33.
17. Academia Historica, *Chiang Kai-shek Papers: Shiluegaoben*, 060100–204, 06–00930, entry of 2 September 1945.
18. Snow 2003, pp. 277–8.
19. Franklin Gimson (n.d.) 'Internment in Hong Kong March 1942 to August 1945', typescript in possession of the author, p. 1.
20. The order for Gimson is in CO129/591/16, Foreign Office to Chungking telegram, 11 August 1945.
21. *British military administration Hong Kong*, p. 1.

22. CO129/591/12, Admiralty to Commander in Chief, Hong Kong telegram of 3 September 1945.
23. MacDougall to his wife, letter of 27 February 1941, *MacDougall Papers*, Rhodes House Library, Oxford University.
24. CO129/594/6, MacDougall to Garter, letter of 5 December 1945.
25. Author's interview with MacDougall at 'Mercers' Finchingfield, Essex on 17 February 1983.
26. CO537/1650, G. E. J. Gent's minute, 21 September 1945.
27. Tsang 2003a, p. 66.
28. Tsang 1988, p. 26.
29. FO371/53632, Minute from Foreign Secretary to Prime Minister dated 8 March 1946.
30. FO371/53632, Prime Minister's minute to the Foreign Secretary dated 9 March 1946; Luff 1968, p. 77.
31. CO129/595/4, Governor's speech, 1 May 1946.
32. South China Morning Post, *Hong Kong Hansard: Reports of the Meetings of the Legislative Council of Hong Kong, Session 1946* (Hong Kong: South China Morning Post, 1946), 63 (Minutes of 5th meeting).
33. Tsang 1988, pp. 186–8.
34. CO129/312, 'Hong Kong, Straits Settlements, and Federated Malay States cadetships', December 1902.
35. Miners 1987, p. 85.
36. Mills 1942, p. 420.
37. Ibid., p. 421.
38. Tsui's personal account of his time as a member of the BAAG can be found on the Internet, at http://www.galaxylink.com.hk/~john/paul/paul.html.
39. Ride 1981.
40. Tsang 2003a, p. 129.
41. Colonial Secretariat 1966, p. 96.
42. Clinton was appointed a cadet in December 1951.
43. Personal communication received from Mrs Ellie Alleyne, dated 19 March 2004.
44. Tsang 1988, p. 27.
45. FO371/46259, 'Notes on Future of Hong Kong' by Keswick, 3 November 1945.
46. FO371/46259, 'Secretary for Chinese Affairs' by Keswick, 24 September 1945.
47. Tsang 1988, p. 188.
48. Snow 2003, p. 289.
49. For the civil war, see Westad 2003.
50. CO882/31, Governor Young to Secretary of State, confidential dispatch, 22 October 1946.
51. Tsang 1988, p. 60.
52. Ibid., p. 74.
53. CO537/5400, minutes of the Smaller Colonial Territories Committee on 20 July 1950.
54. Author's interview with MacDougall at 'Mercers' Finchingfield, Essex on 17 February 1983.
55. For the reversal of the Young reforms, see Tsang 1988.
56. CO537/5400, minutes of the Smaller Colonial Territories Committee on 20 July 1950.

*Notes*

57. *Transcript of interview between Heathcote-Smith and Steve Tsang*, typescript at Rhodes House Library, Oxford University, 7.
58. Grantham 1965, p. 19.
59. Tsang 2003a, 92–101.
60. Grantham 1965, p. 105.
61. Grantham was tremendously successful in this respect. See Tsang 1997b.
62. Grantham 1965, p. 105.
63. Ibid.
64. CO129/611/2, Ruston's minute, 10 April 1946.
65. Ibid.
66. FO371/53634, Secretary of State to Commander in Chief, Hong Kong, dispatch 8, 6 May 1946.
67. CO129/611/2, Ruston's minutes of 31 December 1946.
68. *Transcript of interview between Heathcote-Smith and Steve Tsang*, Rhodes House Library, Oxford University, 6.
69. CO537/5628, Governor to Secretary of State, 230, 5 March 1950.
70. Grantham 1965, p. 112.
71. See Tsang 1997b.
72. Tsang 1988, pp. 168–9.
73. Grantham 1965, p. 104.
74. Ho n.d., p. 5; and Tsang 1995, p. 156 (Report of Public Service Commission Chairman for 1956 and 1957).
75. C. B. Burgess, 'Great Britain and constitutional development in Hong Kong 1945–1952', unpublished paper in author's possession.
76. Rhodes House Library, *Transcript of interviews with David Jordan conducted by Steve Tsang*, pp. 11–12.

## Chapter 5. Expansion

1. Tsang 2003a, p. 148.
2. CO129/597/2, Creech-Jones to Grantham 302, 24 September 1948.
3. CO129/597/3, Bourdillon's minute of 5 July 1949.
4. CO1030/392, Ashton's minute of 10 July 1956.
5. Bray 2001, pp. 51–2.
6. Communication received from P. W. Williams, 16 August 2000, ff.4.
7. Morrison 1962, p. 133.
8. Hong Kong Salaries Commission 1959, para. 167.
9. Paper attached to Michael Wright to Ian Lightbody, personal communication dated 4 March 2001.
10. Hong Kong Salaries Commission 1959, para. 68.
11. Bray 2001, p. 35.
12. Tsang 1995, pp. 157–8.
13. For a short overview of the case in western Europe, see Goldsmith 1998, pp. 25–54.
14. Bartholomew 2004, p. 309.
15. Faure 2003, p. 125 (Governor to Secretary of State, 14 November 1950).
16. Ibid.; and Hamilton 1969, p. 63.
17. Bray 2001, p. 52.
18. Sweeting 1993, pp. 52–4.

203

19. Donohue 1962, pp. 11–12.
20. Sweeting 1993, p. 238.
21. Interview with Burgess in London on 15 June 1983.
22. Ibid.
23. Rhodes House Library MSS Ind.Ocn.s.222, Papers of Sir Franklin Gimson, 'Diary 1 June 1943 to 17 August 1945', pp. 174–5.
24. Ibid., pp. 177–8.
25. Interview with Burgess in London on 15 June 1983.
26. Personal communication from Kenneth Topley, 17 March 2005.
27. CO1030/1386, Burgess (Officer Administering the Government) to I. McLeod (Secretary of State) confidential tel. 354, 18 April 1960.
28. Rhodes House Library, *Transcript of interviews with David Jordan conducted by Steve Tsang*, p. 339.
29. Personal comment received from K. Y. Yeung, dated 23 June 2005.
30. Rhodes House Library, *Transcript of interviews with Sir David Trench, conducted by Steve Tsang*, pp. 97–8.
31. Tsang 2003a, p. 190.
32. Scott 1989, pp. 105–7.
33. Rhodes House Library, *Transcript of interviews with David Jordan conducted by Steve Tsang*, p. 339.
34. Personal communication from Bernard Williams dated 23 March 2005, and conversations with Bernard Williams in Oxford on 17 March 2005.
35. For Holmes's exploits during the war, see Ride 1981.
36. Bray 2001, pp. 79, 93; and personal communication from Kenneth Topley dated 23 March 2005.
37. Rhodes House Library, *Transcript of interviews with Sir David Trench, conducted by Steve Tsang*, p. 97.
38. Ibid., p. 266.
39. Holmes 1969, pp. 2–3.
40. Scott 1989, p. 125.
41. Bray 2001, p. 139.
42. Interview with Cowperthwaite in St Andrews on 4 April 1983.
43. Rhodes House Library, *Transcript of interviews with Sir David Trench, conducted by Steve Tsang*, pp. 202–3.
44. Bartholomew 2004, p. 312.
45. Comments received from K. Y. Yeung dated 23 June 2005.
46. Bartholomew 2004, p. 313.
47. Personal communication received from Eric Ho, dated 2 June 2005.
48. Personal communication received from Kenneth Topley dated 22 March 2005.
49. Bartholomew 2004, pp. 311–12.
50. Personal communication received from Kenneth Topley, 6 June 2005.
51. Bray 2001, p. 118.
52. Rhodes House Library, *Transcript of interviews with Sir David Trench, conducted by Steve Tsang*, pp. 200–1.
53. Rhodes House Library, *Transcript of interviews with Sir Philip Haddon-Cave conducted by Steve Tsang*, 30.
54. Rhodes House Library, *Transcript of interviews with Sir David Trench, conducted by Steve Tsang*, pp. 203–4.

*Notes*

55. Ibid., p. 204.
56. Ibid., p. 205.
57. Ibid., pp. 276–9.
58. Personal communication received from Eric Peter Ho, dated 24 May 2005.
59. Interview with Cowperthwaite in St Andrews on 4 April 1983.
60. Rhodes House Library, *Transcript of interviews with Sir David Trench, conducted by Steve Tsang*, pp. 278–80.
61. Rhodes House Library, *Transcript of interviews with Sir Philip Haddon-Cave by Steve Tsang*, 22–3.
62. Tsang 2003a, p. 190.
63. Tsang 2003b, pp. 225–6.

## Chapter 6. Meeting the challenges of a Chinese community

1. Coates 1975, p. 17.
2. Personal communication from Brian Wilson, 13 January 2006.
3. Ibid.
4. Wilson 2000, p. 23.
5. Hayes 1996, p. 16.
6. Wilson 2000, p. 22.
7. Coates 1975, pp. 92–3.
8. Ibid., p. 95.
9. For an authoritative account of Tsuen Wan's history and genealogies, see Hayes 1983, pp. 115–26, which is written by a former administrative officer.
10. Coates 1975, p. 95.
11. Hayes forthcoming, Chapter 7, section entitled 'Shek Pik 1959–60'.
12. Coates 1975, pp. 95–8.
13. Akers-Jones 2004, pp. 21–2.
14. Hayes 1996, p. 31.
15. Ibid., p. 37.
16. Ibid., pp. 41–2.
17. Wilson 2000, p. 34.
18. MacPherson 2001, p. 117.
19. Communication made orally by Robert Upton on 17 January 2006.
20. Hayes 2001, p. 73.
21. Communication from Patrick Williamson to the author (via Christopher Hui), 23 August 2000.
22. Akers-Jones 2004, p. 46.
23. Response to questionnaire received from Jeremy Marriott, p. 3.
24. Hase 2001, p. 134.
25. Personal communication received from James Hayes, dated 24 May 2004.
26. Rhodes House Library, *Transcript of interviews with Sir David Trench, conducted by Steve Tsang*, p. 97.
27. Clark 2004, pp. 171–2.
28. Tsang 2003a, p. 190.
29. Bray 2001, pp. 133–4.
30. Personal communication received from Robert Upton, 17 February 2006.
31. Ibid.
32. Bray 2001, p. 134.

33. Secretary for Chinese Affairs 1969, p. 3.
34. Bray 2001, p. 135.
35. Ibid., p. 137.
36. Mulloy n.d., pp. 9–10.
37. Ibid., p. 16. See below for a discussion of police corruption in Wanchai.
38. Ibid., pp. 16–17.
39. Bray 2001, pp. 137–8.
40. Mulloy n.d., pp. 11–12.
41. Ho 2005, p. 98.
42. Hase 2001, p. 135.
43. Ibid.
44. Ibid., p. 136.
45. Ibid., pp. 134–5.
46. Mulloy n.d., p. 13.
47. Ibid., pp. 13–15.
48. Ronald Holmes, 'Informal remarks made by Sir Ronald Holmes at a farewell reception held by the Administrative Officers' Association' (private paper in possession of the author: 24 March 1977), p. 3.
49. Rhodes House Library *Transcript of interviews with B. V. Williams conducted by Steve Tsang*, pp. 10–11.
50. Wilson 2000, p. 65.
51. Rhodes House Library, *Transcript of interviews with David Jordan conducted by Steve Tsang*, pp. 97–8.
52. Ho 2005, pp. 15–16.
53. Oral communication received from Robert Upton on 17 January 2006.
54. Clark 2004, p. 162.
55. Rhodes House Library, *Transcript of interviews with David Jordan conducted by Steve Tsang*, pp. 80–1.
56. Ibid., pp. 81–2.
57. Rhodes House Library, *Transcript of interviews with G. C. Hamilton conducted by Steve Tsang*, pp. 72–3.
58. Rhodes House Library, *Transcript of interviews with G. T. Rowe conducted by Steve Tsang*, p. 114.
59. Rhodes House Library, *Transcript of interviews with Sir David Trench, conducted by Steve Tsang*, pp. 81–5.
60. Ian Lightbody, 'Farewell speech at administrative service dinner on 17 July 1980', p. 5.
61. See Chapter 2.
62. Tsang 1995, p. 167.
63. Rhodes House Library, *Transcript of interviews with Henry Heath conducted by Steve Tsang*, p. 187.
64. Rhodes House Library, *Transcript of interviews with Sir Donald Luddington conducted by Steve Tsang*, p. 32.
65. Rhodes House Library, *Transcript of interviews with Henry Heath conducted by Steve Tsang*, p. 186.
66. Rhodes House Library, *Transcript of interviews with Sir Donald Luddington conducted by Steve Tsang*, pp. 30–1.
67. Personal communication received from Eric Peter Ho, 13 January 2006.

## Notes

68. Strictly speaking, Baron was not the first director of Social Welfare. Fellow cadet Kenneth Keen was the first director but he served in this capacity for less than three months before handing over to Baron.
69. Personal communication received from Eric Peter Ho, 13 January 2006.
70. Ibid.
71. Rhodes House Library, *Transcript of interviews with David Jordan conducted by Steve Tsang*, pp. 13–4. Jordan did learn to speak Cantonese while in service in Hong Kong and retained a good knowledge of written Chinese.
72. Rhodes House Library, *Transcript of interviews with David Jordan conducted by Steve Tsang*, p. 446.
73. Ibid., p. 451.
74. Ibid., p. 455.
75. Ibid., pp. 482–4.
76. Ibid., pp. 499–507.
77. Ibid., pp. 506–7.
78. See Ho 2005, pp. 55–8.
79. Personal communication from Eric Peter Ho, 13 January 2006.
80. Ibid.
81. Tsang 2003a, p. 201.
82. Lethbridge 1978, p. 38.
83. MacPherson 2001, p. 108.
84. Rhodes House Library, *Transcript of interviews with G. C. Hamilton conducted by Steve Tsang*, pp. 149–53.
85. CO1030/1386, Officer Administering the Government (Burgess) to Colonial Office, telegram 354, 18 April 1960.
86. Mulloy n.d., p. 17.
87. Ibid., pp. 17–19.
88. Ibid., pp. 19–20.
89. For the legal complexity, see Solicitor General Arthur Hooton's explanations, in Tsang 1995, pp. 181–2.
90. Rhodes House Library, *Transcript of interviews with G. T. Rowe conducted by Steve Tsang*, pp. 158–9.
91. Prendergast joined as deputy commissioner and director of operations and he was knighted for his service at the ICAC. Harknett joined as Prendergast's deputy and succeeded Prendergast when he retired. Within the colonial government, in contrast to the image outside it, it was Prendergast not Cater who personified the ICAC in its first years.

## Chapter 7. Localization

1. Mills 1942, p. 421.
2. Tsui was later reappointed as a cadet in 1948. See Chapter 4.
3. For an assessment of Young as governor and his views on political changes in Hong Kong, see Tsang 1988.
4. Personal communication received from Robert Upton, 16 May 2006.
5. Kirk-Greene 2000, p. 264. The Colonial Administrative Service was superseded by Her Majesty's Overseas Civil Service in 1956, but to avoid confusion, colonial administrative officers instead of Her Majesty's overseas civil servants are used

throughout this book to refer to those who were administrative officers in other British colonies and dependencies.
6. Personal communication from Kenneth Topley, 12 January 2006.
7. Personal communication from Robert Upton, 16 May 2006.
8. Those who were appointed to Hong Kong directly as colonial/chief secretaries are excluded, such as Sir Robert Black or Sir Denys Roberts who is a professional lawyer and not a colonial administrative officer prior to his appointment as chief secretary.
9. Topley 2001.
10. Akers-Jones 2004, pp. 6–7.
11. Personal communication from Roderick MacLean dated 27 February 2001.
12. MacLean n.d., p. 3.
13. Clark 2004, pp. 162–4.
14. MacLean n.d., p. 3.
15. Clark 2004, p. 161.
16. MacLean n.d., p. 5.
17. Rhodes House Library, *Transcript of interviews with G. C. Hamilton conducted by Steve Tsang*, pp. 86–7.
18. Ho 2005, p. 21.
19. MacLean n.d., pp. 7–8.
20. Rhodes House Library, *Transcript of interviews with G. C. Hamilton conducted by Steve Tsang*, p. 81.
21. Miners 1991, p. 93.
22. Ibid., p. 100.
23. This officer, Selwyn Alleyne, had his terms of appointment converted to that of an expatriate officer in March 1961 only after he made a successful appeal to the governor in council. Personal communication from Alleyne, 29 September 2005.
24. Colonial Secretariat 1970, Gen. Est. pp. 2–3.
25. Rhodes House Library, *Transcript of interviews with G. T. Rowe conducted by Steve Tsang*, p. 119.
26. Teesdale transcript, p. 82.
27. Rhodes House Library, *Transcript of interviews with G. T. Rowe conducted by Steve Tsang*, p. 117.
28. Rhodes House Library, *Transcript of interviews with G. C. Hamilton conducted by Steve Tsang*, pp. 84.
29. Names and personal details of unsuccessful candidates are not available.
30. Cell 1999, p. 235.
31. Rhodes House Library, *Transcript of interviews with G. T. Rowe conducted by Steve Tsang*, p. 120.
32. Mrs Rachel Cartland's response to a questionnaire on the administrative service, dated 8 August 2000. She is referring to her own selection interview conducted in 1972.
33. Furse 1962, pp. 219–25.
34. MacPherson 2001, p. 108.
35. Jeffries 1956, pp. 138–9.
36. Ho 2005, p. 88.
37. 'Vision, high ideals of service, fearless devotion to duty born of a sense of responsibility, tolerance and, above all, team spirit' are qualities specified in the

report of the Committee on the System of Appointment in the Colonial Service, Cmd. 3554 (London: His Majesty's Stationery Office, 1930), p. 23.
38. Goodstadt 2005, p. 39.
39. Among the first three local female administrative officers, two came from distinguished local families with exposure to British ways and the colonial establishment. Audrey Chau is a niece of Sir S. N. Chau while Anson Fang is a niece of Dr Harry Fang.
40. Kirk-Greene 2000, p. 242.
41. Ibid., p. 243.
42. Tsang 2003, pp. 170–5, 190–6.
43. G. C. Hamilton, 'Hong Kong Disturbances 1967/8 Twelfth Report', 4 February 1968 (in possession of the author).
44. Scott 1989, p. 105.
45. Murray MacLehose in fact started his career as a member of the Malayan civil service, before he transferred to the British diplomatic service. However, he made it a point to avoid reference to his time in the colonial administrative service and saw himself as a professional diplomat sent to govern Hong Kong. As governor he did not identify with the Colonial Administrative Service, which had by then been renamed Her Majesty's Overseas Civil Service.
46. There were, for example, 2500 members of the CAS (HMOCS) in 1957, but by the mid–1970s, there were only 1500, among whom only 300 were not employed in Hong Kong. Kirk-Greene 2000, pp. 270–1.
47. Attachment to Acting Colonial Secretary (M. D. A. Clinton) to all administrative officers, 15 May 1974 (ref: EBCR 2/4068/73).
48. Comment made by Robert Upton on 17 January 2006.
49. Attachment to Acting Colonial Secretary (M. D. A. Clinton) to all administrative officers, 15 May 1974 (ref: EBCR 2/4068/73).
50. MacPherson 2001, p. 109.
51. Rear 1971, p. 61.
52. Kirk-Greene 2000, p. 243.
53. Clark 2004, pp. 167–8.
54. Ibid., 167.
55. Personal communication received from Eric Peter Ho, 13 January 2006.
56. Attachment to Acting Colonial Secretary (M. D. A. Clinton) to all administrative officers, 15 May 1974 (ref: EBCR 2/4068/73).
57. Ibid.
58. They were Cater (1970), Clinton (1968), Heatherington (1963), Lightbody (1969), Sorby (1968), and Todd (1966). See Chapter 4, 'End of Colour Bar'.
59. The rank of Secretary was introduced after the McKinsey reforms. See the following chapter for the reforms.
60. Clark 2004, p. 168.
61. Interview with Dame Anson Chan, 24 October 2003.
62. The Joint Declaration was agreed and initiated in 1984, and came into effect formally after it was ratified in 1985.
63. Miners 1991, p. 93.
64. Ibid., p. 94.
65. Interview with Dame Anson Chan, 24 October 2003.
66. Personal communication from Selwyn Alleyne, 29 September 2005.

67. Interview with Dame Anson Chan, 24 October 2003.
68. Ibid.
69. Hong Kong Government 1973, p. 210.
70. Kirk-Greene 1999, p. 50.
71. Upon marriage all three officers adopted their married name, viz., Audrey Ho, Anson Chan, and Katherine Fok.
72. Establishment Branch 1967, pp. 16–18.
73. Interview with Dame Anson Chan, 24 October 2003.
74. Ibid.
75. Personal communication from Mrs Rachel Cartland, dated 22 September 1999.
76. Interview with Dame Anson Chan, 24 October 2003.
77. Personal communication from Mrs Rachael Cartland, 13 November 1999.
78. Ibid.
79. Words of Trevor Clark, summing up what Barnett was known to have said. Clark 2004, p. 167.
80. For an examination of how the Hong Kong government delivered the best possible governance in the Chinese tradition, see Tsang 1997c, pp. 62–83.

## Chapter 8. Meeting the challenges of modernity

1. Rhodes House Library, *Transcript of interviews with David Jordan conducted by Steve Tsang*, p. 707.
2. Miners 1991, p. 88.
3. Scott 1989, p. 127.
4. The two countries were South Vietnam and Denmark.
5. Rhodes House Library, *Transcript of interviews with David Jordan conducted by Steve Tsang*, p. 707.
6. Scott 1989, p. 133.
7. Akers-Jones 2004, p. 71.
8. Hong Kong Hansard Session 1973, p. 13.
9. The cost of engaging McKinsey came to HK$ 4.7 million. Hong Kong Hansard Session 1976, p. 104.
10. The words in quotes are from Hong Kong Salaries Commission 1971, p. 7.
11. Deputy Colonial Secretary (M. D. A. Clinton) to heads of departments, confidential circular letter of 13 March 1973.
12. McKinsey & Company 1973, pp. 4–6.
13. Secretaries were soon elevated in rank to ensure that they were senior to heads of even major departments, with the exception of the director of commerce and industry who was given the rank of secretary.
14. McKinsey & Company 1973, p. 16.
15. Ibid., p. 9.
16. Ibid., p. 10.
17. Ibid., p. 11.
18. Ibid., p. 13.
19. Ibid., p. 12.
20. Secretary of the Civil Service (Alan Scott) to all Administrative Officers, circular letter EBCR L/M 310/73, 18 January 1974.
21. Scott 1989, pp. 136–7.

22. Secretary of the Civil Service (Alan Scott) to all Administrative Officers, circular letter EBCR 4/4068/70, 9 October 1973.
23. Scott 1989, p. 136.
24. Bray 2001, p. 179.
25. Ibid.
26. Deputy Colonial Secretary (M. D. A. Clinton) to Heads of Departments, circular letter 13 March 1973, ff.6.
27. Secretary posts were ranked below the chief secretary, which was a rank of its own, and that of the financial secretary, the attorney general and the secretary for home affairs. They were at first Staff Grade A posts but were quickly elevated to a rank above Staff Grade A (equivalent to head of a major department).
28. Rhodes House Library, *Transcript of interviews with David Jordan conducted by Steve Tsang*, pp. 713-14.
29. Rhodes House Library, *Transcript of interviews with David Jordan conducted by Steve Tsang*, p. 710.
30. Ibid., p. 711.
31. Ibid., p. 709–10.
32. The director of commerce and industry was given the rank of secretary (supernumerary) until after Jordan's retirement as its director.
33. Personal communication from K.Y. Yeung, 30 January 2006.
34. Personal communication from Robert Upton, 16 May 2006.
35. Personal communication from K. Y. Yeung, 30 January 2006.
36. Ibid.
37. Scott 1989, p. 138.
38. Ibid., p. 140.
39. Cheung 1997, p. 724.
40. The formal name of the colonial secretariat had by then been unceremoniously changed to government secretariat.
41. For an overview of how Hong Kong differed from other colonies in the process of decolonization in the British Empire, see Darwin 1997, pp. 16–32.
42. Interview with Dame Anson Chan, 24 October 2003.
43. Hall 1997, p. 26.
44. Hall is wrong in asserting that the 'Taxi Strike ended abruptly along with Mr Scott's Hong Kong career', implying that Scott was removed from office and from HK as a result of this blunder (Hall 1997, pp. 26–9).
45. Personal communication received from Robert Upton, 16 May 2006.
46. Government Secretariat *c*.1987, p. 191.
47. Tsang 2003b, pp. 229–31.
48. Wilding 2003, p. 37.
49. Bray 2001, p. 192.
50. Ibid., p. 193.
51. Goodstadt 2005, p. 105.
52. From 1884 to 1973 there was a longstanding practice for the justices of the peace and the Hong Kong General Chamber of Commerce to nominate one candidate each to the governor for appointment as unofficial members of the Legislative Council. This can be loosely described as indirect election, as the convention was that the governor would not normally refuse the nomination of these bodies. This

practice was ended by Governor MacLehose. The 1985 change was therefore a significant departure from the practice at the time.
53. Tsang 1995, p. 92–3.
54. Ibid., p. 93.
55. Cheek-Milby 1995, p. 76.
56. Goodstadt 2005, p. 109.
57. Chung 2001, p. 225.
58. Cheek-Milby 1989, p. 273.
59. Interview with Dame Anson Chan, 24 October 2003.
60. Hong Kong Government 1987.
61. Personal comment made by Robert Upton, 10 May 2006.
62. Cradock 1994, p. 228.
63. For the Patten reform and controversies surrounding it, see Tsang 2003a, pp. 255–65.
64. Patten 1992, pp. 34–5.
65. Dimbleby 1997, p. 148; and Tsang 1997a, p. 192.
66. Dimbleby 1997, p. 147.
67. So 1999, pp. 198–9.
68. Chung 2001, pp. 225–6.
69. *Hong Kong Hansard*, 10 July 1996, pp. 18–19.
70. *Hong Kong Hansard*, 10 July 1996, p. 20.
71. Personal communication from Robert Upton, 16 May 2006.
72. Scott 1988a, p. 6.
73. Letter from the Chief Secretary to all civil servants, 27 September 1984.
74. Annex I of the Sino–British Joint Declaration stipulated that 'The government and the legislature of the Hong Kong Special Administrative Region shall be composed of local inhabitants.'
75. Burns 1988, p. 101.
76. Scott 1988b, p. 27.
77. Burns 1988, p. 101.
78. Cheek-Milby 1988, p. 116.
79. Miners 1991, p. 94.
80. Patten 1998, p. 46.
81. Goodstadt 2005, p. 41.
82. Ibid.
83. Ibid., pp. 87–8.
84. Ibid., p. 88.

## Chapter 9. An elite within the government

1. CO129/80, 'Sketch of a scheme for the establishment of Hong Kong Cadetships', undated, *c.*March 1861.
2. Rhodes House Library, *Transcript of interviews with Sir David Trench, conducted by Steve Tsang*, p. 265 (Tape 4).
3. A very small number of administrative officers, including those at the secretary level, were not in fact graduates. They were mostly recruited from within the Hong Kong government.
4. Burns 2004, p. 118.
5. Colonial Secretariat 1966, p. 59.

*Notes*

6. Personal communication received from Ian Lightbody, 15 January 2006.
7. Clark 2004, p. 162.
8. Burns 2004, p. 132.
9. Rhodes House Library, *Transcript of interviews with Sir David Trench, conducted by Steve Tsang*, p. 265 (Tape 4).
10. Wright 2001.
11. Ibid.
12. Ibid.
13. Ibid.
14. Scott 1988b, p. 37.
15. Ibid., p. 38.
16. Wright 2001.
17. Ibid.
18. Interview with Dame Anson Chan, 24 October 2003.
19. Personal communication from K. Y. Yeung, 13 April, 2006.
20. Rhodes House Library, *Transcript of interviews with Henry Heath conducted by Steve Tsang*, pp. 185–6.
21. Personal communication received from Peter B. Williams, 16 August 2000, pp. 8–9.
22. Rhodes House Library, *Transcript of interviews with Henry Heath conducted by Steve Tsang*, p. 186.
23. Ibid.
24. Rhodes House Library, *Transcript of interviews with David Jordan conducted by Steve Tsang*, pp. 520–1 (Tape 9).
25. The number of aircraft involved was over 80 at first, but 11 left Hong Kong for China with their crews when they defected from the nationalist to the communist government in November 1949, and were therefore not subject to the subsequent litigation. For an analysis of the complex issues involved, see Zeng 1987, pp. 105–24.
26. Steve Tsang 1997b, p. 301.
27. CO537/5628, Governor to Secretary of State, secret and guard telegram 230, 5 March, 1950.
28. Leary 1972, p. 656.
29. CAB129/39, CP(50)61, 3 April 1950 (Cabinet paper 'Chinese Civil Aircraft at Hong Kong', submitted by the Secretary of State for the Colonies and the Minister of State for Foreign Affairs).
30. CAB128/17, CM19(50)2 (Cabinet Minutes), 6 April 1950.
31. Grantham 1965, p. 163.
32. CO537/5628, Governor to Secretary of State, secret and guard telegram 230, 5 March, 1950.
33. CO537/5628, J. J. Paskin minutes of 7 March 1950.
34. CAB128/17, CM19(50)2, 6 April 1950 and CM24(50)6, 24 April 1950.
35. CAB129/39, Annex to CP(50)74 (Opinions of the Attorney-General, 17 April 1950).
36. CAB129/39, CP(50)74, 21 April 1950 (Cabinet paper 'Chinese Civil Aircraft at Hong Kong', submitted by the Secretary of State for the Colonies and the Minister of State for Foreign Affairs).
37. CAB128/17, CM19(50)2 (Cabinet Minutes), 6 April 1950.

38. CAB129/39, Annex B to CP(50)61, 3 April 1950 (Opinions of the Attorney General).
39. CO537/5629, Secretary of State to Governor, secret telegram 481, 4 April 1950.
40. CO537/5630, Governor to Secretary of State, secret and guard telegram 369, 8 April 1950.
41. Personal communication received from Robert Upton, 16 May 2006.
42. Vickers n.d.
43. Rhodes House Library, *Transcript of interviews with Sir David Trench, conducted by Steve Tsang*, p. 229 (Tape 4).
44. Vickers n.d.
45. Goodstadt 2005, p. 215.
46. Miners 1991, p. 219.
47. Vickers n.d.
48. Ibid.
49. Personal communication received from Topley, 27 October 2003 (Ken Topley's 'Memoirs', 2001), p. 34.
50. Personal communication received from Trevor Clark, dated 7 August 2002.
51. Vickers n.d.
52. Rhodes House Library, *Transcript of interviews with Michael Wright*, pp. 253–5 (Tape 5).
53. Bray 2001, p. 200.
54. Rhodes House Library, *Transcript of interviews with David Jordan conducted by Steve Tsang*, pp. 502–3 (Tape 9).
55. Ibid., p. 503.
56. See Chapter 6, 'Life and work in departments'.
57. First two quotes are from Vickers n.d., and the last is from a personal communication received from Kenneth Topley, 27 October 2003 (Ken Topley's 'Memoirs', 2001), p. 34.
58. Bray 2001, p. 200.
59. Personal communication from Robert Upton, 16 May 2006.
60. Bray 2001, p. 200.

## Chapter 10. Inhibited elitism

1. Some of the prewar cadets who distinguished themselves have already been named in Chapter 2 and their names are therefore not repeated here.
2. Personal communication received from Ian Lightbody, 3 April 2006.
3. Ibid.
4. Quote from Rhodes House Library, *Transcript of interviews with G. T. Rowe conducted by Steve Tsang*, p. 120. See Chapter 7 for recruitment criteria.
5. Personal communication from Selwyn Alleyne, 17 April, 2006.
6. Personal communication from Brian Wilson, 21 April, 2006.
7. David MacDougall was the only one who had the capacity to do so but he was an intake of 1928 and was seconded out of the Hong Kong government to serve in the British government in 1937. He was too junior to have been in a position to have made much of an impact before his secondment.
8. For the pressure that Hong Kong came under during the cold war, see Mark 2004; and Tsang 2006, pp. 165–86.

*Notes*

9. Personal communication from Kenneth Topley to Ian Lightbody, 4 April, 2006, made available to the author on 25 April 2006.
10. For the strike-cum-boycott, see Carroll 2005, pp. 131–58; and Tsang 2003a, pp. 92–101.
11. I examined this issue in detail in Tsang 1997c.
12. Personal communication from Brian Wilson, 21 April, 2006. For an enquiry into the limits to judicial independence in early Hong Kong, see Munn 2001b, pp. 19–47.
13. Steve Tsang 1997d, p. 40.
14. Peter Wesley-Smith 1994.
15. Tsang 1997a, pp. 56–7.
16. Tsang 1999, p. 7. This concept is borrowed from Ramon Myers, who defined it in a slightly different way as 'the zone that contains power, symbols, and institutions that allocate and project power' but is 'constrained by the existence of economic and ideological marketplaces' (Myers 1994, p. 172).
17. Tsang 1997d, p. 41.
18. Ibid.
19. Personal communication received from Robert Upton, 16 May 2006.
20. Ibid.
21. Rhodes House Library, *Transcript of interviews with Sir David Trench, conducted by Steve Tsang*, p. 204 (tape 3).
22. Tsang 1997c, p. 78.
23. Personal communication received from Robert Upton, 16 May 2006.
24. Tsang 2000, pp. 44–8.
25. Tsang 1997e.

# REFERENCES

Airlie, Shiona (1989) *Thistle and bamboo: the life and times of Sir James Stewart Lockhart*, Hong Kong: Oxford University Press

Akers-Jones, David (2004) *Feeling the stones: reminiscences by David Akers-Jones*, Hong Kong: Hong Kong University Press

Atwell, Pamela (1985) *British mandarins and Chinese reformers: the British administration of Weihaiwei (1898-1930) and the territory's return to Chinese rule*, Hong Kong: Oxford University Press

Bartholomew, James (2004) *The welfare state we're in*, London: Politico's Publishing

Beales, Derek (1969) *From Castlereagh to Gladstone 1815-1885*, London: Nelson

Bertram, James (1947) *The shadow of a war: a New Zealander in the Far East 1939-1945*, London: Victor Gollancz

Bray, Denis (2001) *Hong Kong metamorphosis*, Hong Kong: Hong Kong University Press

*British military administration Hong Kong, August 1945 to April 1946: report to the secretary of state* (1946) Hong Kong: Government Printer

Burns, John P. (1988) 'Succession planning and localization', in Ian Scott and John Burns (eds) *The Hong Kong civil service and its future*, Hong Kong: Oxford University Press

—— (2004) *Government capacity and the Hong Kong civil service*, New York: Oxford University Press

Cameron, Nigel (1991) *An illustrated history of Hong Kong*, Hong Kong: Oxford University Press

Carroll, John M. (1999) 'Chinese collaboration in the making of British Hong Kong', in Tak-wing Ngo (ed.) *Hong Kong's History*, London: Routledge

—— (2005) *Edge of empires: Chinese elites and British colonials in Hong Kong*, Cambridge, MA: Harvard University Press

Cell, John W. (1999) 'Colonial rule', in J. M. Brown and William Roger Louis (eds) *The Oxford history of the British Empire: the twentieth century*, Oxford: Oxford University Press

Chan, W. K. (1991) *The making of Hong Kong society: three studies of class formation in early Hong Kong*, Oxford: Clarendon Press

Chapman, Richard A. (2004) *The Civil Service Commission 1855-1991*, London and New York: Routledge

# References

Cheek-Milby, Kathleen (1988), 'Identifying the issues', in Ian Scott and John Burns (eds) *The Hong Kong civil service and its future,* Hong Kong: Oxford University Press

—— (1989) 'The civil servant as politician: the role of the official members of the Legislative Council', in Kathleen Cheek-Milby and Miron Mushkat (eds) *Hong Kong: the challenges of transformation,* Hong Kong: University of Hong Kong Centre of Asian Studies

—— (1995) *A legislature comes of age: Hong Kong's search for influence and identity,* Hong Kong: Oxford University Press

Cheung, Anthony B. L. (1997) 'Rebureaucratization of politics in Hong Kong', *Asian Survey,* vol. XXXVII, no. 9, August

Chu, Tung-tsu (1962) *Local government in China under the Ching,* Stanford: Stanford University Press

Chung, Sze-yuen (2001) *Hong Kong's journey to reunification: memoirs of Sze-yuen Chung,* Hong Kong: Chinese University Press

Clark, Trevor (2004) *Good second class: memories of a generalist overseas administrator,* Stanhope: The Memoir Club

Clarke, G. K. (1962) *The making of Victorian England,* London: Methuen & Company

Coates, Austin (1975) *Myself a mandarin: memoirs of a special magistrate,* Hong Kong: Heinemann Educational Books

Collins, Charles (1952) *Public administration in Hong Kong,* London: Royal Institute of International Affairs

Colonial Secretariat (compiler) (1966) *Hong Kong government staff list 1966,* Hong Kong: Government Printer, Part IV

—— (1970) *Staff list Hong Kong government 1970,* Hong Kong: Government Press

Compton, J. M. (1968) 'Open competition in the Indian Civil Service, 1854–1876', *English Historical Review,* vol. 83 April

Cradock, Percy (1994) *Experiences of China,* London: John Murray

Darwin, John (1997) 'Hong Kong in British decolonisation', in Judith M. Brown and Rosemary Foot (eds) *Hong Kong's transitions, 1842–1997,* Basingstoke: Macmillan

Dewey, C. J. (1973) 'The making of an English ruling caste: the Indian Civil Service in the era of competitive examination', *English Historical Review,* vol. 88, April

Dimbleby, Jonathan (1997) *The last governor,* London: Warner Books

Donohue, Peter (1962) 'Education Department', in Hong Kong Government (ed.) *The Government and the people,* Hong Kong: Government Press

Elsbree, Willard (1953) *Japan's role in Southeast Asian nationalist movements 1940–1945,* Cambridge, MA: Harvard University Press

Endacott, G. B. (1964a) *Government and people in Hong Kong 1841–1962,* Hong Kong: Hong Kong University Press

—— (1964b) *A history of Hong Kong,* Hong Kong: Oxford University Press

Endacott, G. B. and Alan Birch (eds) (1978) *Hong Kong eclipse,* Hong Kong: Oxford University Press

Eitel, E. J. (1983) *Europe in China,* Hong Kong: Oxford University Press

Establishment Branch (1967) *Hong Kong Administrative Service 1862–1967,* Hong Kong: Government Printer

Faure, David (ed.) (2003) *Colonialism and the Hong Kong mentality*, Hong Kong: Centre of Asian Studies, University of Hong Kong

Feuchtwanger, E. J. (1975) *Gladstone*, London: Allen Lane

Finer, S. E. (1999) *The history of Government III: empires, monarchies and the modern state*, Oxford: Oxford University Press

Furse, R. D. (1962) *Aucuparius: recollections of a recruiting officer*, Oxford: Oxford University Press

Goldsmith, Michael (1998) 'The growth of government', in Ole Borre and Elinor Scarbrough (eds) *The scope of government*, Oxford: Oxford University Press

Goodstadt, Leo F. (2005) *Uneasy partners: the conflict between public interest and private profit in Hong Kong*, Hong Kong: Hong Kong University Press

Government Secretariat (compiler) (c.1987) *Staff biographies: Hong Kong Government 1986*, Hong Kong: Government Printer

Grantham, Alexander (1965) *Via ports: from Hong Kong to Hong Kong*, Hong Kong: Hong Kong University Press

Gu Weijun (1987) *Gu Weijun Huiyilu*, vol. 5, Beijing: Zhonghua Shudian

Hall, Christopher (1997) *The uncertain hand: Hong Kong taxis and tenders*, Hong Kong: The Chinese University Press for the Hong Kong Centre for Economic Research

Hamilton, G. C. (1969) *Government departments in Hong Kong 1841–1969*, Hong Kong: S. Young ISO

Hase, Patrick H. (2001) 'The district office', in Elizabeth Sinn (ed.) *Hong Kong: British crown colony revisited*, Hong Kong: Centre of Asian Studies, University of Hong Kong

Hayes, James (1983) *The rural communities of Hong Kong: studies and themes*, Hong Kong: Oxford University Press

—— (1996) *Friends and teachers: Hong Kong and its people 1953–87*, Hong Kong: Hong Kong University Press

—— (2001) 'Colonial administration in British Hong Kong and Chinese customary law', in Elizabeth Sinn (ed.) *Hong Kong: British crown colony revisited*, Hong Kong: Centre of Asian Studies, University of Hong Kong

—— (forthcoming) *The great difference: Hong Kong's New Territories, 1898–2004*, Hong Kong: Hong Kong University Press

Ho, Eric Peter (n.d.) *Serving Hong Kong: the memoirs of Eric Peter Ho*, unpublished typescript

—— (2005) *Times of change: a memoir of Hong Kong's governance 1950–1991*, Leiden: Brill

Hobsbawn, Eric (2000) *The age of empire 1875–1914*, London: Phoenix Press

Holmes, R. D. (1969) *The City District Officer scheme: report by the secretary for Chinese Affairs, Hong Kong*, Hong Kong: Government Printers

Hong Kong Government (1973) *Hong Kong 1973*, Hong Kong: Hong Kong Government Press

—— (1987) *Green Paper: the 1987 review of developments in representative government*, Hong Kong: Government Printer

Hong Kong Hansard Session (1973) *Hong Kong Hansard session 1972–3*, Hong Kong: Government Printer, Governor's speech, 18 October 1972

—— (1976) *Hong Kong Hansard session 1975–6*, Hong Kong: Government Printer

# References

Hong Kong Salaries Commission (1959) *Hong Kong Salaries Commission report for 1959*, Hong Kong: Government Printer

—— (1971) *Hong Kong Salaries Commission report 1971*, Hong Kong: Government Printer

Ichisada Miyazaki (1976) *China's examination hell: the civil service examinations of imperial China*, translated by Conrad Schirokauer, New York: Weatherhill

Ireland, W. A. (1905) *Far Eastern topics: studies in the administration of tropical dependencies*, Westminster

Jeffery, Keith (1999) 'The Second World War', in Judith M. Brown and William Roger Louis (eds) *The Oxford history of the British Empire: the twentieth century*, Oxford: Oxford University Press

Jeffries, Charles (1938) *The colonial empire and its civil service*, Cambridge: Cambridge University Press

—— (1956) *The Colonial Office*, London: George Allen & Unwin

Kirk-Greene, Anthony (1999) *On crown service: a history of HM colonial and overseas civil service 1837–1997*, London: I.B.Tauris

—— (2000) *Britain's imperial administrators, 1858–1966*, Basingstoke: Macmillan

Leary, William M. Jr. (1972) 'Aircraft and anti-communists: CAT in action, 1949–52', *The China Quarterly*, no. 52, October/November

Lethbridge, H. J. (1978) *Hong Kong, stability and change: a collection of essays*, Hong Kong: Oxford University Press

Lu Xun (n.d.) 'Luetan Xianggang', in Lu Weiluan (ed.) *Xianggang de Qiuque*, Hong Kong: Huafeng chubenshe

Luff, John (1968) *Hong Kong cavalcade*, Hong Kong: South China Morning Post

McKinsey & Company (1973) *The machinery of government: a new framework for expanding services*, Hong Kong: McKinsey & Company

MacLean, Roderick (n.d.) *Random reflections of a former Hong Kong Gwei-lo retread 1969–1975*, unpublished private paper

MacPherson, Ian F. C. (2001) 'Aspects of crown service', in Elizabeth Sinn (ed.) *Hong Kong, British crown colony revisited*, Hong Kong: Centre of Asian Studies, University of Hong Kong

Mark, C. K. (2004) *Hong Kong and the cold war: Anglo–American relations 1949–1957*, Oxford: Oxford University Press

Mills, Lennox A. (1942) *British rule in eastern Asia: a study of contemporary government and economic development in British Malaya and Hong Kong*, London: Oxford University Press

Miners, Norman (1987) *Hong Kong under imperial rule, 1912–1941*, Hong Kong: Oxford University Press

—— (1991) *The government and politics of Hong Kong*, fifth edition, Hong Kong: Oxford University Press

Morrison, C. G. M. (1962) 'Resettlement Department', in Hong Kong Government (ed.) *The Government and the people*, Hong Kong: Government Press

Mulloy, Gareth (n.d.) 'District Officer Wanchai, 1971–73', unpublished private paper in author's possession

Munn, Christopher (2001a) *Anglo–China: Chinese people and British rule in Hong Kong, 1841–1880*, Richmond: Curzon

(2001b) 'The rule of law and criminal justice in the nineteenth century', in Steve Tsang (ed.) *Judicial independence and the rule of law in Hong Kong*, Basingstoke: Palgrave

Myers, Ramon (1994) 'Transforming the Republic of China's modernisation experience to the People's Republic of China', in G. Klintworth (ed.) *Taiwan in the Asia-Pacific in the 1990s*, St Leonards, NSW: Allen & Unwin

Patten, Christopher (1992) *Our next five years: the agenda for Hong Kong*, Hong Kong: Government Printer

—— (1998) *East and West*, London: Macmillan

Perham, Margery (1960) *Lugard*, vol. 2, London: Collins

Ping-te Ho (1962) *The ladder of success in imperial China*, New York: Columbia University Press

Qian Mu (2002) *Zhongguo lidai zhengzhi deshi*, Hong Kong: Sanlian chubenshe

Rear, John (1971) 'One brand of politics', in Keith Hopkins (ed.) *Hong Kong: the industrial colony*, Hong Kong: Oxford University Press

Ride, Edwin (1981) *BAAG: Hong Kong resistance, 1942–1945*, Hong Kong: Oxford University Press

Sayer, Geoffrey Robley (1980) *Hong Kong 1841–1862*, Hong Kong: Hong Kong University Press

Scott, Ian (1988a) 'Introduction', in Ian Scott and John Burns (eds) *The Hong Kong civil service and its future*, Hong Kong: Oxford University Press

—— (1988b) 'Generalists and specialists', in Ian Scott and John Burns (eds) *The Hong Kong civil service and its future*, Hong Kong: Oxford University Press

—— (1989) *Political change and the crisis of legitimacy in Hong Kong*, Hong Kong: Oxford University Press

Secretary for Chinese Affairs (1969) *The City District Officer scheme*, Hong Kong: Government Printer

Sinn, Elizabeth (1989) *Power and charity: the early history of the Tung Wah Hospital, Hong Kong*, Hong Kong: Oxford University Press

Smith, Carl T. (1985) *Chinese Christians: elite, middlemen, and the church in Hong Kong*, Hong Kong: Oxford University Press

Smith, R. J. (1983) *China's cultural heritage: the Ch'ing dynasty 1644–1912*, Boulder, Colorado: Westview Press

Snow, Philip (2003) *The fall of Hong Kong: Britain, China, and Japanese occupation*, New Haven: Yale University Press

So, Alvin (1999) *Hong Kong's embattled democracy: a societal analysis*, Baltimore and London: The Johns Hopkins University Press

Sweeting, Anthony (1993) *A phoenix transformed: the reconstruction of education in post-war Hong Kong*, Hong Kong: Oxford University Press

Thorne, Christopher (1978) *Allies of a kind: the United States, Britain and the war against Japan, 1941–1945*, Oxford: Oxford University Press

Ting, Joseph S. P. (1990) 'Native Chinese peace officers in British Hong Kong, 1841–1861', in Elizabeth Sinn (ed.) *Between East and West: aspects of social and political development in Hong Kong*, Hong Kong: University of Hong Kong Press

Topley, Kenneth (2001) *Ken Topley's memoirs*, unpublished private paper

Tsai, Jung-Fang (1993) *Hong Kong in Chinese history: community and social unrest in the British colony, 1842–1913*, New York: Columbia University Press

Tsang, Steve (1988) *Democracy shelved: Great Britain, China, and attempts at constitutional reform in Hong Kong, 1945–1952*, Hong Kong and Oxford: Oxford University Press
— (ed.) (1995) *A documentary history of Hong Kong I: government and politics*, Hong Kong: Hong Kong University Press
— (1997a) *Hong Kong: appointment with China*, London: I.B.Tauris
— (1997b) 'Strategy for survival: the cold war and Hong Kong's policy towards Kuomintang and Chinese communist activities in the 1950s', *Journal of Imperial and Commonwealth History*, vol. 25, no. 2, May
— (1997c) 'Government and politics in Hong Kong: a colonial paradox', in Judith M. Brown and Rosemary Foot (eds) *Hong Kong's transitions, 1842–1997*, Basingstoke: Macmillan
— (1997d) 'The Confucian tradition and democratization', in Yossi Shain and Aharon Klieman (eds) *Democracy: the challenges ahead*, Basingstoke: Macmillan
— (1997e) 'Changes in continuity: government and politics in the Hong Kong Special Administrative Region', *American Asian Review*, vol. XV, no. 4, winter
— (1999) 'Transforming a party state into a democracy', in Steve Tsang and Hung-mao Tien (eds) *Democratization in Taiwan: implications for China*, Basingstoke: Macmillan
— (2000) 'Political developments in Hong Kong since 1997 and their implications for mainland China and Taiwan', *American Asian Review*, vol. XVIII, no. 1, spring
— (2003a) *A modern history of Hong Kong*, London: I.B.Tauris
— (2003b) 'The rise of a Hong Kong identity', in Taciana Fisac and Leila Fernandez-Stembridge (eds) *China today: economic reforms, social cohesion and collective identities*, London and New York: RoutledgeCurzon
— (2006) *The cold war's odd couple: the unintended partnership between the Republic of China and the UK, 1950–1959*, London: I.B.Tauris
Vickers, Simon (n.d.) 'Governing Hong Kong in the late 20th century: a maverick's memorandum', an unpublished paper provided to the author by Simon Vickers. There is no page numbering in this long paper
Wesley-Smith, Peter (1983) *Unequal treaty, 1898–1997: China, Great Britain and Hong Kong's New Territories*, Hong Kong: Oxford University Press
— (1994) 'Anti-Chinese legislation in Hong Kong', in Ming K. Chan (ed.) *Precarious balance: Hong Kong between China and Britain, 1842–1992*, Hong Kong: Hong Kong University Press
Westad, Odd Arne (2003) *Decisive encounters: the Chinese civil war, 1946–1950*, Stanford: Stanford University Press
Whitfield, Andrew J. (2001) *Hong Kong, empire and the Anglo–American alliance at war, 1941–45*, Basingstoke: Palgrave
Wilding, Paul (2003) 'Hong Kong: legacies and prospects of development', in Benjamin K. P. Leung (ed.) *Hong Kong: legacies and prospects of development*, Aldershot: Ashgate
Wilson, Brian (2000) *Hong Kong then*, Edinburgh, Cambridge and Durham: The Pentland Press
Woodhouse, Diana (1997) *In pursuit of good administration: ministers, civil servants, and judges*, Oxford: Oxford University Press

Wright, Michael (2001) 'The administrative service in Hong Kong as seen by a professional officer', an unpublished paper in the author's possession, dated 1 March

Zeng, Ruisheng (1987) '"Lianghang shijian" neimu', in Lu Yan et al. (eds) *Xianggang Changgu*, vol. 11, Hong Kong: Guang Jiaojing chubenshe

Zhou Hongtao (2003) *Jiang Gong yu Wo*, Taipei: Tianxia Wenhua

# INDEX

Africa, 76, 117
Akers-Jones, David, 90, 116, 117
Alleyne, Selwyn, 120, 128
American Flying Tigers, 173
American War of Independence, 51
Amery, Leo, 51
Anglo–Chinese War, 2, 11, 13, 16
Anstey, T. Chisholm, 5
Asia, 1, 18, 48, 51

Bank of England, 83
Barnett, Kenneth, 22, 37, 127, 137
Baron, David, 105
Beijing, 30, 115, 187, 194
Bevin, Ernest, 174
Black, Wilsone, 41
Blake, Sir Henry, 41
Bombay, 37
Borneo, 21, 22
Bowen, Sir George, 36
Bowring, Sir John, 5, 11, 13, 15, 16, 17
Bray, Denis, 95, 144, 179, 180
Bridges, W. T., 5, 6
British Army Aid Group (BAAG), 50, 56, 57, 79, 114
Burgess, Claude, 22, 65, 75, 76, 111

Caine, William, 6
Caldecott, Sir Andrew, 56
Caldwell, Daniel, 5, 6, 11, 15, 16
Cambridge, 18, 19, 61, 122, 123
Canada, 179
Canton, 9, 15, 29–31, 35–6, 38
Cartland, Rachel, 134

Cater, Sir Jack, 23, 56, 112
Cayman Islands, 149
Central Air Transport (CAT), 173
Central Air Transport Corporation (CATC), 173
Central Intelligence Agency, 173
Central Policy Unit, 159
Ceylon, 17, 35, 41, 45, 46, 55, 59
Chamberlain, Joseph, 40, 46, 47
Chan, Anson, 23, 130, 134–5, 159, 169
Chau, Audrey, 133
Cheng Hon-kuen, 111
Cheng Tung-choy, 120
Chennault, General Claire, 173
Cheung Chau, 54
Chiang Kai-shek, 52, 172, 173, 189
Chiang Kai-shek, Madam, 54
China, 3, 15–18, 20, 24, 27, 31–3, 37, 40, 42, 48–52, 54, 56, 58–9, 62–4, 67–8, 75, 79, 85, 90–1, 109, 120, 131, 134, 136–7, 150, 156, 173, 176, 177, 180, 189, 191, 193–95; People's Republic of China (PRC); Republic of China
China National Aviation Corporation (CNAC), 173
Chinese Affairs, 58, 62, 63, 73, 77, 78, 95, 101, 103, 164
Chinese Civil War, 60, 187
Ching, Henry, 146
City District Officer (CDO), 78, 79, 80, 85, 87, 94, 96–100, 103, 111, 125, 140, 190
Civil Service Abuses Inquiry, 16

*Governing Hong Kong*

Clark, Trevor, 101, 118, 119, 127
Clarke, Arthur, 82
Clinton, Michael, 56
Coates, Austin, 87, 88, 89, 92
cold war, 173
Colonial Air Regulations Order, 175
Colonial Office, 13, 17–19, 35, 45, 46, 47, 50, 52, 53, 54, 55, 62, 65, 76, 81, 170, 178
Colonial Secretariat, 32, 117, 130, 140, 142, 144, 164
Commerce and Industry Department, 79, 106, 107
Confucius, 31
Cotton Advisory Board, 106
Cowperthwaite, John, 65, 75, 80, 81, 82, 83, 84, 106, 168, 182
Crimean War, 14
Crown Lands Resumption Ordinance, 97
Cultural Revolution, 79, 85

Dalian, 42
Davis, Sir John, 1, 3, 4, 5
Deane, Walter Meredith, 19, 21, 24, 25
Democratic Party, 155
Department of Trade, 108, 178, 179
Department of Trade and Industry, 108
District Watch Committee, 38, 39, 40
Donovan, General William (Wild Bill), 173
Dunn, Lydia, 135

East Asia, 52, 187
East India Company (EIC), 14
Edinburgh, 35
Europe, 51, 72, 73
Executive Council, 20, 83, 100, 101, 155, 186

Fang, Anson, 77, 133
Federated Malay States, 45
Festival of Hong Kong, 165
Fiji, 22
First World War, 47, 61, 137
Fisher, Sir Warren, 47, 48

Fletcher, Sir George, 22
Foreign and Commonwealth Office, 108, 178, 180
Foreign Office, 17, 54, 62, 63, 108, 122, 140, 178, 179, 180
Furse, Ralph, 123

General Agreement on Tariffs and Trade (GATT), 106, 107, 109
Geneva, 106
George Watson's College, 35
Gimson, Franklin, 53, 76
Gladstone, William, 3, 14
Godber, Peter, 110
Goodstadt, Leo, 159, 160
Government of India Act, 14
Grantham, Sir Alexander, 22, 30, 60–6, 73, 85, 173–5
Gu Weijun, 52
Guangdong, 2, 10

Haddon-Cave, Philip, 82, 116, 146, 157, 159, 178
Haileybury College, 14
Hamilton, Geoffrey, 101, 125
Hancock, Alfred, 38
Harcourt, Cecil, 43, 53, 58, 76
Harknett, G. A., 112
Hase, Patrick, 98
Hawkins, Brian, 105
Hayes, James, 89, 90, 93, 182
Heath, Henry, 105, 170
Heathcote-Smith, C. B. B., 63
Heatherington, Robert, 56
Heung Yee Kuk, 88
Ho, Eric Peter, 119, 120, 127, 128, 144
Holmes, Ronald, 50, 65, 69, 75, 78, 79, 80, 85, 95
Hong Kong Regiment, 49, 50
Honolulu, 51
Hotung, Robert, 38, 54
House of Commons, 152, 155
Hulme, J. W., 5

Imperial Defence College, 76, 79
Independent Commission Against Corruption (ICAC), 112
India, 14, 19, 46, 51, 54, 121

*Index*

Indian Civil Service (ICS), 14, 18, 35, 46, 182, 191
Indian Mutiny, 121
Indo-China, 36, 51
Ip Chi, 120
Ireland, 50
Isle of Man, 35

Japan, 50, 51, 162; Japanese, 30, 48, 49, 50, 51, 52, 53, 56, 57, 59, 65, 68, 76, 77, 79, 80, 120, 187, 192
John Swire & Sons, 135
Johnston, A. R., 6
Johnston, Sir Reginald, 22
Jordan, David, 101, 106–9, 145, 146, 171, 172, 179, 182, 184

*kaifong* associations, 77
Kennedy, Sir Arthur, 26
Kennedy-Skipton, G. S., 50
Keswick, John, 38, 58, 61, 62
King William's College, 35
King, T. H., 26
King's College, 29, 35
Korean War, 67, 68
Kowloon, 6, 13, 15, 32, 82, 87, 88, 92, 94, 96; Kowloon City, 97
Kuomintang, 59, 62, 64, 172, 174
Kwun Tong, 92

Labour Party, 178
Lee, Thomas C. Y., 105
Legislative Council, 148, 150, 152, 153, 155, 156, 170
Li Fook-kow, 120, 128
Lightbody, Ian, 56, 104, 163
Lister, Alfred, 22, 23
Lo, Katherine, 133
Lockhart, Sir James Stewart, 22, 24, 29, 31, 33, 34, 35, 36, 37, 38, 39, 40, 41, 42, 43, 44, 75
London, 4, 13, 18, 29, 35, 52, 53, 57, 58, 61, 68, 73, 79, 81, 108, 109, 115, 120, 140, 149, 167, 170, 171, 173, 174, 175, 177, 178, 179, 180, 188, 192, 194
London School of Economics, 117
Loo Aqui, 8

Lu Xun, 31
Luddington, Sir Donald, 23, 104, 105, 111, 170
Lushun, 42

Macau, 156
MacDonnell, Sir Richard, 25
McDouall, John, 75, 77, 78, 79, 95, 103
MacDougall, David, 22, 43, 49, 50, 52, 53, 54, 55, 56, 58, 59, 60, 61, 62, 63, 64, 65, 81
McKinsey & Company, 86, 140, 141, 142, 143, 144, 145, 146, 147
MacLean, Roderick, 117, 118, 119
MacLehose, Sir Murray, 22, 83, 86, 92, 125, 140, 141, 144, 148, 150, 151, 180, 192
Macmillan, Harold, 115
MacPherson, Ian, 126
Major, John, 176
Malaya, 17, 30, 46, 55, 115
Man Mo Temple, 8
Mao Zedong, 173
Marshall Plan, 172, 174
Martin, Robert Montgomery, 4
Matheson, Jardine, 38, 58
May, Charles, 6
May, Francis Henry, 22, 44, 46
Medical and Health Department, 74
Mencius, 31
Mok Man Cheung, 38
Mulloy, Gareth, 97, 98, 99, 111, 112
Mutual Aid Committees (MACs), 98

New Territories (NT), 31–3, 37, 40–3, 56, 79, 87–9, 91–5, 99, 101
Newcastle, Duke of, 17
Nigeria, 101, 118
Northcote, Stafford, 14, 16

O'Rorke, Bridget, 76, 133
Office of Strategic Services, 173
Oxford, 18, 57, 107, 121, 122, 123, 126

Pacific War, 22, 30, 42, 51, 80, 120, 163, 167, 173
Pan American Airways, 173

225

Part, Sir Antony, 108, 109, 179
Patten, Chris, 131, 153–5, 159, 192
Peak, 38, 54
Peak District (Residence) Repeal Bill, 55
Pearl Harbour, 51
Pembroke College, 61
People's Republic of China (PRC), 155, 156, 172, 173, 174, 176, 189, 194; *see also* China; Republic of China
Pottinger, Sir Henry, 1
Prendergast, John, 112
Public Service Commission, 124, 165
Public Works Department, 73, 169

Qing period, 28, 33

Republic of China, 173
Resettlement Department, 69, 74, 79, 98
Rider, Edith Louise, 38
Roberts, Lord Goronwy, 178
Robinson, Sir Hercules, 15, 16, 17, 18, 19, 21, 26, 30
Robinson, Sir William, 39, 41
Rowe, George, 122, 123
Rowlands, Martin, 69
Royal Navy, 54
Royle, Anthony, 178
Russell, Lord John, 15
Russell, Sir James, 22, 23

Sandhurst, 61
Sarawak, 21, 22
Sassoon, Frederick, 37
Sassoon family, 38
Sayer, Geoffrey, 22
Schofield, Walter, 22
Scott, Alan, 149
Second World War, 67, 87, 114, 124, 133, 140, 189
Secretariat for Chinese Affairs, 79, 85, 105
Selborne, Lord, 47
Sham Shui Po, 98
Shamian, 31
Shandong province, 42
Shatin, 92
Shawcross, Sir Hartley, 174
Shek Kip Mei, 69, 70, 73
Shek Pik reservoir, 90
Shiu-ching Lo, 77
Shuet-yeng Chau, 77
Sierra Leone, 80
Simla, 54
Singapore, 51, 115, 117
Sino–French War, 36
Smith, Adam, 81
Smith, Norman, 22
Smith, Sir Cecil Clementi, 19, 21, 22, 26, 31, 37, 46, 75, 186
Social Welfare Department, 73, 95, 98, 105, 169
Solomon Islands, 23
Sorby, Terence, 56
South Africa, 115
Southeast Asia, 117
Southeast Asia Command, 58
Special Administrative Region (SAR), 23, 109, 154, 157, 194
Special Operations Executive, 79
Stanley Fort, 99
Stanley internment camp, 50, 53, 66, 76
Star Ferry riots, 78
Starkey, R. G., 23
Stewart, Frederick, 36
Straits Settlements, 17, 21, 22, 30, 45, 46
Sui dynasty, 18
Swaine, John Joseph, 120
Sweetman, James, 117

Tai Po, 88
Tai Po Kau, 92
Taipei, 173
Taiwan, 64, 172
Tam Achoy, 8
Tan Boon-cheok, 120
Teesdale, Edmund, 22
Thailand, 51, 156
Tiananmen Square massacre, 153, 176
Todd, Alastair, 56
Tonnochy, Malcolm Struan, 19, 21

*Index*

Topley, Kenneth, 117, 178
Transport Department, 82, 165
Trench, Sir David, 23, 78, 79, 81–3, 95, 102, 103, 116, 125, 140, 141, 162, 177, 192
Trevelyan, Charles, 14, 16
Trinidad, 22, 121
Tsang, Donald, 23, 159
Tsuen Wan, 89, 90, 92
Tsui, Paul Ka-cheung, 56, 57, 65, 114, 128, 129
Tun Mun, 92
Tung Wah Hospital, 38, 39, 40

United Kingdom, 10, 16, 105, 108, 109, 124, 171, 172
United Nations, 67
United States (USA), 67, 106, 155, 174
Upton, Robert, 180

Vickers, Simon, 176
Victoria, 4, 21, 31, 32, 40
Victoria Harbour, 76, 82
Victoria, Queen, 1, 2, 121
Vietnamese boat people, 177

Wall Street crash, 55
Wanchai, 97, 98, 99, 111

Wardle, Charles, 176
Wei Yuk, 37
Weihaiwei, 22, 42
Wellington College, 61
Western Pacific, 23, 78, 95
Whitehall, 133, 137, 177, 178
Whitehead, T. H., 39
Williams, Bernard, 100
Williams, Peter, 69, 170
Wilson, Brian, 92
Wilson, Sir David, 159
Wodehouse, H. E., 24
Wong Lam, 151
Wong Machow, 11, 16
Wong, David T. K., 106
World Trade Organization, 109
Wright, Michael, 167, 169, 178, 180

Yau, Carrie, 155
Yeung Kai-yin, 133
Yeung Wing-tai, 120
Youde, Sir Edward, 148, 180
Young, Howard, 155
Young, Sir Mark, 50–1, 54–6, 58–61, 63, 64, 66, 114, 192
Yuen Long, 88

Zhongqing, 58
Zhoushan, 5